WAITING ON A TRAIN

The Embattled Future
of Passenger Rail Service

James McCommons

Foreword by James Howard Kunstler

Chelsea Green Publishing Company
White River Junction, Vermont

Project Manager: Emily Foote
Developmental Editor: Jonathan Cobb
Copy Editor: Cannon Labrie
Proofreader: Helen Walden
Indexer: Christy Stroud
Designer: Peter Holm,
      Sterling Hill Productions

Printed in the United States of America
First printing October 2009
10 9 8 7 6 5 4 3 2 1   09 10 11 12 13 14

Chelsea Green Publishing is committed to preserving
ancient forests and natural resources. We elected to print
this title on 30-percent postconsumer recycled paper,
processed chlorine-free. As a result, for this printing, we
have saved:

17 Trees (40' tall and 6-8" diameter)
7,752 Gallons of Wastewater
5 Million BTUs Total Energy
471 Pounds of Solid Waste
1,609 Pounds of Greenhouse Gases

Chelsea Green Publishing made this paper choice because
we and our printer, Thomson-Shore, Inc., are members
of the Green Press Initiative, a nonprofit program dedicated to supporting authors, publishers, and suppliers
in their efforts to reduce their use of fiber obtained
from endangered forests. For more information, visit:
www.greenpressinitiative.org.

Environmental impact estimates were made using the Environmental Defense Paper Calculator.
For more information visit: www.papercalculator.org.

Our Commitment to Green Publishing

Chelsea Green sees publishing as a tool for cultural change and ecological stewardship. We strive
to align our book manufacturing practices with our editorial mission and to reduce the impact
of our business enterprise on the environment. We print our books and catalogs on chlorine-
free recycled paper, using vegetable-based inks whenever possible. This book may cost slightly
more because we use recycled paper, and we hope you'll agree that it's worth it. Chelsea Green
is a member of the Green Press Initiative (www.greenpressinitiative.org), a nonprofit coalition
of publishers, manufacturers, and authors working to protect the world's endangered forests and
conserve natural resources.

    Waiting on a Train was printed on Natures Book Natural, a 30-percent postconsumer-waste
recycled paper supplied by Thomson-Shore.

Library of Congress Cataloging-in-Publication Data
McCommons, James, 1957–
  Waiting on a train: the embattled future of passenger rail service / James McCommons;
foreword by James Howard Kunstler.
    p. cm.
  Includes index.
  ISBN 978-1-60358-064-9
  1. Railroads--United States. 2. Transportation--United States. I. Title.

  HE2741.M196 2009
  385'.220973--dc22

                  2009030142

Chelsea Green Publishing Company
Post Office Box 428
White River Junction, VT 05001
(802) 295-6300
www.chelseagreen.com

CONTENTS

Amtrak routes and corridors

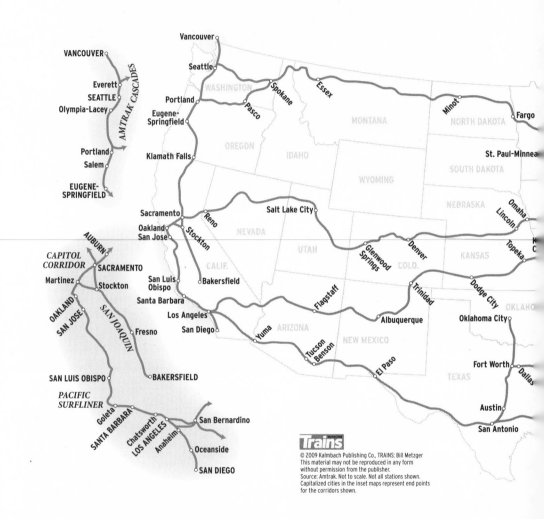

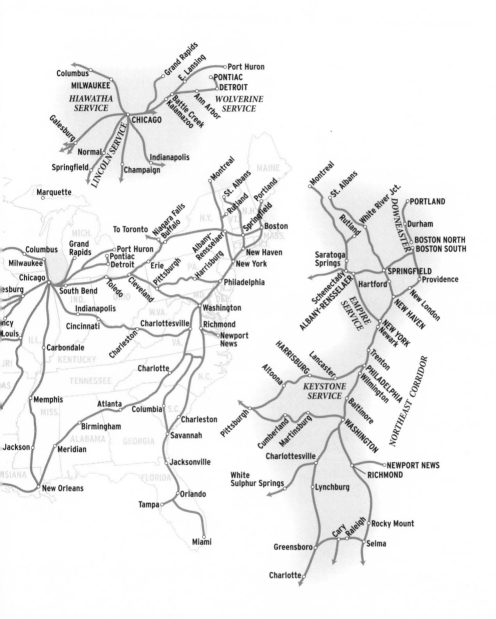

FOREWORD

The world economic fiasco, which I call "The Long Emergency," may be speeding us into a future of permanent nostalgia in which anything that is not of the present time looks good. I say this to avert any accusations that I am trafficking in sentimentality where the subject of railroads is concerned. For the moment, any suggestion that a railroad revival in America might be a good thing is generally greeted as laughable for reasons ranging from the incompetence of Amtrak, to the sprawling layout of our suburbs, to our immense investment in cars, trucks, and highways—motoring culture now overshadowing all other aspects of our national identity.

This said, I will hazard to engage in a personal sentimental journey to the memory bank of my many adventures on trains, starting with the best: my yearly journey from New York City to summer camp in New Hampshire, which I repeated for several years beginning in 1959. Apart from my delirious joy at getting out of the city for two whole summer months, the trip itself was magical. The camp rented two Pullman sleeper cars. They smelled deliciously of machine oil and freshly washed linens, and were air-conditioned to arctic levels of temperature. Whatever wasn't luxuriously plush was polished to a high sheen, including a lot of chrome and brass.

We departed from Pennsylvania Station about 9:00 p.m. for the overnight trip. Most of us stayed awake until the wee hours terrorizing the porter with our water guns, visiting in each others' berths (sharing troves of Zagnut bars, Raisinets, and sometimes even booze filched from our parents' liquor cabinets), and watching the cavalcade of the New England landscape scroll through the window in the moonlight, past the tobacco-growing sheds of the Connecticut River valley, the ghostly switching yards, and the quiet streets of nameless small towns. Eventually, the rocking train lulled most of us to an hour of sleep.

We pulled into our destination, White River Junction, Vermont, near the crack of dawn, and then we bleary little insomniacs were stuffed into an old U.S. Army–surplus troop truck for the last leg of the journey across the river to New Hampshire—then a wonderfully backward corner of the country with no interstate highways and lots of men with beards. The reverse trip home at the end of August was fun, too, in the same way, except for our tragic fate of having to return to the rigors of school.

I rode the Long Island Railroad commuter line a lot in the 1960s because I lived in Manhattan with my mom and stepfather and was exported on Saturdays twice a month to visit my father in the suburbs. While it became routine, it was never dull watching the endless lumpenprole precincts of Queens County, with their unimaginably dreary asphalt-shingled shoebox houses, numberless auto scrapyards, and chaotic shopping boulevards of colorful folks from foreign lands. I often rode back Monday mornings with my father, along with a thousand other identical men in suits and hats. Up until 1963, the great old Pennsylvania Station still existed, and one rose out of the transportation bowels of the city, with those ranks of suited and hat-wearing executives, like a conquering legion through a set of triumphant vaults to the great global engine that was New York in the postwar decades.

Train service went straight to hell by the late sixties. In college, I took the old New York Central from Rochester to New York City a few times, but by then the rolling stock had developed the ambience of a lavatory, with trash everywhere, and the upholstery rotting, and odoriferous men snoring across the rows of seats. There were mysterious delays all along the way. The old Beaux Arts train stations in Syracuse and Albany had not yet been turned into banks, but you could no longer buy so much as a stick of gum in them. The inducement to drive, instead, on the brand-spanking-new New York State Thruway, was huge.

By the mid-1970s, American passenger rail, in near total disarray, fell under the baleful sway of Conrail and Amtrak, both apparently created on a Soviet-management model, with an extra overlay of Murphy's Law[1]* to insure maximum entropy of service. In 1974 I took the San Francisco Zephyr from New York to Oakland, California. It was, of course, uncomfortable, filthy, and cold, with worn-out rolling stock, iffy linens, and onboard food consisting of mystery-meat sandwiches prepared solely in a "Radar Range." The most remarkable thing about this journey was how we managed to avoid anything scenic. The initial run was overnight from New York to Chicago in the November darkness. In Chicago, we had such a long layover—all day, really—that I was able to tour the Art Institute, the Field Museum, and even take in a movie before we resumed our journey on a different train. We rolled through Iowa and Nebraska all night and I woke up somewhere along the bleak prairie outside of Denver. In that city, we parked on a siding near a stockyard all day long for reasons never explained, and departed again at dusk for the leg through the Rockies. Things finally got interesting the next morning in Sparks, Nevada, when we entered the Sierras, but the Radar Range cuisine had introduced some malign flora into my guts and I spent most of that final leg in the bathroom.

---

1 * Murphy's Law: Anything that can go wrong, will go wrong.

Since then, train travel in the United States has become a pretty bare-bones affair. Amtrak has become the laughingstock of the world. Most Americans now living have never even been passengers on a train—for them it's as outmoded as the stagecoach. The final three-decade blowout of the cheap fossil-fuel fiesta led to the supremacy of the automobile and the fabulous network of highways that provided so much employment and so many real-estate development opportunities. This is all rather unfortunate because we are on the verge of experiencing one of the sharpest discontinuities in human history.

We're heading into a permanent global oil crisis. It is going to change the terms of everyday life very starkly. We will be a far less affluent nation than we were in the twentieth century. The automobile is now set to become a diminishing presence in our lives. We will not have the resources to maintain the highways that made Happy Motoring so normal and universal. The sheer prospect of permanent energy-resource problems has, in my view, been the prime culprit behind the cratering of our financial system for the simple reason that reduced energy "inputs" lead inexorably to the broad loss of capacity to service debt at all levels: personal, corporate, government. It's quite a massive problem and it's not going away anytime soon, which is why I call it "The Long Emergency." There are many additional pieces to it, including very troubling prospects for agriculture, for commerce, manufacturing, really for all the "normal" activities of daily life in an "advanced" civilization.

I think we're going to need trains again desperately. Among the systems in trouble (and headed for more, very soon) is commercial aviation. In my opinion, the airline industry as we know it will cease to exist in five years. Combine this with the threats to our car culture—including resumed high fuel costs and the equal probability of scarcities and shortages, along with falling incomes and lost access to credit—and you have a continental-sized nation that nobody can travel around.

Rebuilding the nation's passenger railroad has got to be put at the top of our priority list. We had a system not so long ago that was the envy of the world; now we have service that the Bulgarians would be ashamed of. The tracks are still lying out there rusting in the rain, waiting to be fixed. The job doesn't require the reinvention of anything—we already know how to do it. Rebuilding the system would put scores of thousands of people to work at meaningful jobs at all levels. The fact that we're barely talking about it shows what an unserious people we have become.

Rebuilding the American passenger-railroad system has an additional urgent objective: we need a doable project that can build our confidence and sense of collective purpose in facing all the other extraordinary challenges posed by the long emergency—especially rebuilding local networks of commerce and relocalizing agriculture. There's been a lot of talk about "hope" in our politics lately. Real hope is generated among people who are confident in their ability to contend with the circumstances that reality sends their way, proving to themselves that they are competent and able to respond intelligently to the imperatives of their time. We are, in effect, our own generators of hope. Rebuilding the American railroad system is an excellent place to start recovering our sense of purpose.

—JAMES HOWARD KUNSTLER

PROLOGUE

Baltimore
on the oldest railroad in america

Patches of snow lay along the tracks. The late afternoon sun, flickering strobe-like through the trees, momentarily froze each image, as if slowing down the reel of a movie. Through the bare branches streamed red brick warehouses, graffiti-marked retaining walls, parking lots ringed with razor ribbon, and tiny backyards littered with barbecue grills and play sets. Wisps of smoke vented into the cold air from the chimneys atop the row houses. From its backside, Baltimore looked worn and forlorn.

The wheels clattered away on the rails below as John Hankey, a historian and one-time locomotive engineer, talked into my ear, pausing whenever the locomotive's whistle blasted—two long, one short, another long—at road crossings. Once, when the horn sounded especially insistent, even frantic, John gripped his seat and said, "That's not good." A moment later, we passed some bushes on a trash-strewn hillside and saw kids scrambling upslope away from the train.

The commuters dozed and chatted, most of them on their way to Washington's Union Station. A man sitting nearby opened the *Washington Post* to a story of the president-elect, holed up in Chicago, naming new cabinet members and conjuring up economic remedies. At the end of this crazy year, we certainly needed to take the cure.

John and I had boarded the MARC (Maryland Rail Commuter) train at Camden Station, next to Oriole Park, the site of one of the country's earliest railroad terminals. Camden Yards was once a major passenger station with a sprawling complex of warehouses and loading docks, freight terminals, repair shops, and switching yards for the Baltimore and Ohio Railroad (B&O). Prior to the Civil War, the Camden Line had been the only rail link to the capital. Abraham Lincoln passed this way en route to Gettysburg and then again when the funeral train took his body back to Springfield, Illinois, for burial.

And here on this stretch of track, I was nearing the end of my own long journey. Over the months of 2008, I'd ridden some 26,000 miles by rail researching and writing about the future of passenger railroading in America. I was on the Camden Line this bright December day for the chance to pass over the oldest continuously operated piece of railroad in North America. Passenger trains have run this route for 179 years.

CSX Transportation, one of the giant freight railroads, now owns the Camden Line, but it was built by the B&O. After the war of 1812, the country had expanded westward. Goods and people moving to and from the interior could not easily reach Baltimore and other East Coast cities, so trade shifted to the Ohio and Mississippi rivers and, ultimately, New Orleans.

Seeing their commercial business dwindling, most East Coast cities gambled on new, westward canals—following New York's success with the Erie in 1825—but Baltimore decided to build a railroad. In 1828, no one in America knew much about railroading; the technology was still developing in Britain. Steam locomotives didn't exist here, and there was no steel to speak of. The first rails were fashioned from stone and wood; the track bed cut by hand using Irish, German, and slave labor.

Many hills around Baltimore contain large amounts of clay. Black powder had been so ineffectual in moving the soil—"the charges just kind of went poof in the clay," said John—that crews working day and night had to dig with just hand tools. One day in 1828 a hill gave way, and one of Hankey's Irish ancestors was buried alive. Death while working on the railroad wasn't uncommon. I, too, had an ancestor who had been killed on the job.

For the first few miles from Camden Station, we followed the original 1830 railroad bed. The right-of-way had been widened, more ballast added and modern tracks and signaling put in, but this was where the concept of railroading in America had first proved itself.

The tracks sashayed sharply to the left and then to the right. "This is 1830 railroading," Hankey explained. "Steam locomotives weren't yet available, so they initially ran with horses pulling a car. They optimized for a level grade and didn't care about curves, which is precisely the wrong equation. Better to go as straight as you can even if you have to climb a grade."

In a few minutes, we dropped down to the Patapsco River valley and passed Vinegar Hill where, in 1829, Irish laborers went on strike and rioted because their bosses had skipped out with their pay. The railroad asked for the militia to put down the rebellion and arrest the leaders, an early example of the heavy hand railroads were to play for many decades in business and labor history.

Seven miles from Camden Station, the line split. The old B&O mainline veered off to the northwest and our MARC train ran southwest toward the capital. And then we were crossing the Patapsco on the Thomas Viaduct, a spectacular stone bridge more than six hundred feet long, built in 1835 on a curve and constructed of Roman arches. Talk about infrastructure—it was an engineering marvel of its day, and heavy freight and commuter trains still pass over it today. A fifteen-foot obelisk, dedicated to the B&O president, board of directors, and the bridge architect, Benjamin Latrobe, stood at the east end of the bridge.

"They had just opened up the line to Washington and already were putting up monuments to themselves," Hankey remarked.

And so they should, I thought, because in the next few decades, the United States became the greatest railroad nation on earth, building on and contributing to an empire of capitalism. Trains penetrated the wilderness, moved goods and people, tied together a nation, helped win a civil war and later two world wars, and created a modern, mobile industrial society. Railroads were the engines of economic growth in the late nineteenth century. By the 1920s—when the railroads were at their peak with more than 1,000 companies operating over a network of 380,000 miles of track—they carried 1.27 billion passengers annually. The Pullman Company, which invented and operated the "sleeper" cars, was the largest hotel operator in the world, catering to 40,000 guests every night. "The railroad was a reliable, efficient, high-capacity, all-weather, and democratic mode of transportation," said Hankey. "It enabled America to become one nation and expand on a continental basis."

Then, about fifty years ago, unlike the rest of the world, the United States decided the country didn't need trains anymore or the infrastructure of rail lines that reached out to nearly every town, every factory, and every citizen. It wasn't so much a conspiracy as a happenstance of neglect, poor planning, and the usual messiness of democracy and capitalism. The U.S. was the only industrialized country in the world to have an entirely private rail system and when the private business model didn't work anymore, we just let the railroad go to seed, not knowing what we had until it was nearly gone. The rise of the automobile and assembly line, the discovery of cheap oil in Texas and Oklahoma, and the government's drive to subsidize and build a sprawling road network enticed Americans from the railroads. There was psychology at work as well. For a headstrong country that saw itself as the epitome of modernity and technological innovation, trains seemed old-fashioned, passé.

At Union Station, Hankey and I got off the commuter and walked over to America's fastest train, Amtrak's Acela Express, waiting to be boarded for the run north to New York and Boston. In 1999, Amtrak bought twenty Acela train sets—meaning locomotives and cars—which were designed and built overseas. Though capable of 200 mph, Acela rarely hits 150 mph, and on a typical trip averages only 88 mph—no faster than many steam locomotives running between major cities eighty years ago.

Acela is the best America can do at present, which isn't very good at all when compared to the French, the Germans, and the Japanese, and now the Chinese and the South Koreans and Taiwanese and Spaniards—all of whom have been building high-speed trains and infrastructures for years.

How this state of affairs had come to pass and what we can do to improve upon it had taken me a good amount of time to sort out. I read extensively, interviewed dozens of experts like Hankey, and spent weeks on the rails traveling the country, talking as I went with the people who ride and work the trains.

There was much to discover. Although I had family connections to railroading, I knew little of the industry, its history, and the reasons why Amtrak emerged as the sole operator of intercity passenger trains. My travels on Amtrak sometimes fulfilled my low expectations of a railroad run on a shoestring, but I also went to places where its services work quite well.

I experienced the difficulty of getting around the country without a car and also came to understand that our modes of travel—rail, aviation, and highway—are ridiculously separated from one another. Connectivity matters.

And finally, despite the popular zeitgeist that Americans won't ride trains, are in love with their cars, and the United States is just too big for rail travel, I sensed the country was at a turning point with passenger trains and ready to rediscover rail.

As it turns out, that was truer than I could have imagined.

PART I
Through the Rockies and Sierras

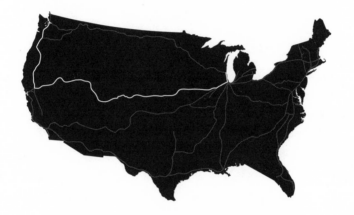

California Zephyr
here come your game boys and microwaves

The odyssey began in early 2007 when I got a magazine-writing assignment that would take me from my home in Michigan's Upper Peninsula to Seattle, Washington. I could have flown, but I asked the editor if she would pay for a train instead. Sure, she agreed, if the cost didn't exceed a jet. It was a bit more, but I made up the difference because it was a chance to climb aboard a long-distance train again.

I also wanted to bring along Kelly, my oldest son, then thirteen, to introduce him to the landscapes of the West and to train travel, too. He barely remembered the trip we had taken from Toledo to Harrisburg when he was five, and I had not been on a train since.

When we boarded the California Zephyr at Chicago's Union Station that March, I didn't know this one trip would encompass so much of the promise in, and the trouble with, passenger-train service in the United States today. Having ridden Amtrak for some thirty years, I knew we would likely encounter some poor service, missed connections, long waits, and run-down equipment. Still, the train offered great scenery, the camaraderie of fellow passengers, a reprieve from driving or flying, a great safety record, and an exotic experience.

So few intercity passenger trains run today that most Americans have never boarded one. Amtrak doesn't come through their town, or it comes just once a day—perhaps in the middle of the night—or every other day. Rarely is the train on time, and more recently, it's often been filled and with no available seats. Where I live in the Upper Peninsula is isolated, and no matter how great a renaissance rail may undergo in this country, I don't expect a passenger train will come that far north again for a long time.

Until 1969, the Chicago and North Western Railway's Peninsula 400 ran between the Upper Peninsula and Chicago, making the trip in about six hours, an hour quicker than I can drive it doing the speed limit. But no more. The nearest railhead for a passenger train to me today is Milwaukee, 273 miles to the south. There, I could pick up the Hiawatha, an Amtrak success story. Making seven trips daily to downtown Chicago and back, the Hiawatha is a corridor train between major cities that are too close for efficient air service and connected by a deteriorating interstate highway filled past capacity.

The departments of transportation in Illinois and Wisconsin subsidize the Hiawatha service and have spent millions building stations and helping the Canadian Pacific expand its track system to accommodate both freight and passenger trains. The DOTs want to lure some commuters off the roadways, and also give people another mode of travel. The trains run on time. They are clean, filled with passengers, and increasingly popular since gas prices skyrocketed in 2008.

We boarded the train at the Amtrak station near Milwaukee's airport, Mitchell Field, having left our automobile in long-term parking. Commuters jammed the Hiawatha, tapping on Blackberries and yakking on cell phones. An attendant wheeled a cart down the aisle, and I bought a coffee and opened a newspaper. Frozen farm fields rolled past the window. Now, all we had to do was sit back and ride—first to Chicago, then to Sacramento by sleeping car, and then, after a few days in California visiting a childhood friend, north through the big woods and Coast Ranges to Seattle. Thousands of miles, eighty-plus hours on the rails, a panorama of western landscape, and a melting pot of human characters to encounter along the way—the trip guaranteed adventure. I told Kelly, "By the time we get home, you'll know you've been somewhere."

I had pulled him from school for ten days. He carried a knapsack of comic books, an iPod and Game Boy, school texts, and a thick folder of homework. But he was too excited that morning for algebra and instead peered out the window looking for the Sears Tower and Chicago skyline.

At Union Station, we checked our bags at the Metropolitan Lounge, reserved for first-class sleeping-car passengers, and went upstairs to the Great Hall with its Romanesque columns and hard, wooden railroad benches.

Because of its central location in the Middle West, Chicago has long been a railroad town. At one time, the city had five railroad terminals, but Union Station was the busiest. In the 1940s, it handled more than 300 trains and 100,000 passengers a day. Today, it's still busy, with commuters riding Metra and a few thousand passengers traveling on one or another of Amtrak's 50-odd trains that run in and out of Union Station each day.

The Great Hall was cut off from the regular flow of passengers when Amtrak remodeled the station in 1989 and moved its waiting areas and lounges belowground. Amtrak constructed the comfortable, classy Metropolitan Lounge for first-class passengers, but herded its coach passengers into the unimaginatively named Lounges A and B, which are frequently jammed with passengers and luggage, and claustrophobic in comparison to the airy, cavernous Great Hall. Veteran passengers flee to the hall and wait up there for their trains, but unsuspecting newbies, who want to stay close to the boarding areas, miss one of America's great indoor spaces.

Kelly and I sat on the benches, tilted our heads back and looked at the winter light filtering through the overhead skylights. Homeless people slept on nearby benches, their faces and hands obscured beneath soiled jackets, sweaters, and blankets. They resembled long piles of unwashed laundry. They smelled, too. Train terminals offer refuge during the day, and in my travels I encountered homeless lying in Oakland's Jack London Station, sleeping upright in the art deco chairs of the L.A. terminal, and squatting in corners of New York's Penn Station. Kelly's sad expression and stolen glances at those men were disquieting. What could I say?

We boarded the train as an ice storm whipped into the city, jamming up rush-hour traffic on the Dan Ryan Expressway and delaying flights out of O'Hare and Midway. Sleet pelted the train as it gathered speed through the western suburbs and onto the frozen cornfields of northern Illinois.

After the conductor punched our tickets, we walked forward to the dining car and ordered dinner. While we ate, the storm morphed into a full-blown midwestern blizzard. Looking into the blur of snow, I told Kelly stories about other train journeys.

His mother, Elise, and I, were once aboard a train traveling from Detroit to Chicago. The locomotive stalled for hours in a sweltering cornfield. And there was that cold night we spent riding across Kansas when the heat failed in the sleeping car. As compensation, the sleeping-car attendant brought us bottles of red wine, which we drank in sleeping bags zipped up to the neck.

In the early 1970s, Amtrak ran the "Rainbow Trains." The *consists*—a technical term railroaders use as a noun to describe the composition or arrangements of the locomotive and cars—were a hodgepodge of old, hand-me-down equipment inherited from a dozen different railroads. The toilets, known as "holes in the floor," flushed right onto the tracks, and you could watch the wooden ties rushing by underneath. In 1978 on the Sunset Limited in west Texas, I watched cooks working over smoky stoves fired by charcoal briquettes. The air-conditioning and exhaust fans had broken down, and the dining attendants threw open the windows at the ends of the car to clear the smoke. Heat from the Chihuahuan Desert blasted through the windows, and I ate with an old railroader who reckoned the engineer had the train running 95 to 105 mph.

I was in college then, on my way to Arizona to drive an elderly aunt and all her belongings back to a retirement home in Pennsylvania. In the lounge car, I met Sigrid, a blue-eyed, freckled blond running away from a possessive boyfriend in Florida. A friend had gotten her a job in California on a sprawling farm in the San Joaquin Valley, where she was to stand at the row end of a broccoli field and vector in crop-dusting planes.

"I'll need to wear an aluminum suit with a mask. You know, because of the pesticides. And I have to wave these flags to signal the pilot."

"Those are semaphores," I said, remembering a vocabulary word I'd picked up in an English class.

During a fueling stop in El Paso, we stepped onto the oven heat of the railroad platform and took pictures of one another standing outside the stucco-covered station. We drank cold beer in the lounge car as the train ran through Deming and Lordsburg.

In Arizona, right at dusk, we reached the ranching town of Benson. I was the only passenger getting on or off. The conductor looked me over and said, "Young man, this will be easy. We're going to slow the train to a crawl—but not stop. When I say 'now'—you step off. Take a big step forward and then turn around and I'll toss your knapsack."

When I caught the pack, he gave me an approving nod and then windmilled his arm at the engineer leaning out from the locomotive. The train throttled up toward Tucson. These days, Amtrak employees aren't allowed to step on or off moving trains, but back then a lot went on, including running trains 100 mph over tracks rated at 50. Nowadays with global positioning systems on every locomotive and central dispatch—where a person thousands of miles away can track a rolling train like an air-traffic controller—there's less freelancing.

When I looked up, Sigrid had her face pressed against the back window of the train. She waved good-bye. A dust devil scurried along the tracks. My aunt was nowhere in sight. I glanced across the street to a feed store where some good old boys sat on a bench regarding me as another long-haired curiosity.

Sigrid got smaller and smaller and then disappeared into the desert. And I knew I should have stayed on the train. Even now, I wish I had.

When the Zephyr with my son and me aboard crossed the Mississippi at Burlington that night, it was snowing hard. For a time in central Iowa, we paralleled Route 34, and I peered over to see cars spun out in ditches and tractor trailers creeping along. On a portable radio, Kelly tuned in the AP news, and we heard that airports in Chicago, Detroit, Minneapolis, and Des Moines were closed, thousands of passengers sprawled in the concourses, and the effects on air traffic were rippling across the nation.

It mattered not at all to the Zephyr. The tenor of the locomotives seemed to deepen. It built up speed and sliced into the storm. That evening, we turned out the cabin lights and gazed out at snowdrifts piling up in the empty main streets of small towns. Pickup trucks sat in driveways and television lights flickered from the windows of passing farmhouses.

All evening, our train braked into stations right on time. The conductors and attendants hustled folks aboard and we sped away into the countryside. This was how a train was supposed to run—on time, efficient, and with only enough "dwell" in the stations to get folks off and on. The countryside reeled past. We were making progress.

Kelly changed into his pajamas, boosted himself into the upper bunk, and I latched the safety netting to catch him if the train made a sudden jerk. He was tired and giddy. A few hours out of Omaha, the train punched through the back side of the storm and into the clear skies of the Great Plains. Muted light of a full moon filled the cabin, and I sat up to see black, treeless land rolling away and the red line of dawn on the eastern horizon. The attendant had a coffee pot going and a fresh stack of the *Omaha World Herald*.

In the empty lounge car, I read, drank coffee, and watched the day come to light on the plains. Mornings are always magical on a train—going to sleep in one town and waking up hundreds of miles down the line. When the Zephyr pulled into Denver that morning, we were five minutes early.

Day two also went well. The train climbed the Front Range and plunged into black tunnels that emptied into magnificent snowy valleys. Along the Colorado River, we watched deer and elk bound away from the tracks. A historian gave short lectures over the speakers about characters like Doc Holliday, the tubercular dentist, gambler, and gunslinger who succumbed in a Glenwood Springs sanitarium. In the evening, the train descended the western slope, running along arroyos and beneath red buttes saturated by the setting sun.

But that night, in the Union Pacific yards outside of Salt Lake City, troubles began. While most passengers slept, the train idled for nearly four hours blocked by freight trains and hampered by switching problems. Behind schedule and out of sync with oncoming traffic, the Zephyr was at the whim of Union Pacific dispatchers in Omaha. Time and again the next day we were shunted onto sidings to make room for eastbound freights that rolled past laden with shipping containers off the docks of the West Coast.

"Get out of the way because here come all your Game Boys, microwaves, and cheap Wal-Mart crap," a conductor grumbled.

We'd gotten jammed up in a supply line that stretched all the way back to Asia. The big railroads love this "hook and haul" business, in which goods coming off container ships are put on trains and hauled cross-country. At the time, before the great economic downturn in the late months of 2008, this stream of stuff produced by cheap labor abroad, sold by big box stores, and fueled by consumer credit seemed endless. The shipping containers sported logos in Chinese characters and English—Maersk, China Shipping, and Cosco.

Other trains pulled triple-decker car carriers loaded with Daewoos, Nissans, and Toyotas.

No matter what these trains hauled, the Zephyr—filled with nearly three hundred people—pulled over to let them pass, sometimes waiting at a lonely siding for thirty minutes. Such stops mystify the Europeans who ride the trains.

"We're stopped because of a bloody freight train?" one told me. "Unbelievable."

In 1971 when Union Pacific and other freight railroads turned their passenger operations over to Amtrak, they agreed to give passenger trains preference over freights. It frequently doesn't happen that way—sometimes because dispatchers purposefully sideline passenger trains, but more often because the existing infrastructure is just overwhelmed by too many trains. The truth in America is freight matters more than people, and nearly all the track belongs to the big railroads not to Amtrak.

Amtrak pays incentives to the freight railroads to deliver its passenger trains on time, but those payments are miniscule as compared to the profits earned by hauling freight. In other words, the incentives don't provide much incentive.

In 2007, the Zephyr arrived in California on schedule only about 20 percent of the time, the next-to-worst performance in the Amtrak system. By summer 2009, when the recession cut freight traffic by nearly 25 percent, thus loosening some of the bottlenecks, and the big railroads made a political decision to do a better job of delivering Amtrak trains, the on-time performance of the Zephyr improved to nearly 60 percent.

"The other railroads hate Amtrak—just hate us. We're in the way," the conductor told me. He was being impolitic. It's rare to hear Amtrak officials be as blunt. Passenger trains and freights run on a shared right-of-way, meaning they are on the same tracks. Outside of the Northeast Corridor, Boston to Washington, D.C., and a few other places, Amtrak doesn't own any track. It is a guest, and the freight railroads are the reluctant hosts.

American freight railroads are not now the overregulated, bankrupt basket corporations they were in the 1960s and '70s. They have several competitive advantages over the other transportation modes—air, road, and water—when it comes to hauling coal, grain, chemicals, and consumer goods, and their business has thrived in recent decades.

Stand on a hillside in the open country of Wyoming's Red Desert or the Mojave Preserve in southern California, and run your eyes along the length of a mile-long freight train loaded with 200-plus shipping containers and you get a sense of the efficiencies. Known as intermodals—because the containers are easily moved between ships, trains, and trucks—these trains are greener than trucks and good at moving items across the continent. The problem has been a lack of rail capacity. In the merger mania that permeated the industry after deregulation in 1980, the railroads ruthlessly gobbled one another up, combined operations, abandoned redundant and little-used routes, and ripped out tracks. Today, most of the country's rail infrastructure is controlled by only seven major railroads, also known as the Class 1 railroads, categorized by generating more than $250 million in revenues annually. Most of the country is divided up by the big four: BNSF, CSX Transportation, Norfolk Southern, and Union Pacific. Smaller shares, but still big pieces, are taken up by Canadian National, Kansas City Southern, and Canadian Pacific. As well, there are regional railroads and short lines.

Much of this contraction was, from a corporate and efficiency point of view, necessary and good management, but there also were boneheaded decisions that realized short-term gains without looking ahead. Critics say the railroads got so good at downsizing, they forgot how to grow. Since the 1960s, nearly half of the nation's rail infrastructure was abandoned or removed.

The freight railroads could use those tracks. And even though they are spending more than $3 to $4 billion a year to restore and improve the tracks, it's not enough to keep pace. The Great Recession has offered some breathing room, but gridlock on the railroad will likely return when the economy picks up, unless government steps in and also invests in infrastructure.

With all the delays, it took us all day to cross Nevada. In Winnemucca, the Zephyr got stuck behind a slow-moving freight, and we made just fifty miles in three hours. Then, because we'd been unable to reach Reno before federal safety rules required a new crew, we stopped in the desert for ninety minutes until another crew was driven out from the city.

And it got worse. The dining car ran out of food, the lounge out of beer. Passengers who had missed connections or were fretting about relatives waiting for hours to pick them up barked at the crew. The chagrined workers threw up their hands, almost as if to say, "What did you expect from Amtrak?"

Veteran riders of Amtrak's long-distance trains just assume the train will be late. They don't book tight connections. They tell friends and relatives to call ahead and check arrival times. And they try to stay patient. Yet even by Amtrak standards, our progress that day had been ridiculous. It reached absurdity in Sparks—just outside of Reno—where Amtrak tried to hook on a private railway car of gamblers bound for San Francisco. The car wouldn't couple, and every time it bumped the Zephyr, the automatic brakes engaged on the train and threw passengers against the seats and walls.

We finally crossed the mountains into California at midnight, and when the Zephyr inched into Sacramento sixty-two hours after leaving Chicago, it was fifteen hours late. It was an ignominious end to a trip that had had some transcendent moments.

Sacramento
all you got now is amtrak

For the next two days, we stayed at a motel across the street from the station. Sacramento is a railroad town, and we heard the whistles and rumbles of the trains day and night. On Sunday, we walked downtown to mass at the Cathedral of the Blessed Sacrament and on the way back passed the palatial home of Leland Stanford, one of the politically powerful "Big Four" who had built the eastbound section of the transcontinental railroad. As California's governor, Stanford made sure the railroad received massive land grants and public funding, actions that were as corrupt as they were bold.

He later founded Stanford University, became president of the Central Pacific and a big stockholder in the Southern Pacific. He lived the lavish lifestyle of the railroad baron. It was folks like Stanford who made railroads indispensable to life in the nineteenth and early twentieth centuries and who made the railroads one of the most hated institutions in the land.

"Railroads were like the tobacco companies, big oil, and child pornographers all rolled up in one. They were considered to be bastards that needed to be kept under the government's thumb," John Hankey remarked. "What went on during the 1800s poisoned the atmosphere for the next century."

Kelly and I walked into Old Sacramento to see the California Railroad Museum with its detailed dioramas and massive artifacts—steam locomotives, passenger cars, and the refrigerator cars that first hauled Central Valley produce to the eastern United States. Steeped in nostalgia for the golden age of railroading, the museum displayed an old and elegant dining car, fitted out with silverware and china plates. After World War II, the Union Pacific and Santa Fe ran fast "streamliner" trains with dining cars like this one, fine appointments, and grand names: Super Chief, El Capitan, and the California Zephyr.

In the back of the dining car, a grumpy docent stiffly unfolded from his chair and came toward us, hands in his back pockets and chest pushed out, ready to answer some questions.

Kelly told him we'd come out from Chicago on the Zephyr.

"Zephyr," he said. "That is what they call it, don't they?"

I said it wasn't quite like a Zephyr. We were fifteen hours late into Sacramento.

"Doesn't surprise me; it's always late," he said.

He told us he had ridden the streamliners as a young man, and now he occasionally takes Amtrak's Coast Starlight to L.A.

"Amtrak's food is better than the airlines, but it's all plastic plates and microwave food—nothing like this," he sniffed. "You'll never see any of this again. Just won't happen. All you got now is Amtrak." He spoke it like a slur.

In the bookstore, there were baseball caps, hundreds of books, toys—many emblazoned with the emblems of bygone railroads, swallowed up in mergers, gone defunct from lack of traffic—all the trivia a rail fan, a model railroader, or a child could lap up. There was little of Amtrak to be seen, and it certainly wasn't celebrated, yet it's now the only intercity railroad in the United States.

On our last day, we caught the city's new light-rail train up to Folsom to have dinner with friends before returning to the station to pick up the Coast Starlight to Seattle. Sometimes, these light-rail systems, powered by electricity rather than diesel, can be built on old right-of-ways previously traversed by trolleys before they were ripped out in favor of city buses. But when a city has to retrofit rail into suburbs and commercial strips designed around the automobile, it's an expensive, tedious process. Sacramento opened its first light rail in 1987 but it took twenty more years until the line reached the train station where residents can connect up with Amtrak.

We boarded the Coast Starlight that night at 1:30 a.m., the train being ninety minutes late from L.A. We rode coach, slept in our seats, and awoke when the train stopped in Dunsmuir and then climbed a grade near Mount Shasta, passing rock fields of basalt extruded eons ago from the caldera. A fresh snow lay like frosting over the black rock. Rain drenched the forests all the way north to the Oregon border. Even though we pressed our faces against the windows as we passed over trestles in the big woods, we couldn't see their supports below but only the frothy rivers over which we passed. North to Eugene and then Portland, the valleys were wide, fecund, and green, but shrouded in winter fog. Masses of snow geese rose off lakes and irrigation canals and swirled into the sky. We reached Seattle in twenty-one hours traveling 828 miles. I covered my story for the magazine and we got on a flight back to Milwaukee, leaving Seattle just as a Pineapple Express—a warm and wet Pacific weather front—drenched the Northwest.

All during the flight, I kept thinking about the train. And the questions I'd been asking myself for two or three decades—probably every time I got off a train—came back stronger than ever.

When are we again going to have a decent passenger-train system in this country—one that moves people efficiently between major cities and provides Americans with a true alternative to airplanes and automobiles?

What happened to the passenger-rail system that existed decades ago—the one remembered only through museums or in the reminiscences of our oldest citizens? Why was this system allowed to fall apart and be discarded in favor of other modes of travel?

And why has Amtrak not gotten any better? Sure, its toilets don't flush onto the track anymore, but some of its equipment is now older than the run-down stuff it inherited from the other railroads back in 1971. How did Amtrak end up as the nation's only intercity passenger service? And would those freight railroads ever consider running passenger trains again?

Train World
foamers and trainspotters

The year 2008 turned out to be an extraordinary and volatile one to be riding across the land with a cross section of Americans, many of whom were perplexed, angry, or resigned in the face of what they saw happening in their country. From day to day, it was hard to keep up with the news, and the effects much of it had or will have on transportation.

Consider the following: gas prices that hit $4 a gallon and seemed to make a deep impression on consumers that the days of endless supplies of cheap fuel may be over; the meltdown of a U.S. auto industry ill prepared for the future; an airline industry whose level of service declined as prices rose; the highest ridership ever in Amtrak's history; the passage of the most generous funding bill in Amtrak's history and the election of the first administration actually friendly to passenger rail; a crash between a commuter and freight train that killed twenty-five people on a shared right-of-way that led to new calls for better safety technology; the passage of a bond issue in California that may lead to America's first bullet train, an economic stimulus bill that puts $8 billion into developing high-speed rail and grants Amtrak another billion to fix up railcars and begin repairs on the Northeast Corridor; and, finally, a recession and financial crisis that threatens the country's economic stability and may eventually show us that we live in an age of limits where energy efficiency may triumph over convenience. Something had truly changed.

Does all this mean we're soon going to have passenger trains running all over America again, and multitudes will quickly abandon their cars for the train? No chance.

What it may mean is that the United States will develop a more robust and balanced public transportation policy. That it will invest in rail—as it has in highways and aviation—to move more people and more goods between major cities. In the next forty years, the nation's population is expected to increase by another one hundred million citizens; with that prospect, it's absurd to believe we can have an effective transportation system dependent only on highways and air.

If green technologies really are the future of America—if we really are moving into an age of constraint where energy is no longer cheap and carbon outputs must be limited—then rail has clear advantages and will be critical to the country's economic future.

Passenger trains consume 17 percent less energy than airplanes and 21 percent less than cars for every passenger mile, according to the Department of Energy. The average inter-city passenger train produces 60 percent less carbon dioxide per passenger mile than a car and 50 percent less than an airplane.

Already, trains are green in comparison to other transportation modes and do not depend on technologies that have yet to be developed. We only need to build more tracks, improve the tracks we have, and run more trains—restoring some of the rail capacity that was abandoned for highways, cars, and planes.

Perhaps this all sounds like wishful thinking, the rant of a rail fan who loves trains and train travel and is nostalgic for the golden days of railroading.

I do like riding trains, but I am not a rail fan. I don't collect old timetables, rusty railroad lanterns, and other memorabilia. I don't take vacations to ride special excursion trains or to see refurbished steam locomotives. I don't chase trains along highways or stand on overpasses snapping photos of passing diesel locomotives. I don't hang around stations and railway yards with a handheld scanner so I can listen to the crew's chatter. I don't put together model trains. The folks who do—mostly men—are true rail fans. In England, they're called "trainspotters"; in the United States, railroaders call them "foamers"—people who metaphorically foam at the mouth when it comes to trains.

On a train in Iowa, I met Tom Landolt, a retired Union Pacific engineer who had been visiting old friends in Nebraska and was on his way home to New Mexico by way of Chicago and New Orleans—a route necessitated by the peculiarity of Amtrak's network.

We ate eggs in the dining car and then lingered over coffee, talking about railroading. He leaned forward, "Would you like to see some pictures?"

I knew what was coming.

He slipped a package of shots from his vest and placed them on the table. I thumbed through shots of freight locomotives, double-stacked intermodals in west Texas, and a head-on picture of Amtrak's Sunset Limited. They were all taken from the cab of his locomotive. I explained that my book was more about transportation than trains.

"You know what a foamer is?" Tom asked.

I nodded.

"Well," he said with a sly grin and a stage whisper. "Some of us are closet foamers."

I directed him to a retired factory worker I had met in my sleeping car who was monitoring the crew chatter on the radio, checking time schedules, and making sketches for his model railroad back home. Later, I saw the two of them in the lounge car huddled over the pictures. As I went around the country and talked to lobbyists and advocacy groups working for increased passenger-train service, they were wary of being identified as rail fans, I learned.

I interviewed Al Runte, who had written a book about the way railroads helped to open the West and establish several national parks. For the first twenty minutes, he leaned back in his chair, arms crossed over his chest, regarding me with suspicion.

At some point, as I was explaining the purpose of the book, I got around to using the word "transportation."

Suddenly, Runte slapped his palms on the table.

"Geez. I am so relieved. For a moment, I thought you were just another goddamn foamer."

Runte is a strong critic of Amtrak and the government's decision to relieve the big railroads of their common-carrier obligation to run passenger service. His solution is to nationalize the freight railroads and/or the infrastructure. Then the public would own the tracks as it currently owns the road system. That's the only way America will get more passenger trains that move large amounts of people on time and efficiently, he said. The incremental approach of running Amtrak on the infrastructure of the freight railroads hasn't worked and won't in the future. Most rail fans, he said, make excuses for Amtrak instead of demanding real change.

"What we have now is a rail-fan approach to transportation, and it's ridiculous. Rail fans say just give us more Amtrak. We'll take anything. Please, please just give me a train. Let me suffer, beat me, bruise me, let the dining car run out of food, let the kitchen catch on fire, I don't care . . . it's a train. I'm happy."

Rail fans reside in what historian John Hankey refers to as "train world," which can be quite different from "real railroad world." Hankey himself had moved in and out of real railroad world: he had alternated between getting a Ph.D. in history and being at the controls of coal trains for the Baltimore and Ohio Railroad. He never quite got the Ph.D., largely because the lure of running big locomotives took time away from school, but eventually he found a niche as a railroad historian and curator.

In Hankey's parlance, real railroading world is the bare-knuckled business of moving goods, coal, grain, and people across the landscape using big equipment that is inherently dangerous—especially when it is handled carelessly by railroaders or not respected by pedestrians and motorists. At the executive level, it's about cutthroat corporate politics, national transportation policy, and hard-assed decision making based on profit.

And then there is train world, a softer place populated by all the folks who have a stake or passion in railroading—the foamers and trainspotters, historians and museum personnel, passenger interest groups and lobbyists, model railroaders, memorabilia collectors, train-magazine staffs, academics and transportation think-tankers, and, yes, even people who sometimes have a foot in both worlds.

I sat down with Jim McClellan, a former director of strategic planning at Norfolk Southern. In the 1970s, he had been one of the architects of Amtrak and Conrail—two interventions by the federal government that saved crucial parts of the railroad network—and he's been involved in many of the big mergers and other railroad-policy battles of the last thirty years. Now retired, he still works as a consultant and gives speeches to investors, executives, shippers, and other real railroaders.

What I also discovered was a man who is an accomplished railroad photographer and an amateur painter—but only of pictures of trains running through American landscapes. He also has built himself a room-sized model railroad layout, and he arranges his travels around the world so he can ride trains.

McClellan and I had a good laugh after we finished several hours of interviews and he dropped me off at my Virginia motel. He leaned out of the car and shook my hand,

"I think you're on to something with this book. When you called, I thought you were just another railroad nut."

Later that week, when Hankey and I were on the MARC train in Maryland, I remarked that McClellan was a full-blown foamer.

"An unapologetic one, too" said Hankey. "That has been a rarity in real railroad world. For a long time, it wasn't OK for executives of big freight railroads to get up and say I love trains. If you were at Ford or General Motors, you were allowed to say I love cars. It was even expected. But to say 'I love trains' was to be nostalgic, and nostalgia was anathema."

When I spoke with Gil Carmichael, formerly the federal railroad administrator under George H. W. Bush and the head of a commission that had tried to "reform" Amtrak in the 1990s, he indicated that there are a fair number of closet foamers among the people who run the big freight lines. "Those freight boys might tell you that they don't like passenger trains, but they just love riding around their systems on those executive trains they own," he said. "If you scratch 'em deep enough, you'll find out that underneath, they're foamers, too."

For many decades—prior to the creation of Amtrak—passenger service was a money-losing proposition for railroads. This legacy makes freight railroads reluctant to say or do anything that might indicate they have any interest in carrying passengers on their infrastructure. Passenger advocates, meanwhile, don't want to be too closely identified with rail fans, who legislators might view as nostalgic dreamers.

I don't use the term "foamer" pejoratively. Early in my research, rail fans taught me a great deal. Whenever I wondered why my train was stopped or late or what type of freight was rolling by, I'd look around the lounge car or the platform and find a rail fan with a radio and notebook. I'd get my answer and a whole lot more. Sometimes my eyes glazed over at the minutiae and nomenclature, but I was grateful for the information.

I'd call myself a train rider, though more than a casual one. I like geography. I like the people I meet on the train and have ridden Amtrak on and off for nearly thirty five years. I also grew up in a railroad family, in Albion, Pennsylvania, in what used to be a railroad town. My father spent forty-some years on the Bessemer and Lake Erie Railroad (B&LE), a short line Andrew Carnegie created to haul iron ore from freighters on Lake Erie to his steel mills in Pittsburgh. On the return trip, the trains brought Appalachian coal to ship out through the Great Lakes.

For nearly a century, while American-made steel was king and the coke ovens and blast furnaces of Homestead and Hazelwood darkened the skies of southwest Pennsylvania, the economics worked in favor of the Bessemer. Trains rumbled through my hometown; the switchyards and car-repair shops employed hundreds of men. The Bessemer, like nearly all railroads in America before 1960, hauled people as well as commodities. Townspeople could board a southbound for Pittsburgh or head north to Erie for a day of shopping and from there make connections to the rest of the country.

By the time I was a boy in the 1960s, however, the passenger depot had long been shuttered. I was raised in a car culture fueled by cheap gas, auto advertising, and heavy government subsidies for new highways. When my parents took us into Erie to shop at the new malls we drove our Chevrolet on Interstate 90, the big highway my parents called "The Super."

The Bessemer's business model began to fail in the late 1970s when foreign steelmakers flooded the market, and the domestic steel mills—some a century old and unable to comply with new pollution standards—closed down. The repair shops, switchyards, and dispatching services in Albion closed, too. The yards that once held 3,000 hopper cars went feral with weeds, rabbits, and woodchucks. The double set of tracks through town was reduced to one. The railroad was sold, and only two trains now come through town each day. None stop.

When I was growing up, though, I'd lie in bed and fall asleep to the sounds of trains being assembled in the yards—the grumbling of switch engines and the thud of cars coupling together and the succession of sounds as that impact rippled down the length of the train.

My father, Herbert, was a clerk in the car department, a pencil pusher who walked two or three miles a day through the yards, writing out the paperwork on the cars and locomotives being repaired. Dad hired onto the Bessemer as a callboy at age sixteen. Back then, he would run through the town to roust engineers and conductors out of bars, knock on the doors of homes and boardinghouses, and shake men awake at the railroad rest house, telling them they were needed to take a train down to Pittsburgh. Many of these men had known his father, Frank, and knew what had happened to him.

On November 6, 1919, my grandfather was working as a brakeman on a huge steam locomotive pulling a string of heavy iron-ore cars up a grade near Lake Erie—a process known as pulling drag. For some reason, the boiler ran low on water and the locomotive exploded, killing my grandfather and everyone else in the crew.

Frank was just thirty-four, my father eight years old and the eldest of four children. The family got a small pension but it wasn't enough and at the beginning of the Depression, Dad quit school and hired on at the railroad, just like nearly all the men in town.

His uncles worked in the car-repair shops until—in my father's vernacular—they "got canned" for going on strike to unionize. My great-grandfather, a Union draftee during the Civil War and a farmer, also ended with a railroad connection. He moved into town and spent his last few years lowering and raising the crossing gates on Main Street.

My dad, having had his fill of the railroad, retired at age sixty-two. He lived to be eighty-nine, long enough to see it disappear from town. None of his children went into railroading. By the 1970s, when we came of age, it was a dying industry everywhere. There appeared to be no future in it.

Real Railroad World
the birth of amtrak

I stepped aboard my first train in 1975 when I was eighteen and rode Amtrak's Lake Shore Limited back and forth between Erie and college in Boston. Later, I bought rail passes, slept in the coaches, and circumnavigated the country by train. I took trains for business, to get home to visit family, to take vacations. Always it was on board Amtrak trains, because those were the only passenger trains that were running.

Few living Americans have set foot on an intercity train—only about 2 percent. And just 3 percent of Americans use light rail and commuter trains to get to and from work—although the percentage is much higher in the Northeast and other select cities that have mass-transit rail. In most places, rail just isn't an option. For most Americans, a train is a lumbering freight that comes into town, halts road traffic for several minutes, and then goes clickety-clack off somewhere else—but who knows where.

The median age of the U.S. population is thirty-seven, so it's not surprising we would have so little experience with railroads, which includes the politicians and government bureaucrats who formulate the nation's transportation policies. A train is just not part of everyday life for most of us.

That wasn't always so.

In 1946, just prior to the great rise in automobile and air travel and the conversion of the railroads from steam to diesel power, about 1.5 million Americans out of a population of 132 million worked for railroads. Everyone had a relative or an acquaintance in the industry. Tens of thousands of trains crisscrossed the country each day. People rode trolleys, interurbans, and streamliners. One gauge of the decline in passenger-rail use is employment. Between 1947 and 1972, the industry lost 40,000 jobs annually; some years losses reached 150,000. There were many reasons: diesels usurped steam locomotives, buses replaced trolley systems, trucks wrested freight from railroads, and people increasingly took to the interstates and airways.

Not until 1990s did the industry stabilize and begin to grow again. Bill Withuhn, curator of Transportation History at the Smithsonian Institution's National Museum of American History, offered this telling anecdote of the popular decline.

The museum acquired a 4-6-2 "Pacific"-type steam locomotive. These heavy engines were used throughout the Carolinas during the 1930s. Painted the distinctive green of the Southern Railway, the locomotive could pull twelve to fifteen steel passenger cars at 80 mph.

Withuhn held a training session with docents so they could talk to visitors about the locomotive. "I'm waxing rhapsodic about this locomotive's power and speed, and this young man raises his hand and asks, 'Mr. Withuhn, why is this locomotive so important to transportation? I mean what's it doing here in the Smithsonian?' And I think for a second and come up with an analogy—a pretty good one I thought—and said, 'Well, think of it as the 747 of its day.' The young man liked that and immediately writes it down, and then raises his hand again and asks, 'But where did all the people sit?'"

Withuhn laughed and slapped his knee, "And that's why there is a model of a passenger train in the exhibit, so kids can look at that model and see that a locomotive pulled passenger cars. And inside the model of each passenger car, we have fifty-two little people."

Out on the rails, passengers discuss all types of topics while traveling, but because they are on a train, conversations often return to railroading and the state of passenger service. You hear a lot of theories: Amtrak is a private railroad; passenger trains are supposed to get out of the way of freight trains; passenger trains would be profitable if just run correctly; Amtrak is always at fault when a train is late, or, conversely, the freights are to blame; Democrats support passenger trains; Republicans hate them; the United States could have trains like Europe and Japan in ten years; and General Motors, Greyhound, and the airline industry, acting in conspiracy, killed the passenger train. Some theories are ridiculous; others contain slivers of truth. A rail fan, if so inclined, could spend all day in the lounge car correcting crackpot notions.

Just what did happen to passenger service in America and how Amtrak ended up the nation's only intercity passenger-rail service isn't a simple story. To begin to understand that, it helps to know something of Amtrak's origins.

Amtrak is a quasi-public–private entity created in 1971 by the federal government to take over passenger operations from railroads in an effort to save the industry from collapse. Passenger trains had been bleeding buckets of money for decades, but the railroads were tightly regulated by the Interstate Commerce Commission. As an industry with common-carrier obligations, railroads were required to run passenger trains. They could not easily abandon routes—even though some trains ran with just a handful of passengers—and had to go through elaborate "train off" proceedings that included public hearings. Some railroads tried to hasten the end by closing stations, running dirty trains, and treating passengers poorly. A few offered subsidies to riders if they would find other transportation.

A group of railroad executives, Department of Transportation bureaucrats, and elected officials sat down to figure out what to do with passenger trains. On one side, passenger-train advocates and some congressional members were intent on keeping, even expanding, passenger service, partly because they saw the Japanese and Europeans moving ahead with fast, so-called bullet trains. The railroads, which were barely holding on by hauling freight, and members of the Nixon administration just wanted passenger trains to fade into the economic sunset, seeing them as obsolete in the age of jet travel and interstate highways.

The decision by Congress and the Nixon administration to create Amtrak came down to compromise, and some odd, unworkable business arrangements became law. In exchange for getting themselves off the hook of carrying passengers, the railroads made cash payments to capitalize Amtrak and turned over some of their passenger equipment. Significantly, the railroads also agreed to play host and allow Amtrak trains to run on their infrastructure for a user's fee. Even today, Amtrak retains these rights, which gives it a huge advantage over private companies that might want to run passenger trains. Railroads aren't required to allow other entities to run on their tracks, but they cannot refuse Amtrak. As part of Amtrak's creation, dozens of trains were cut, and the nation's passenger network reduced by half. Some cities that had service for more than a century suddenly were without trains.

Shed of money-losing passenger trains, the railroad's bottom lines improved, and the savings in costs allowed some companies to survive a few years longer, only to be devoured in the merger mania and restructuring of the industry that took place in 1980s and '90s. Congress gave Amtrak two major, but mutually exclusive mandates—run a nationwide system and create efficiencies that would turn a profit and enable the railroad to wean itself from government subsidies as soon as possible. In other words, Amtrak was supposed to make passenger trains profitable, something the existing railroads had not been able to do. Unrealistic perhaps, but it was that profitability language that convinced the Nixon administration and conservative members of Congress to support the bill. The money Congress appropriated for the new enterprise was insufficient from the start.

Amtrak was an invention, an untested model, really a pipe dream with big contradictions. Its creators knew it was flawed, or were just hopeful it would work. The railroads signed on because they saw Amtrak as a stopgap measure, a way to ease America into a future without passenger trains, and it removed a burden from their balance sheets. They didn't think it would last. Passenger advocates accepted Amtrak because the political alternative at the time seemed to be no trains at all. Politicians went along because the railroads were in such poor financial shape that the only alternative appeared to be nationalization. Ironically, just three years later, the federal government did nationalize several bankrupt freight railroads to create Conrail.

Then came a surprise upturn in Amtrak ridership, sparked by the Arab oil embargo of 1973 and the first run-up in gas prices. Some Americans got out of their gas guzzlers and boarded trains. Airlines had yet to be deregulated and were still rather expensive. A few congressmen found they could curry favor with voters by keeping trains running through their districts, and Amtrak earned some powerful friends in Congress. In 1976, Amtrak was given ownership of the Northeast Corridor, the electrified tracks running from Washington, D.C., to Boston. Now it had its own infrastructure in the busiest passenger corridor in the nation and one capable of running trains at relatively high speeds.

In 1991, the DOT designated eleven high-speed rail corridors of 100 to 600 miles in length, but put forth very little money to make these corridors a reality until Barack Obama made high-speed rail (up to 125 mph) one of his transportation goals and began sending billions into their development in 2009.

Meanwhile, the freight railroads made a comeback. The Staggers Act, signed into law by President Jimmy Carter in 1980, deregulated the railroads and enabled them to set their own rates according to market conditions. Through the 1990s and into the first decade of this century, freight railroads merged, trimmed their infrastructure, lowered costs, and came back strong.

Amtrak, which had the luck to survive its early years, and the attempts of presidents and congressional members to fiscally starve it to death, continued to limp along. For thirty-eight years, it has lurched from one fiscal crisis to another. It has never made a profit and hasn't weaned itself from federal government subsidies, which is no surprise to informed observers of the rail industry. No passenger-rail service in the world makes a profit. However, that statement, too, depends on how profitability is measured. Some trains in Europe and Japan do earn an operating surplus, but government subsidizes the construction and maintenance of the infrastructure, which is publicly owned.

Even now, Amtrak does move millions of people, and some of its trains and services work quite well. On the Northeast Corridor, it has the largest market share of business travelers between New York, Philadelphia, and Washington and has outcompeted the shuttles run by the airlines. The Acela trains offer

Americans a glimpse of the high-speed corridor service now being promoted by the Obama administration.

In many ways, Amtrak is three different railroads: the Northeast Corridor, the long-haul, or overnight, trains, and the corridor trains that are subsidized by states that want intercity passenger trains. One of the best examples of the last is in the Pacific Northwest, where Amtrak operates the Cascades Service between Victoria, British Columbia, and Eugene, Oregon. Lush in European styling and designed to lure business travelers with creature comforts, the Amtrak Cascades trains are unlike any others on Amtrak's system, as I soon found out.

PART 2

Pacific Northwest

North Dakota
across on the hi-line

On a snowy March afternoon in 2008, I drove five hours from northern Michigan to Columbus, a town of 4,500 on the Crawfish River in south-central Wisconsin. By the luck of its location on Canadian Pacific tracks, this little town is served by the Empire Builder, the long-haul train that runs between Chicago and the cities of Portland and Seattle. I booked a roomette—an economy sleeper on the second level of the double-decker Superliner car. After I settled in, the attendant stuck his head in, "You know how all this works?"

I did, but I had been prepared to listen to an orientation of sorts. Instead, he just looked at me expectantly, so I just nodded.

"Good," he said, appearing relieved. "Let me know if you need anything."

No demonstration of the air controls in the room, nothing about the location of the ice bucket, the free juice and coffee, and no explanation of dinner reservations or wine tasting—all the perks of traveling first class. Over the next two days, he was around but not really friendly or helpful. All I can say is, he wasn't the best Amtrak attendant I encountered in my travels—or the worst.

The conductor came by and punched my ticket, noting my first destination—Essex, Montana.

"Staying at the Izaak?" he said.

"For a couple of days, then I'm on to Seattle."

"You a skier or rail fan?"

"Skier mainly."

As we passed the frozen lakes of the Wisconsin Dells, I arranged the essentials—notebooks, radio, binoculars, MP3 player, a novel, and a road atlas. I poured a coffee from the communal urn down the hall and took a *Milwaukee Sentinel* from a stack of newspapers. Now I was on train time. A thousand miles to sit back and relax.

Afternoon turned to evening; darkness fell quickly over the bare woods and snowy fields. At La Crosse, we went over the Mississippi River and headed north on the Minnesota side.

I always take late dinner reservations. Then, if the company is good, I can sip another glass of wine or linger over a coffee, chatting with my tablemates. The staff doesn't need the table, so they don't try to rush you off.

Dining cars practice community seating. No one sits alone, and whom you break bread with is the luck of the draw. This night, the attendant brought over a lumbering, middle-aged man with a cookie-duster mustache. He reached a meaty hand across the table, "Hi, I'm Mort."

Mort Berkowitz's New York accent was unmistakable. He didn't look at the menu, but ordered a glass of red wine and the flat iron steak—rare. The flat iron is the most expensive item on the menu, and since meals are included in the price of a sleeper, those in the know always go for the best. I had a steak, too.

Mort was on a two-week business trip. He had boarded the Lake Shore Limited at Penn Station and was on his way to Seattle for business, and then on to L.A. aboard the Coast Starlight. His wife would fly in for a few days, but Mort was coming back across the country alone on the train. He was a veteran, having crossed the Rockies four times on the California Zephyr and once on a Canadian train.

"I love the train," he said "Here you have the time to kibitz with strangers. I meet people I never would in the city."

Berkowitz has an office on Times Square where he manufactures political buttons. He was going west to meet with vendors and using train time to conjure up new button ideas.

He slipped one across the table with a picture of a grinning Chelsea Clinton saying, "Don't Tell Mamma. I'm voting for Obama." There was one of McCain as Methuselah and a button depicting George W. Bush with the caption "The Flaw in the White Conspiracy Theory." When we exchanged business cards Mort pulled out two—one said "Your Republican Campaign Headquarters" and the other, "Your Democratic Campaign Headquarters."

"I'm really a Democrat, but when it comes to buttons, I'm an equal opportunist. I'll make and sell them to whoever is paying."

We compared notes on Amtrak. He lamented the decline in food service, the substitution of plastic plates for dinner china, the move to eliminate dining cars and observation lounge cars with the new Cross Country Diner, a kind of combination car that doesn't offer much space to sit back and socialize with other passengers.

"Across Amtrak, the level of service is really uneven. It depends on the disposition of the onboard service chief of that train," he explained. "If that person is people-oriented, you have a great experience. But just as often you can end up with a surly Amtrak waiter who isn't very pleasant."

Sleeping car passengers tend to get better treatment but they pay a premium. Depending on the time of year and the route, roomettes can run between $100 and $500 extra. Like airline seats, the fewer left, the higher the price.

I had spent many a night sleeping in the coaches in my adult life and would do so again in the coming months, but not on this chilly winter evening. I returned to my sleeper, put on pajamas, wrapped myself in the blankets, and left the curtains open to the land.

Before dawn, I took my laptop and stagger-stepped my way through the rocking coaches. The passengers resembled a litter of puppies snuggled together for warmth. A mother snored with her little girl against her chest, both their mouths agape. Beneath blankets and winter coats, young women sprawled across their boyfriend's laps, their arms and legs jutting into the aisles.

At mid-coach sat a straight-backed heavy-set fellow in bib overalls. He held no book or magazine, wore no ear phones, had no distraction of any kind. The windows were still black with the night. His palms on his knees, he looked forward in a thousand-yard stare. He seemed to be waiting out this train ride. Maybe he was a farmer or a truck driver whose back hurt, or he was accustomed to his own bed and just wanted to get home. I nodded to him but he looked right through me.

In the empty lounge, I sipped coffee, wrote, and watched the day come on. There was no sun, no red line on the horizon, just a diffuse brightening, as if an artist had used a no. 2 pencil to shade in the sky and differentiate it from the snowy prairie. We were crossing the Red River valley, which is not a valley at all, but the bottom of ancient Lake Agassiz. Ten thousand years ago when ice sheets melted, Agassiz sprawled wider than all the Great Lakes combined. Today, its dry and fertile bed is some of the flattest land anywhere in America, a place where you can experience the curvature of the earth by watching, as you approach a town, the slow rising of grain elevators from the horizon. It was all geometry—the sky hemispheric, visible out both windows. Roads scored into the land, and shelterbelts—each tree lovingly planted—running off to vanishing points. Somewhere out there, I could believe, was the edge of the world.

The lounge eventually filled with passengers buying juice and sweet rolls at the café. I went up to the dining car for a sit-down breakfast. Dining-car stewards bemoan the decline in dress and decorum of passengers. In the heyday of trains, people washed up, shaved, brushed their teeth, did their hair, and put on clean shirts before coming down for a meal. A few still do, but a lot of folks stumble in, still wiping sleep from their eyes. So I wasn't surprised to see a young couple come into breakfast wearing matching flannel pajama bottoms decorated with cupids and love hearts. She carried a baby and her nursing blouse was half unbuttoned. He sported a buzz cut, a sleeveless Semper Fidelis T-shirt, and muscled, tattooed arms.

At breakfast, I sat with Gary and Linda Wagenbach of Northfield, Minnesota, who were on their way to Washington to visit a son. She's a retired college administrator; Gary's a biology professor on sabbatical.

Their family-sized bedroom in the lower level of the sleeping car had windows on both sides, and they'd spent the hour before breakfast watching for birds. From the dining car windows we could see all around us tufts of grass and brush sticking out of frozen prairie potholes, which would be lush with snowmelt in spring. But even now there were birds on these plains, and as the train rushed along they shot from their hiding places like so many BBs from a scattergun.

"Partridge?" asked Linda.

"Hungarian, I think," replied Gary.

We passed vast snow-covered fields whose furrows formed a rippled texture beneath the snow cover. Along fencerows sat piles of rocks and fieldstone, a harvest no doubt of many years of spring plowing.

A thin bespectacled man with white hair and a thick mustache curving down to his upper lip slipped into the seat next to mine. Trygve Olson told us he had boarded the train at Fargo and was going to Idaho.

"Do you know if this is durum wheat country?" Gary asked.

Olsen nodded, "Yes it is. Back in the valley, it was red wheat, but not here. It's drier."

"Are you a farmer?" I ask.

No, an art professor at Minnesota State–Moorhead on spring break. He and his wife planned to get off around 2:00 a.m. when the train stopped at Sandpoint, Idaho, hang around the station for a couple of hours, and then catch the eastbound back home. Last year, Olson rode the train to the Mississippi Delta and stayed just a day before returning.

"Trains are a way for me to refocus. I like to zone out on the landscape," he said.

Gary observed that train trips induce a type of resting wakefulness. "It's like camping in the woods," he added. "There's not a lot to do and that's the whole point. Meals are a big event. You spend most of the time looking out the window. It's hypnotic."

Olson draws editorial cartoons for the *Fargo Forum*, and was well versed on North Dakota politics and economics. Over omelets and railroad toast (French toast, actually), we talked about the oil boom in the Badlands, which was being overrun with drilling rigs and transient roughnecks. The previous fall some North Dakota farmers ran low on diesel fuel and couldn't bring in all their grain, so the state was planning to build a refinery near Bismarck to process its own crude. In this land of populism, grange halls, and farmer cooperatives, where there is suspicion of big business, Wall Street, and the Chicago Board of Trade, it was not a surprising move. North Dakota still operates its own bank, the only state-owned depository in the nation.

It was out here on the Plains and on the farmsteads of the Midwest that a populist backlash against American railroads took hold more than a century ago. In the closing decades of the nineteenth century—what Mark Twain dubbed "the Gilded Age" of robber barons and banking magnates—the railroad industry was the most powerful force in the country, more formidable than government, which set no rules for business behavior during this period of laissez-faire capitalism. Railroads and financiers acted badly because there was no one to stop them.

Organized on a military model and based on martial discipline, nineteenth-century railroad companies took no prisoners. Many of the top officers had come out of the Civil War and were expert in moving goods long distances and controlling large groups of men. They put together sprawling, sophisticated business organizations not yet seen anywhere else in the world.

In prior years, American businesses had largely been capitalized by wealthy individuals and families, but railroads needed enormous resources for land, infrastructure, labor, and equipment. When they couldn't raise it ethically, railroads floated worthless stock, promoted agriculture in western lands unsuitable for farming, corrupted politicians and institutions, and bypassed towns unwilling to pay bribes or buy stock. They took land for railbeds, and, when there was no competition, charged outrageous prices to haul goods. Among farmers who had no other way to get their crops to market, the railroads made few friends.

The animosity came to a head in the financial panic of 1873 that politicized the National Grange of the Patrons of Husbandry, which had been founded years earlier as a sort of agrarian Masonic Order. Its purpose was to spread scientific practices to farmers and provide them with an intellectual and social life. Grangers generally had eschewed politics and religion, though they promoted co-ops and other mild forms of socialism.

Grangers wanted cheaper transportation to markets, and when they saw that government was controlled by the big railroads, they began running their own candidates for office. By 1875, the number of grange halls in America had soared from 3,000 to 21,000. When the grange-backed politicians gained control of several state legislatures—Michigan, Illinois, and Minnesota—they began passing "granger laws" to regulate the shipping rates that railroads could charge farmers and established state railroad commissions to act as watchdogs.

Railroads fought back in courts. Though there were conflicting court decisions and precedents set throughout the latter decades of the nineteenth century, the Supreme Court generally upheld as constitutional the right of government to regulate private businesses that serve the public interest.

A railroad wasn't just a business; it was a business that had a public responsibility. Railroads functioned as natural, or technical, monopolies, meaning it was difficult, even impossible, for them to compete against one another by lowering prices. Rarely could a railroad afford to build and maintain an infrastructure parallel to a competitor. One railroad tended to win out in a region, and when competition was removed, the survivor became monopolistic and set prices accordingly. And because they ran goods and people across state lines and were critical to the country's well-being—they were the only real national transportation network for decades—they could not be allowed to operate unfettered.

Although the grange movement led to government regulation of railroads and to the establishment of the Interstate Commerce Commission, the ICC didn't get its teeth until the Progressive Era and the presidency of Theodore Roosevelt. Eventually, government came to control railroads to an astonishing degree, and by the mid-twentieth century, their regulations, coupled with broad government antipathy to the railroads, would nearly crush the industry and contribute to the demise of passenger service.

As we rolled west, past Rugby, North Dakota—proclaiming itself as the geographical center of North America—the land got higher and drier. Fields morphed into rangeland that sprouted cattle rather than crops. What had been a gray day turned brilliantly blue. I sat in the sightseer lounge car with its big windows and watched the shortgrass prairie—snowless and brown—reel by in a mesmerizing monotony. Sometimes, the train paralleled U.S. Route 2—the east-west motor route across the state's northern tier—but mostly the train veered off into a landscape absent cars, billboards, and towns. Out there, the eye locked onto small details—two deer bounding from a copse of trees, derricks puncturing an oil patch near Stanley, and curtains fluttering from the broken windows of an abandoned homestead.

We passed intermodal trains racing east, their shipping containers stacked two high. As a result of the nation's trade deficit, a lot of these containers return to Asia empty or are filled with recyclables. We buy their stuff and send them our garbage.

The train pushed west, past Havre, Glasgow, and then to Shelby, all fifty miles or so from Canadian border, thus this rail route carries the moniker the Hi-Line. All the Dakota cold was now behind us, replaced by strange, Chinook-like warmth flowing down from the Continental Divide. Most of the passengers joined the smokers on the platform at Shelby and reveled in the sunshine and mild air.

A pack of semi-inebriated grandmothers exited a coach at Shelby and crossed the street to the Oasis Bar and Casino, a weathered, wind-blasted establishment displaying a big "Welcome Amtrak" sign. It looked like a shitkicker of a place with four-wheel-drive pickups in the parking lot and rangy ranch dogs pacing back and forth in the truck beds. One grandmother—who actually wore a shirt saying grandma—stood as lookout, listening for the "all aboard" shout. Her companions crowded the bar, threw back shots, and stuffed bottles of beer in their purses. Only first-class passengers are allowed to bring liquor aboard.

Back on the train, with the Rockies rising up on the horizon, the first-class passengers filled the dining car for a wine tasting—cheese and crackers and glasses of two reds and two whites from Oregon and Washington vineyards. I sat with Mort and a rail fan I met back in Shelby. He lived in Seattle and was headed home after visiting Civil War battlefields in Virginia.

Mort cocked his thumb at the dining-car steward, who was reading aloud from the back of a bottle before pouring out samples.

"Are you listening to this guy?"

The steward, no wine connoisseur and apparently farsighted, too, held the bottle up at eye level and squinted hard. He stumbled so badly over the lingo on the labels that Mort finally waved impatiently for the bottle and took over the presentation.

Afterward he confided, "When the guy pronounced Sauvignon 'sav-in-jon,' I couldn't take it anymore."

The last time I saw Mort he was in the hallway outside the roomette of Trygve Olson, the art teacher and political cartoonist. They were passing buttons back and forth, giggling.

Essex, Montana
at the izaak walton inn

After Cut Bank, the mountains closed in and cut off the sun. I packed my gear as the train climbed through the black forests to the Continental Divide at Marais Pass. At 5,213 feet above sea level, Marais is the lowest railroad pass through the Rockies, and its existence enabled the Great Northern Railway to open up the country's northern tier—from the Iron Range in Minnesota to the fruit growing valleys of Washington—to settlement and development.

James Jerome Hill, a one-eyed tycoon from St. Paul who was nicknamed the Empire Builder, assembled the Great Northern in 1889 from several smaller roads and used those to construct the Hi-Line route across the continent. The railroad promoted the establishment of Glacier National Park and underwrote the construction of massive resort hotels. It chose a Rocky Mountain goat as its symbol and, during the height of passenger service ran a luxurious streamliner train, the Empire Builder, named after Hill.

The little hamlet of Essex is a flag stop; there's no station. Unless someone gets on or off, the train doesn't stop. I detrained ("detrain" is a great railroad term) with Ron and Ila Erickson of Bethel, Minnesota. The warmth of lower elevations was gone; we were back in winter. The snow banks stood head high and big flakes floated down. The Izaak Walton, a three-story wooden structure, glowed warmly beneath the black, scalloped shapes of the mountains.

As a chauffeur loaded our bags into a shuttle van, we watched the Amtrak pull away.

"Those lights on the side," Ron said. "They'll change when the train is about to go forward. See . . . the conductor is radioing the engineer, and now the lights change."

The train crept forward, and a line of faces peered down at us from the coaches.

"You a rail fan?"

"Engineer," he said. "Retired."

Early in his career, Erickson had worked in Whitefish, Montana, and crossed the Continental Divide more than forty times behind the controls of a locomotive. In retirement, he operates the Hustle Muscle, a vintage diesel engine for the Great Northern Railway Historical Society back in St. Paul.

As we rode over to the inn, Ron told me he testifies as an expert witness on derailments and other railroad accidents. I told him about my grandfather and the boiler explosion.

He sucked in his breath. "My God, when one of those explosions happened, they were just huge. Those engines ran at extremely high pressure."

Inside the inn, it was easy to see why rail fans love the place. Bedspreads, lamps, iron railings, stained-glass windows, and napkin holders all bore the Great Northern's image of Rocky, the mountain goat. A length of welded rail serves as the foot rest in the bar. Old diner menus, yellowed route maps, rusty lanterns and oil cans, advertising posters from the 1950s, and black-and-white photographs of derailments and monumental snowstorms line the walls of the hallways. Near the hotel, four cabooses have been converted into cabins.

I had taken a trackside room, which was comfortable but utilitarian—after all, these were crew quarters for railroad men. Even today, there are no phones or televisions. Cell phones don't work either. The Izaak is all about unplugging. You ski, watch trains, read rail-fan magazines in the lobby in front of a fire, or eat in the restaurant. There's really nowhere else to go.

I had skied at the inn years ago, and remembered shouldering skis and threading our way in front of idling locomotives and around standing cars to reach the trails on the far side of the tracks. It was a dangerous arrangement, which the BNSF and state of Montana rectified by building a steel pedestrian bridge.

The bridge is the catbird's seat for rail fans. Small openings had been cut along the bridge's wire mesh sides for fans to poke out a camera and telephoto lens. The next morning I went out there to see the arrival of the eastbound Empire Builder. A big, bearded fellow puffing on a pipe was already pacing on the bridge. When he saw me, he staked out one of the openings, which offered the best angle to shoot the train and the inn.

The train came in quick, announcing its arrival with a whistle.

The Empire Builder was pulled by GE Genesis Locomotives, built for the long-haul passenger market. The Genesis styling—a sheath of rectangular sheet metal that looks somewhat aerodynamic—was at first disconcerting for some rail fans who longed for the traditional snub nosed look of a diesel-electric locomotive.

Amtrak trains often run with two locomotives, but it's not because the train needs that much motive power—the railroad terminology for locomotives—to pull the loads. The additional engine is more for protection in case one or the other fails on a long trip. It also helps generate the electricity required to run the onboard systems—air-conditioning and heat, light, refrigeration and micro-wave ovens, toilets and showers, and outlets to power all those DVD players, cell phones, and computers that passengers bring along.

Diesel locomotives do not have mechanical or hydraulic transmissions like diesel-powered cars and trucks; the massive diesel engine turns a powerful alternator to supply high current to electric motors mounted on the axles. The world's fastest trains—including Amtrak's Acela—get their power from overhead wires, eliminating the need to carry fuel or heavy generators. But long-distance lines lack the overhead wires to accommodate that kind of electric service.

Diesels were first introduced in the 1920s by the American Locomotive Division (ALCO) and its partner, General Electric. But it was production and marketing aplomb by General Motors that made diesel engines part of the American scene and led directly to the demise of steam power.

In 1930, General Motors purchased Electro-Motive Corporation, a manufacturer of gas-electric cars, and began building diesel engines to pull lightweight stainless-steel car bodies made by the Budd Company in Philadelphia. Their most famous early creation was Burlington's Pioneer Zephyr, which in 1934 ran the 1,015 miles from Chicago to Denver in just thirteen hours, five minutes, averaging 77.6 mph and topping out at 112. People turned out by the thousands to watch it fly by their towns; radio networks tracked its progress live. Railroads embraced the technology, and fast, diesel-electric trains appeared on several routes. It was the beginning of the streamliner era.

World War II interrupted everything as GM retooled to make tanks, airplanes, and other armaments. Railroads concentrated on moving millions of soldiers and huge amounts of raw materials and arms across the country, which they accomplished with steam power. At war's end, there were still 40,000 steamers in existence and hundreds of thousands of people in the nation—pipe fitters, boilermakers, and shop mechanics—employed in their operation and maintenance.

But the railroads were worn down by the war service, their equipment and physical plants in need of investment and replacement. Diesel offered them the opportunity for a huge leap forward when they came to retool.

First, diesels were all-purpose, more fuel-efficient machines that could be run as units. If you needed more power, no need for a bigger locomotive, simply add a unit. Maintenance costs were reduced. Diesels were built of components that could be swapped out in the shop. No need to have a small army of boilermakers and pipe fitters to fashion and custom-fit parts. Steam engines required fuel every 100 miles, water every 50 miles. Diesels didn't. Diesel locomotives had a lower center of gravity and thus could handle curves better. They provided high torque for pulling uphill and high horsepower under several ranges of speeds. They could pull longer trains, and longer trains meant fewer crews and reduced labor costs. And there was dynamic braking. Using the same principle of "regenerative braking" now common in hybrid and electric automobiles, the engineer could switch the motors on the locomotive's axles into generators and convert the force of a moving train into electricity.

As well, an engineer could reduce the electricity going to the traction motors and slow the train—an essentially frictionless braking system that reduced parts wear. Dynamic braking had been available on electrified tracks before but never on the open road. It was a great safety feature, especially in places like the Rocky Mountains.

The major steam manufacturers—the Baldwin Locomotive Works in Pennsylvania and the Lima Works in Ohio—improved their trains to compete with the new diesels and sheathed them in art deco coverings to make them look more modern. Some steam-powered passenger trains—such as the Hiawatha of the Milwaukee Road—sped along at 100 mph.

But it was to no avail. GM purchased the Winton Engine Company, which built gasoline and diesel engines, and in 1941 merged it into Electro-Motive to create the Electro-Motive Division (EMD) of General Motors. GM produced and marketed its new machines with the competitive strategies and economies of scale it brought to the automobile industry. While manufacturers of steam locomotives had produced customized machines for each railroad and allowed railroads a hand in the design, GM mass-produced its engines and didn't offer many options beyond the paint job—which in itself was a remarkable idea. Railroads shifted away from the flat black and gray of the steamers and experimented with color and designs that identified their brands.

GM also used its muscle and its ability to extend easy credit terms to convince railroads that had electrified their infrastructures and were already running powerful electric locomotives, to tear down their overhead electrical wires and run diesels, instead. Later, this made those railroads less able to compete efficiently against trucks and automobiles by limiting their ability to run high-speed trains. At the time, it seemed like a good economic decision because diesels were a cheaper alternative to building or maintaining an electrical infrastructure. The same rationalization held true for electric trolleys. Many cities turned to buses rather than replacing older trolley systems and lines.

While other countries kept or added to their electrified infrastructure networks, America dieselized. There are few electrified lines in America today.

GM went after the end customer, too, by running image-building ads in consumer magazines. Under the slogan "Better Trains Follow General Motors Locomotives," the ads touted the absence of smoke and steam to obscure the passenger's view, and smoother acceleration and braking at stations that didn't jerk passengers around. Steamers were just old news, and passengers wanted modern trains. Millions of soldiers and citizens had come out of the war with bad memories of riding crowded, worn-out trains.

The changeover to diesel-electrics was stunningly swift. The last steamer was made in 1949. By 1960, steam engines were all but gone. Nearly 500,000 railroaders lost their jobs because water and fueling stations and steam-engine repair shops were no longer needed. The Lima Works and Baldwin Locomotive Works, manufacturers nearly a century old, did not survive the transition. General Electric and GM came to dominate the diesel industry. Later GM spun off EMD as an independent company.

The future may be bright, especially for GE, which has now surged far ahead of EMD in units produced. Diesel-electrics in the future will incorporate hybrid technology, biodiesel fuels, and regenerative braking to capture energy and recharge batteries.

But it is the electrified grid, now only installed on the Northeast Corridor, that offers the ultimate power option for running really fast trains. As more freight and passenger trains are needed in America, experts predict a return to electrification in high-traffic corridors. And if that electricity is generated by a cleaner technology rather than a coal-fired power plant, environmental benefits will accrue.

Back at the inn, I rented a pair of skis and spent the afternoon on groomed forest trails. It was mostly quiet in the woods except for the periodic sound of diesels powering up on the track or whistles echoing back and forth between the valley walls. When I came back across the pedestrian bridge, I found Ron Erickson, leaning on a railing, looking down at two idling BNSF locomotives. A mile-long string of low-slung well cars, designed to hold two shipping containers one atop the other, trailed behind. Out of sight, a pusher engine positioned itself at the rear of the train. The locomotives in front were powerful enough to pull the cars over the pass, but on the uphill climb, the combined weight of the cars would put too much stress on the couplings and the train could pull apart, Erickson explained. Better to push it over than pull.

"It can be a dicey bit of coordination; the crews need to talk to each other," he said.

I glanced over at the hotel. Pacing along the tracks, puffing his pipe, was the rail fan I'd seen earlier. He had a scanner in his hand, listening to the crew chatter. Minutes later, the diesels gave out a throaty roar and the train began to move between the mountains.

The Cascades
locomotive problems

I boarded the westbound Empire Builder at 10:00 p.m. the following evening to continue my journey, relieved to find two empty seats where I could stretch out.

The train descended the western slope of the Rockies and reached the Flathead Valley at Columbia Falls, Montana, where veneer and particle-board plants pumped out huge billowing clouds of steam and humidity. The attendant came down the aisle handing out pillows. I was sandwiched between members of an extended family traveling from North Dakota to a funeral in Tacoma. The woman to my back, the daughter of the deceased, taught kindergarten and reeked of perfume. Well dressed for a train ride—especially in the coaches—she stuck out in a silky black pantsuit, bright lipstick and painted nails, armfuls of bracelets, and matching hoop earrings.

An elderly aunt and uncle, the dead woman's brother, sat to my front. Across the aisle were some cousins. The funeral was the day after tomorrow; the obit that ran in that day's *Tacoma News Tribune* had contained several mistakes. I heard all this as she yapped on her cell for forty-five minutes to the relatives gathered at her brother's house in Tacoma.

The uncle couldn't sleep, and walked up to the lounge. Before he left, the kindergarten teacher, a veteran traveler of this route, counseled him in a tone honed on five-year-olds, "Now don't you go to sleep anywhere but in this car tonight. The train splits in the middle of the night and part of it goes to Portland. You don't want to end up in another state."

We all slept across the Idaho panhandle. In Spokane, at 2:00 a.m., the train was indeed broken in two, some cars bound for Portland, others for Seattle. I felt a bump as the locomotive uncoupled and the head-end power (HEP) shut down. The air system went silent. Ten minutes later, another locomotive bumped us and coupled, but the HEP didn't surge back on. The conductor and assistant came through our car several times, radios crackling. Something was wrong.

We had neither electricity nor heat, and the winter chill seeped into the car. The Portland train was long gone. I checked my watch, 3:35 a.m. A long time later, another locomotive bumped into the cars, and the heat and air returned.

The Spokane passengers, who had waited all this time in the station, finally boarded and filled most of the empty seats, but thankfully, no one joined me.

The next time I awoke, we were out in the country, on a siding, waiting while a train loaded with freshly cut Douglas fir 2 × 4s and 2 × 8s ambled by a few feet away. The land beyond was mostly treeless and bare, sliced open by dry washes and pocked with sagebrush.

We were in the scablands near the Grand Coulee Dam. Around fifteen thousand years ago, floodwaters several hundred feet high and moving at 50 mph swept over eastern Washington when an ice dam in the Rockies broke, releasing Lake Missoula, which was swollen with glacial meltwater. It may have happened more than once. Those floods scoured the land, peeled off layers of rock, cut wide channels, and dropped enormous boulders onto the barren plains. The consequence is a spare, even spooky-looking landscape with enough soil to grow a bit of grass and sagebrush, but the area didn't prosper until water stored by the Grand Coulee Dam enabled ranchers to irrigate.

The dining car was empty, and I ate breakfast alone, watching out the windows as the train entered the Trinidad Loop, a horseshoe curve that—depending on your direction of travel—either descends to, or ascends from, the Columbia River valley. Either way, it's a spectacular piece of railroad engineering and a rare opportunity to see the locomotive and the rear cars of the train simultaneously. Trains typically do not climb grades greater than 2 or 3 percent, so the only way to gain elevation in a short distance is a loop or a horseshoe curve.

As we nosed into Wenatchee, called the apple capital of the United States, the train passed sprawling orchards of carefully pruned trees, their trunks and some branches propped up with wooden bracing to support the coming season's bounty. Empty apple bins as large as pickup trucks surrounded the Bluebird Packing Plant.

Wenatchee was a twenty-minute smoke stop. The folks in my car's lower level, devoted to seating for people with disabilities, limped or rolled their wheelchairs onto the platform and lit up. Sorry to say, they were a tough-looking bunch, with swollen limbs, braced knees, and cheeks and noses exploded with veins. The cook from the dining car stepped out of the kitchen and shook a cigarette from his pack. From the street, a young man rode his bike onto the platform and said to the cook.

"You guys running late?"

"Yeah, locomotive problems. We had to put on another engine. It was pointed the wrong way in Spokane, so it took time to get it around some freights."

The bicyclist said, "I was on this train on February 13 when it killed somebody. It was the second day in a row that happened."

The cook flicked an ash and shrugged.

"Man, it's a terrible thing," the bicyclist said. "What's wrong with people?"

It's an awful truth that trains run over people and cars with some frequency. In 2008, 286 people died at grade crossings when a train hit their vehicle. In a train-auto collision, the motorist is at fault more than 90 percent of the time and is twenty times more likely to die when hit by a train than another car. Another 483 people die annually in trespass incidents away from grade crossings. The average trespasser is a thirty-eight-year-old white male under the influence of alcohol and/or drugs. The fact is people do foolish things around railroad tracks.

A few weeks after this trip, the Empire Builder hit a seventeen-year-old girl walking on the tracks while talking on her cell phone. A man in California never heard the train because he was plugged into his iPod. Motorists and pedestrians try to beat approaching trains to crossings by gunning their cars or breaking into a run. They go around gates, ignore flashing lights, or blow through unguarded crossings. In July 2009, five teenagers in Michigan were killed by the Wolverine, an Amtrak train, when the driver went around a stopped car and lowered crossing gate and entered the right of way. Sometimes, people get drunk or stoned and pass out on the tracks. Some scofflaws park vehicles on crossings, hoping to collect insurance money. And then there are the suicides.

Any engineer with a long career probably has the unfortunate experience of running over some object or some person. There are about 139,000 highway-rail grade crossings in America. Tens of thousands do not have gates; they are guarded only by black-and-white signs and the blast of a whistle from an approaching train. In many instances, the tracks were there long before the roads. The highway departments chose the cheaper option to cross the tracks at grade rather than building an over- or underpass.

The number of fatalities of motorists has dropped since the railroads and the Federal Railroad Administration started Operation Lifesaver, a program to improve warning devices at grade crossings and better educate people to the dangers. In 1981, there were nearly 10,000 collisions and 728 fatalities. In my hometown where there were three main crossings, a railroad safety officer came to our school each year and showed us frightening films to drive the point home—you do not mess with trains.

While crossing deaths are down to about 300 per year, the number of trespass deaths (500 annually) has remained about the same for decades. Because most right-of-ways are unfenced, railroads wage an unending battle to keep people off the tracks. No Trespassing signs and chained access roads don't prevent illegal incursions or dumping—a problem I was reminded of as we left Wenatchee.

Ravines and ditches along the tracks and river were littered with broken drywall and old asphalt shingles, bags of leaves, tires, auto parts, washing machines, and plastic toys. Americans wouldn't tolerate this amount of trash along the highway, but railroad tracks are considered inherently bad neighborhoods, backing up to scrapyards, recycling centers, factories, and warehouses. Homes and lots next to the tracks aren't the choicest residential real estate either, so prices are lower, and as a result the poor often concentrate there.

As we climbed into the Cascades and the Wenatchee National Forest, signs of human civilization disappeared. In the mountains it was slow going and took nearly four hours to reach Everett, 178 miles away on Puget Sound. The train sliced into a deepening snowpack that rose prodigiously on both sides of the tracks, and we saw evidence of snowslides, places where stands of trees had halted the advance and the avalanche's debris piled up in humps like viscous soft ice cream.

We were approaching Stevens Pass and the Cascade Tunnel, at 7.8 miles the longest tunnel in the United States and a storied and tragic location in railroad history.

In the 1890s, thousands of Great Northern workers built a series of eight treacherous switchbacks to enable trains to get over the divide, but avalanches so often blocked the tracks that the railroad bored a tunnel in 1900. Two miles long, the tunnel was problematic from the start. There was no ventilation, so the fumes and smoke from the steam engines built up inside and sickened the train crews. Furthermore, the tunnel was located high on the mountain so the avalanche danger remained.

In February 1910 a series of storms and poor judgment led to the Wellington train disaster, which killed ninety-six people and remains the worst avalanche disaster in American history.

A Seattle-bound passenger train and a mail train passed through the tunnel and then stalled out in a blizzard in the tiny town of Wellington, just outside the tunnel's west portal. Snow fell for a week; eleven feet in just one day. Drifts along the tracks towered one hundred feet. Passengers and railroad workers, who were forced to sleep on the trains, sensed danger. They asked to be moved back into the tunnel for protection but the local railroad superintendent refused.

Finally the cold weather broke, only to be replaced by a thunder and lightning storm and warm winds rushing down the valley. At 1:00 a.m. on March 1, a snow shelf broke loose, and a wall of snow, soil, and trees engulfed the trains, pushing them a thousand feet into Tye Creek and burying them under forty feet of debris. The power of the avalanche was enhanced by the bare slopes of the mountains, which had been denuded by logging and forest fires sparked by passing steam engines. Afterward, the Great Northern built concrete snowsheds to protect the trains, but the ultimate solution was another tunnel further down the mountain.

In 1929, the railroad opened the Cascade Tunnel and switched to electric locomotives to avoid the fumes problem. When diesels arrived in the 1950s, electrification ended, and the railroad installed exhaust fans. Even today, it's no small matter to pass through the tunnel. There's just one track and the tunnel has to be aired out for twenty to thirty minutes before the next train enters.

When we exited the west portal, we passed an idling BNSF intermodal awaiting its turn, and for the next hour, we ran downslope between the mountains toward Everett. There, the train turned south and ran along Puget Sound for twenty miles on a narrow ledge of land wedged between bluff and shore. What a view, better than from the highway above. Railroads, of course, established their right-of-ways long before paved roads and always took the path of least resistance, so builders tended to hug river courses and shorelines.

Seattle
the "n" word: nationalization

In *Allies of the Earth: Railroads and the Soul of Preservation* the historian Al Runte wrote that railroads, unlike highways, generally respected landscape, following the contours of the land, creating smaller footprints, and, as a result, offering travelers more intimacy with nature and place. Highways, on the other hand, can mount grades of 10 percent, so their builders frequently plowed or blasted through obstacles rather than going around them.

After I detrained at Seattle's King Street Station, I met Runte at a hotel restaurant for lunch. A big blunt man who has dabbled in politics, coming in second after spearheading a populist campaign for mayor of Seattle in 2004, Runte was once a professor of environmental history at the University of Washington. He was denied tenure and sued the university, so he doesn't have warm feelings toward academics. "So you're going to write a book about trains, about the romance of trains. Maybe get people interested in taking one and then they are going to have this crappy experience on Amtrak and they'll think, 'well, what a jerk you are.'"

Runte is an unrelenting critic of Amtrak and believes the funding and governance structures set up in 1971 are flawed—even a fraud. Shared use of the infrastructure by freights and passenger trains, he said, is unworkable because the freight railroads have no incentive to promote Amtrak's success. The freights and Amtrak have been making excuses for one another for thirty-plus years, and he doesn't see it getting any better.

"Amtrak is a creature of the railroads. You can't understand its management, corporate structure, its culture, until you understand that it was set up to be mediocre," said Runte. "It was a mediocre enterprise to begin with, and it's been a self-fulfilling prophecy. It's never even reached the low standards it has set for itself."

When I told him about our delay in Spokane, the three hours it took to get a new locomotive, he threw up his hands. "That's typical—for America anyway," he remarked. "In Europe, it's unlikely a bad locomotive would have been hooked up at all, and it would have changed out in minutes, not hours."

Although Amtrak will get significantly more funding in the coming years, Runte isn't optimistic its performance will commensurately improve. Amtrak will buy a few hundred more cars and locomotives, he predicts, maybe put on some additional trains—especially in regions and states where congressional supporters live and where states are kicking in subsidies. Congress will legislate better performance standards for Amtrak and the freight railroads, but those will fail to be met, he said. There won't be an efficient national system that resembles what is in place in Europe or Japan as long as the freight railroads are still in charge of the infrastructure and the dispatching, determining whether freight or people get priority, Runte believes.

"Until my train has at least equal status with a freight train, passenger rail in this country is not going to work."

Then he leaned forward and tapped his finger on the table.

"So, I'm ready to say the 'N' word."

He paused to give weight to what he was about to say.

"Nationalize the bastards and get it over with because that is what it's going to take," he said. "This incremental approach is a load of crap because it doesn't get around the basic problem—the railroads don't want passenger trains. It's how we got Amtrak in the first place."

I would hear the "N" word a number of times in my travels, but never with the same conviction. Some people suggested nationalizing the dispatching, creating a system akin to air-traffic control. Other folks suggested a takeover of the infrastructure. The public would own and maintain all of the rails—as we do the interstate highway system—and charge the railroads to run on them.

My conversation with Runte occurred months before the Bush and Obama administrations took huge chunks of ownership in the banking, mortgage, and auto industries and before Congress poured billions into bailouts, so what I said next should be placed in that context. Nationalization, I countered, sounded impossible in a political and cultural climate that seemed to believe government can't do anything right and certainly not better than private enterprise.

Runte didn't want to hear it.

"You know that's an argument you hear all the time from corporations and politicians. But government can do things well—or at least as well as corporations—and it will do things that corporations won't even go near," he said.

Transportation is a public good. Government built the highway system, constructed airports, and provides security and air-traffic control. In the nineteenth century, government gave away millions of acres of land to the railroads and provided low-interest loans and grants to encourage the laying of track. Although railroads may like to think of themselves as private businesses that are not beholden to the public, said Runte, they are like utilities, and they control transportation corridors that are absolutely vital to the nation.

There is also precedent for railroad nationalization in our history, he went on. Railroads were nationalized during World War I. Again, in the 1970s, government stepped in, restructured bankrupt railroads, created Conrail, turned it into a profitable enterprise, and reprivatized it to Norfolk Southern and CSX. And government created Amtrak.

So it isn't out of the question to imagine a railroad government owned and operated, said Runte. If money and profit are the only motivations for a railroad, goods will always win out over people, however. The fact America doesn't have a decent passenger-rail system is emblematic of a cultural meltdown, he said.

At this point, he was nearly shouting, passionate and outraged.

The waitress came over, "Are you guys doing all right?"

"More coffee please," I said.

Runte continued in a softer voice, "If we turn health care, transportation, national parks, and education into profit centers, we don't have a country any more, we just have a business. Culture needs things that are outside the economic model. So do we defend these things—like the right to transportation—or do we go down together?"

That night I took a long walk along the rainy streets ruminating about what Runte had said. Why hasn't the country been willing to invest in a rail system when it has spent hundreds of billions on superhighways, airports, and waterways? In its nearly forty years of existence, Amtrak has gotten about $30 billion and only grudgingly from administrations—both Republican and Democrat. It's not considered money invested, but money squandered. I ended up at Seattle's Public Market, where I ate salmon in a restaurant overlooking Puget Sound. Out on the water, two container ships lay at anchor, their decks stacked with hundreds and hundreds of shipping containers. In few other places is America's globalized economy more on display. The port of Seattle is the fifth largest in the country. At the shipping terminal, gantry cranes zipped back and forth, working under bright spotlights. In the railroad yards, thousands of FFE (forty-foot equivalent units) and TEU (twenty-foot equivalent units) containers were piled up like stacks of Lego blocks. These rectangular steel boxes, first used about fifty years ago, revolutionized the transportation of freight by standardizing the size and shape of the container, enabling it to be moved seamlessly from boat and barge to rail or truck. Workers and truckers call them tin cans, and they have been the salvation of railroads and the lifeblood of Wal-Mart and other big box stores.

Amtrak Cascades
it's all about frequency

On my way to the train station the next day, the taxi driver held up that morning's *Seattle Times*. "You see this? What's with these people?" he asked.

A headline screamed, "Suspicious Fires Destroy 3 'A Street of Dreams' Homes." The accompanying photo showed a burning trophy home in the foothills of the Cascades.

Developers had advertised these so-called McMansions—as big as 10,000 square feet—as green and environmentally sensitive. The arsonists disagreed. Theirs was a fringe and criminal response to the urban sprawl creeping out from the metroplex, but it reflects the intensity of the issue. King County has smart-growth policies and promotes denser development but has not been able to halt new roads and sprawling neighborhoods designed around the automobile. Its light-rail system, Sound Transit, and Sounder commuter trains have grown significantly in recent years, and voters in November 2008 approved a big expansion. Still, planners predict a 30 percent increase in highway traffic by 2030.

After I bought my ticket for the 7:45 a.m. Amtrak Cascades train south from Seattle, I sat on a plastic chair because all the railroad benches were taken. King Street Station had deteriorated to a dingy cavern because its owner, BNSF, really had no use for a passenger station. The railroad mounted microwave dishes on the landmark 242-foot clock towers. It chopped up the station with sheet rock and false walls and put a faux ceiling over the original ornate ceiling. Cracks and imbedded dirt marred the ceramic mosaic floor. Just days after my visit, however, Seattle purchased the station and announced a $30 million restoration.

If King Street was dingy, the Cascades train was opulent, or at least civilized, in ways other American passenger trains are not. Manufactured in Spain by the Talgo Company, the cars have movies, business–class seats, regional dinner menus, and a bistro offering gourmet coffee, newspapers, and freshly cooked oatmeal. Pastel color schemes, wide seats, and a walk space between cars add to the comfortable ambience. A screen in each car displays the train's exact location as fixed by GPS and gives an estimated time of arrival. On the outside, the train wears a bold color scheme of forest green and cappuccino hues on a cream background.

The Talgo makes a statement when it pulls into a station, and it's no accident that this modern, European-styled train was chosen for corridor service. Washington wanted to capture business travelers and lure in folks unaccustomed to trains.

My train fairly flew out of downtown, running on new welded rail attached to concrete ties. We passed the stacked containers at the shipping terminal, and then minutes later ran by Boeing Field where big cargo jets awaited takeoff. Mount Rainier wasn't far away, but obscured behind a wall of clouds and misty rain.

After we passed beneath the Narrows Bridge in Tacoma, we entered a single-track tunnel and a series of sharp curves along the shoreline, an area known as Port Defiance. The car leaned—or more accurately, tilted—into the turn. Tilt technology enables the Talgo to negotiate curves at a faster speed—much like a motorcyclist leaning into a turn. The Acela trains on the Northeast Corridor also tilt.

The Talgos are capable of running more than 100 mph, but never reach that velocity because of infrastructure problems in places like Port Defiance. The state is spending nearly $60 million to bypass Port Defiance and reroute passenger trains to a straighter more inland route along Interstate 5, which will enable faster running times and cut six minutes between Seattle and Portland. When the project and three others are complete, the state also plans to add more trains for additional round-trips.

I wasn't going far this time, just seventy-six miles to Olympia. Lloyd Flem, government and corporate affairs director for All Aboard Washington, an advocacy group for passenger trains, met me at the station and drove me into the capital to meet with Ken Uznanski, the then passenger rail chief of Washington's Department of Transportation. Months later in a controversial move laced with political overtones the DOT reorganized the rail division and eliminated Uznanski's position.

Flem lobbies legislators in both Olympia and Washington, D.C. Fortunately, rail has gotten some traction with many state politicians. The state of Washington DOT has an active rail division that's focused on moving both freight and people more efficiently along the corridor that runs from central Oregon to British Columbia. Because of the mountain topography—the Cascades to the east and Coastal Mountains to the west—the natural travel corridor in the Northwest traces the low-lying land that includes the Willamette Valley and the Puget Sound lowlands. Railroad builders naturally laid track in the valleys, and the highway builders followed suit. Consequently Interstate 5 and the mainline tracks run quite close together.

Seven of ten Washington residents live within fifteen miles of the I-5/rail corridor, and another million or more people will move there by 2020. The ports of Tacoma, Bellingham, and Portland, already some of the busiest in the world, are likely to expand as well despite the current economic downturn. All this growth in population portends a crisis in transportation: I-5 is near capacity, and to build more lanes or new highways—turning rich farmland into asphalt—will be expensive as well as unpopular.

The Cascades corridor is one of eleven rail corridors of 100 to 600 miles in length that were designated in 1991 by the U.S. Department of Transportation as "high-speed corridors" where passenger trains might someday run at speeds of more than 100 mph. The designation enabled states in these corridors to apply for funds to begin planning for that day. Washington has been one of the few states actually investing its own money in trains and infrastructure. Some of the corridors still don't carry any passenger trains at all, let alone high-speed service.

The Pacific Northwest is emerging as a mega-region where its large and small cities, even rural areas, function as more integrated economic and social units. Efficient transportation and one that leaves a smaller footprint on the land will be needed to move people and goods, Uznanski was explaining to me. We sat in a cubicle crowded with maps, strategic studies, and reams of planning documents. Uznanski pointed out the window to the capitol building.

"Look, there really isn't anyone across the street who is saying that we should not invest in rail. It's more about how much investment we can afford," he said.

Although Amtrak is a creature of the federal government, and partly subsidized by Congress, it also partners with a handful of states that want additional "corridor service" between in-state or regional cities. Sometimes this results in creating new service—the Amtrak Cascades train was initiated in 1993 with one round-trip—or adding frequencies to a service that already exists. The states negotiate with the freight railroads for access, pay for improvements to the infrastructure, and purchase or lease the equipment. Amtrak runs the trains and staffs the stations. Washington was the first state I visited that "partnered" with Amtrak, and it was in these states that I discovered Amtrak runs a pretty fair service when it is given the resources.

In the past ten years, Washington has put more than $120 million into the Cascades Service, purchasing three Talgo train sets ($10 million each) and funding the construction of additional track, new signals, sidings, and safety equipment on the BNSF mainline tracks. These capital improvements have increased the track's capacity and created additional "slots" for passenger trains.

"It's the price of admission to their infrastructure. In return, the railroad allows us to run our trains with the frequency and on-time performance we want," said Uznanski.

The Cascades make four round-trips daily between Seattle and Portland. Two of the trains continue onto Eugene, Oregon, and one train makes a round-trip between Seattle and Vancouver. The goal by 2023 is to run thirteen trains a day for hourly daylight service. Traveling up to 125 mph, the trains would run two and a half hours between Seattle and Portland and three hours between Seattle and Vancouver. In order to run the train above 100 mph, the state must construct 185 miles of passenger-only tracks, however.

Infrastructure improvements may cost $6.5 billion. It is a stunning amount, but not surprising considering the age and configuration of the infrastructure, which dates back to 1914.

The sharp curves, tunnels, and grades may be OK for slow, heavy freight trains, but they aren't suitable for running fast modern passenger trains, said Uznanski.

Whether such investment takes place depends on the availability of matching funds from the federal government and the willingness of the freight railroads to expand their systems for passenger trains. The Rail Safety and Amtrak Funding Act, passed in October of 2008, included some matching monies for states, and Washington, because of its aggressive program, should be able to snag some of that money, but it needs much, much more. The American Recovery and Reinvestment Act (the 2009 federal stimulus package) designated an additional $8 billion for development of high-speed rail, and many rail experts I spoke with felt some of those funds should be channeled to states like Washington. "We need to be more aggressive to get these trains moving, but it's hard when we're the only ones doing all the investing," Uznanski said.

When the state has money, BNSF has been willing to work with Washington, but the railroad isn't anxious to make shared investments that do not benefit its freight operations, said Uznanski.

"The railroads are really in the driver's seat—they can take their toys and go home. But overall, BNSF has been a good partner, not like some other railroads." It was a sly reference to Union Pacific, the only other Class 1 railroad in the Northwest.

The Stampede Pass tunnel, a choke point for freight traffic going over the Cascades north of Seattle, is a good example of the state's private-public partnership.

BNSF's predecessor, Burlington Northern, closed this east-west line to through traffic in 1984, against the advice of rail experts who said the railroad would need the line. Ten years later, as traffic increased, BNSF reopened the pass but the tunnel, built in the 1890s, wasn't high enough to accommodate double-stacked intermodal trains; those trains still have to go down the north-south main line and then over Stevens Pass. So Washington and BNSF are now enlarging the Stampede Pass tunnel.

"Once those intermodal trains can go through Stampede Pass, it will take some traffic off the main line and free up more room for additional passenger trains," said Uznanski.

By bringing the number of trains up to eight a day between Vancouver and Portland, ridership and ticket revenue will increase significantly. Currently, ticket sales—what's known as the farebox—cover 43 percent of the Amtrak Cascades' operating expenses; the state subsidizes the remainder. Run eight trains daily; however, the farebox recovery goes up to 70 percent.

It's all about frequency. When trains are convenient and frequent, ridership—particularly business travel—grows dramatically, said Uznanski.

It was a mantra I was to hear from experts all across the country—frequency builds ridership, and only frequency significantly increases farebox recovery. Sure, it's great to have trains running more than 100 mph in a corridor, but if there are only a couple of trains a day, they just aren't convenient enough to move people off the highway or away from the airport.

After the interview at DOT, Flem and I went off to eat oysters overlooking a finger of Puget Sound. He has a degree in economic geography. When I asked if rail travel will relieve the congestion on I-5, he shook his head no.

"Traffic on I-5 will grow because population is growing. Trains aren't going to cure congestion but neither will more roads. What trains will do is change some settlement patterns and plant seeds for developers who will build higher-density development closer to the tracks. Rail can promote a more conservative use of the land because infrastructure influences settlement."

Why not jump-start the process, bypass the freight railroads, and build separate tracks for passenger trains?

It would be preferable, he admitted, but not practical because there's no political will to build a passenger-rail system apart from the freight infrastructure. It would be a project on the scale of the interstate highway system, which would require the purchase and condemnation of land, tunnel building, environmental permits, and a ton of dollars. Only California was moving forward on such a project, in its plans to build a bullet train between Los Angeles and San Francisco, and it will need billions in federal assistance to complete the work. What America is stuck with for the time being is a shared infrastructure, he said.

Many of the proponents who want dedicated passenger rails are the same folks advocating for super-high-speed trains, he said. They don't live in the real world.

"These are the same folks who stomp their foot and say, 'I want maglev, and I want it next week,'" he added. "They look at the cover of a *Popular Science* magazine and say that's what needs to be done."

Maglev, or magnetic levitation, elevates and propels a train forward with the use of electromagnets. There are no wheels. The only commercial use of such a train is in Shanghai, where it runs from downtown to the airport. It has reached a speed of 361 mph. Experts say these trains will one day exceed 1,000 mph, maybe even faster if run through tubes evacuated of air so there's no drag. But mag-lev technology is in its infancy, and the trains are expensive.

America doesn't need a quantum leap in technology now, Flem said. Steel-on-steel technology, running flanged steel wheels on steel track, can serve America's needs. It's the same technology the French and Japanese have used to run trains more than 200 mph.

"Right now we just need more trains going 80 and running on the shared right-of-way. It's what we have to work with. I wish it wasn't, but that's the real world."

Then he added, "Advocating for more at this point only makes us look like a bunch of foaming rail fans."

Flem dropped me back at the station and I boarded an afternoon train to Oregon's capital city, Salem. This time, I had a business-class seat, a little roomier with a nice table for my laptop. We continued south past Centralia and through a fecund and stunningly beautiful mosaic of green farmland. The coastal mountains lay to the west, rounded black bumps lit occasionally by great fans of light diffracting through breaks in the cloud cover. I took my free $3 drink ticket—a bonus for being a business traveler—went down to the Bistro car and got a beer.

When the Cascades Service first began, it operated with Amtrak's double-decker Superliner equipment, but the state of Washington wanted something classier and faster. Before it could purchase the Talgos, the state asked the Federal Railroad Administration (FRA) for a variance from crashworthiness standards. European trains have lighter-weight car bodies for energy efficiency and fast acceleration and deceleration. American coaches are much heavier and stronger, designed to survive a hit. But European trains also run with positive train control, an electronic system that automatically slows or stops a train if an engineer misses a signal or passes out while at the controls. Few American trains have such controls today, although they are mandated to be installed on all trains by 2015.

The Talgo has a push-pull configuration, meaning it has a locomotive on one end and a cab car on the other. The engineer sits in the locomotive to pull the train. Rather than turning the train at the end of the line, the engineer moves to the cab car and remotely controls the locomotive, which then pushes the train. The motive power for the Cascades Service is a 3,200 horsepower snub-nosed General Motors diesel-electric, designed for freight but adapted for passenger use. A more efficient passenger locomotive would weigh less and have a lower center of gravity to take curves at a higher speed. The cab cars, which now carry a block of concrete as a kind of balancing ballast, could be equipped with batteries to capture and store electricity from the locomotive's dynamic braking.

The Talgos may have other issues as well, especially with increasing ridership. The entire train holds just 250 people, and the coaches, at forty-four feet, are half the length of a single-level Amtrak car. Because the Talgo cars are not compatible with other Amtrak equipment, it's impossible to tack on more cars and expand the train's capacity. For this lack of versatility and compatibility, some critics call the Talgo trains orphans. Still, they are comely orphans, and if they help create a train culture in the Northwest, they will have done their job.

Oregon
funding rail with vanity plates

I got off at Salem late that evening. The next morning, I went to the Oregon DOT where I had hoped to meet with Uznanski's counterpart, Kelly Taylor, administrator of the rail division. Over the phone, she had been quite honest regarding Oregon's efforts.

"We don't have as good a story to tell you as Washington. We just haven't had the money to put into the trains, and the real problem is where to put the money we have," she said.

When the Cascades Service was first initiated, Oregon envisioned running five trains a day to Eugene, 111 miles south of Portland, but it hasn't come up with the money. By statute, the state cannot use any portion of its gas taxes for rail. Those revenues must go toward highways, so DOT has used lottery-backed bonds, a tax on lawnmowers, and some general funding to run just two Amtrak Cascades trains on to Eugene. Amtrak does not have the money to help with funding. In 2007, Taylor was able to convince the legislature at least to channel income from the sale of vanity license plates into passenger rail and bus service.

I met with Bob Melbo, a rail planner who had been president of the Willamette & Pacific Railroad, a short-line freight railroad, before coming to DOT. Melbo put the issue simply: "There has not been a lot of political support for trains."

Instead, Oregon has subsidized buses between Eugene and Portland to make connections with the remainder of the Talgo trains going north to Seattle. Through the summer of 2008, when gas prices were high, the buses ran full. The overall ridership on the Amtrak Cascades service in both Washington and Oregon rose 14.4 percent in 2008.

"People are moving to the trains and the bus services. Something has to be done because what we offer today is not adequate," admitted Melbo.

Whether Oregon would buy or lease its own trains had yet to be determined. The Talgo, in Melbo's words, is "a nice piece of equipment but it isn't what Oregon needs." There are few curves in the mainline tracks south of Portland so the tilt technology isn't needed. Also, Oregon wants an easily expandable train set, something like the bi-level coaches on California's Capitol Corridor; each coach, depending on its seating configuration, can carry nearly 100 passengers and can hook up to an Amtrak Superliner car.

But there's a further financial problem: Oregon cannot run any more trains until it pays for additional slots on the Union Pacific main line. Although Union Pacific has cooperated with Oregon on some projects, it essentially wants what Melbo described as "megabucks" to expand the infrastructure's capacity. Between Portland and Eugene the main line is single track, and though there are eleven passing sidings, the track already is jammed with freight trains. In the next ten years or so, freight-rail volume in Oregon is expected to double. If the state wants to run five or six round-trips daily between Portland and Eugene, he said, Union Pacific wants it to finance a second set of tracks.

However, Oregon may have an alternative. The Portland and Western Regional Railroad has 500 miles of track in northwest Oregon and it runs a line that largely parallels I-5 between Eugene and Portland.

"And it's all low-density rail," said Melbo. "By going there, we won't have to deal with twenty-five freight trains a day."

The Portland and Western (P&W) has already worked with TriMet, Portland's public transit system, and has shown a willingness to accept public money to upgrade its infrastructure. A big question would be Amtrak's participation. States that subsidize train service typically choose Amtrak to run their trains. Amtrak has experience in the business, it runs a national, centralized ticketing operation, and, most importantly, it has a statutory right to run on the tracks of railroads that originally signed the Amtrak agreement.

In other words, to get access to the tracks of any Class 1 railroad, a state really has to go with Amtrak. Not so on the P&W. Oregon could choose another operator or even contract with the short line to operate the passenger trains. However, until there is money and momentum it's all academic. Oregon, like Washington, will add another million residents by 2020 and most of those people will reside along the I-5 corridor where highway traffic will get worse.

"If we start running trains up to 80 mph and getting the time between Eugene and Portland down to two hours, we're going to move a lot of people off I-5," Melbo said. "We know there is a market there."

The next morning, I rode a Talgo to Portland, just fifty-two miles to the north of Salem. I had a few hours before I caught the Empire Builder back to the Midwest and had arranged to stop at the café in Powell's City of Books to meet Fred Nussbaum, a director with the Association of Oregon Rail & Transit Advocates (AORTA), a rail advocacy group. Nussbaum holds an urban studies degree from Portland University and a planning degree from MIT and has worked as a rail planner for transit agencies.

He placed a city bus schedule on the table and told me we had an hour to talk before he had to catch the bus home to give a music lesson. He plays cello as a member of the Pacific Northwest Contra and English Country Dance Band.

When it comes to mass transit and intercity rail, Oregon, like much of the country, is at a crossroads, he said. Although it has established the Cascades Service and aided construction of Portland's new light-rail system, the state so far has been too timid to make the types of investments needed for the future, he said.

"Why does Washington have more trains than Oregon? Money talks. Oregon can only muster $10 million while Washington has spent more than $100 million," he said.

AORTA would like to see Oregon create a passenger system capable of running six to eight trains a day at speeds of 125 mph along the corridor. The Union Pacific main line between Portland and Eugene should be double-tracked—in some sections triple-tracked—to enable the fast passenger trains to go around freights, said Nussbaum.

All of these proposed improvements have been studied and costed out at around $2 billion. Big money, yes, but big payoffs, said Nussbaum.

"You get that many trains going back and forth between here and Eugene and then tie that into what Washington is doing and it would start making a major difference," he said.

I asked Nussbaum about the chances of Union Pacific's cooperation or the possibility of moving to the P&W infrastructure. It didn't matter which was chosen as long as the freight railroad was presented with a business plan that buys the slots needed for passenger trains, he said.

"With all the growth that is coming in the Northwest, both freight and passenger, we need to move much more aggressively. It's really time to act, but in Oregon it's just not happening."

Empire Builder
the best kept secret in america

Shadows were long when the eastbound Empire Builder left Portland, crossed the Hayden Island Railroad Bridge to Vancouver, and then headed up along the Columbia River on the Washington side. I showered and then came back to my roomette for dinner. The Portland section pulls only a snack/café car, but first-class passengers receive a fully prepared, but cold meal. I had roast chicken, a Caesar salad, and glass of white wine.

My roomette was on the river side of the car, sometimes just a few feet from the water. The Columbia is a mighty river, but it has been tamed by dam after dam. We passed Bonneville, among the largest, with its spillways shooting out jets of water and the high-voltage lines running into the hills. Irrigation pipes came down like giant straws from the vineyards and orchards perched on the steep hillsides.

Away from Portland, the sky had turned gray. The sun was a dim, white bulb, like a flashlight with wax paper over the lens, its diffuse light softening the edges of the volcanic rock that poked out of the landscape like piles of blackened scrambled eggs.

Near Bingen, little tugs towed rafts of logs, strung together with cables. By the time we reached The Dalles, it was dark. In the longer days of summer, the scenery on that stretch of railroad beneath the towering cliffs of the Columbia Gorge is one of the most scenic on Amtrak.

Sleep came easily that night. In Spokane, we connected up with the Empire Builder from Seattle and got a full-service dining car for the return trip east. We crossed the Idaho Panhandle and then Montana's Flathead Valley before climbing into the Rockies. At Whitefish, I had a breakfast of oatmeal and then went down to the sightseer lounge, or observation car, to watch the crossing of the Rockies.

While the outside view was sublime—trestles over rivers, broad valleys and bowls of snow where mule deer and elk foraged along the forest edges—the interior of the car was hideous. Done up in a garish brown, orange, and blue motif, the car looked like the interior of a fast-food restaurant or a 1970s shag carpet gone bad. Even when these cars were new—thirty years ago—they were ugly.

We came out of the mountains at Browning and struck out across the snow-less prairie, through Shelby, Glasgow, Havre, Wolf Point, and Minot. I returned to my room, wrote and napped, and, yes, zoned out on a landscape of cattle, grain elevators, and empty plains. Winter sun filled and warmed the roomette.

At the wine tasting, I ate cheese and crackers and drank with a home builder from St. Cloud and a farmer from Rugby. The dining car steward—obviously not the same one on the earlier train—gave long, erudite explanations about clarity and taste and showed us how to swirl each sample to bring out the bouquet.

We didn't listen. Just threw back a glass and held it up for more.

The farmer told us he lives in town, but he and his sons own 6,000 acres and seed 4,000 more rented acres with soybeans, sunflowers, and rapeseed (canola). Much of the land is in sight of the railroad tracks.

"I drive the tractor all the time, look up and watch this train go by," he said. "Thought I ought to get on it."

He and his wife had been vacationing in Seattle. Two years earlier, he had a heart bypass.

"Doctor who did my surgery. Two weeks later, he had his own heart attack and died," he said. "Can you believe that?"

"Got to take care of yourself," the builder, a strong and limber guy but with all gray hair, replied. "I'm fifty-three, on my second marriage, and I got a six-year-old. I need to stick around a while."

He was coming back from a skiing vacation with his brother, their wives, and several children.

"The train is the best kept secret in America. It really is," he said. "This is the second year we've done this trip this way." Turning to the farmer, he asked, "How's the price of wheat?"

"Down eight dollars since Saturday."

"Has it been cold in Rugby?"

"Twenty-two below yesterday—probably colder when we get in tonight."

"I got some cattle myself. Twenty head," said the builder.

"Hobby farmer, eh?" It wasn't a put-down, just a fact.

Perhaps it was the empty plains or a man with a patched-up heart or the wine or the way train travel can just make a person feel suspended from life, adrift on the landscape, looking on like a spectator. Like a lot of conversations I've had on trains, this one turned philosophical.

The farmer said he had run a farm-implement business and found it tough to compete with the "big boys" in town who had million-dollar inventories.

"A farmer came in one day and said to me, 'You don't have the part I need.'

I said, 'Maybe you ought to buy this place and run it yourself.' And damn if he didn't," he said.

"So, I've been retired twelve years now. But I farm and work to keep my mind active. I know guys that retired. They sat down in the easy chair and next place they went was the funeral home."

He jerked his thumb back toward the sleeping car.

"My wife is lying back there on the couch, and I'm up here meeting people. I said, 'We're just sitting back here talking to each other. We can do that at home.' We ain't meeting people and that's half the fun of the trip. Now I met you guys."

That night I had dinner with a home-economics teacher from Williston and a veterinarian from Colorado who had worked as a meat inspector for seven years on the kill floor of a plant in Greeley. Now he's supervisor with the USDA, and recruits at veterinary schools for new inspectors.

"I tell students, 'You're thinking no way I'm working in a meat plant, but keep it in mind, because maybe later you might see it as a place you can do some good.'"

He had his own epiphany, "I was doing work for the Humane Society and they'd bring me a sick or old dog to put down. One day, it was this black lab. At each door in the facility, the dog stopped, sat down, waited, then got up and walked through. It was a well-trained dog, seven or eight years old; but no one wanted it anymore. So they brought it to me, and I killed it. And that was it. I couldn't do it no more so I went to work for the government."

The teacher said she once took her classes to a slaughterhouse, and some kids freaked when a cow's tail continued to move even though the animal was hanging from a hook, its throat slashed open.

"It was dead. That's just nerves, like a chicken with no head," said the vet.

A school trip to the slaughterhouse? I thought. Only in farm country.

He advised us to eat only lean ground beef—even better if it's organic, grass-fed. Stay away from fast food.

"It's worn-out dairy cows. They shoot them full of bovine growth hormone, milk 'em until they are old and sick, and ship them to the meat plant."

I was having chicken that evening, but I asked, "What about the flat iron steak?"

"Good meat. Absolutely."

When I went to bed that night, ice crystals tens of thousands of feet overhead refracted a rainbow of colors around the moon. The moon dog threw a steely gray light over the flattened land.

In the Twin Cities the next morning a bank thermometer read seven below.

The sun glinted off Minneapolis' skyscrapers as hard-edged as icicles. So much steam rose and billowed from a gas-fired power plant that the cooling towers resembled rockets lifting off from the pad.

At breakfast, I was reminded that the Empire Builder is a lifeline of sorts to the people on the Hi-Line. An elderly couple, ranchers from Wolf Point, Montana, was catching a quick bite before getting off at Winona. She was weathered, desiccated from a life spent outdoors. He was a barrel-chested man with a snap-button western shirt and bolo. His Stetson sat on the seat next to the aisle, and he and his wife had pushed close together against the window. I sensed they still rode around town in their pickup like two teenagers.

"At Winona, there's a bus," she said. "We're going over to Rochester."

"Relatives there?" I asked.

"Personal business," he grunted.

She smiled sweetly at him and touched his arm—an intimate gesture. He bit his lip and looked out the window, suddenly interested in the river bluffs, as if ciphering out their geology. I studied my eggs and didn't ask any more questions. Gradually, she revealed it was their third trip in the past eight weeks, and the train made it so convenient to get there from Montana.

One of them, I realized, was very ill. The Mayo Clinic is in Rochester.

The train rattled over the Mississippi on an old bridge. The back bays of the river were frozen. Fishermen in blaze orange walked between shanties on the ice. It was one of those brilliantly frigid days in the upper Midwest when a high-pressure front moving south from Canada sweeps out the clouds and all the heat radiates into space.

When I got off at Columbus, Wisconsin, I was grateful for dry roads to drive back north. It felt strange to be on a highway riding so low to the ground. The last I saw of the train, it was headed across a frozen field perpendicular to the highway—making its own way across the land.

PART 3
The Midwest

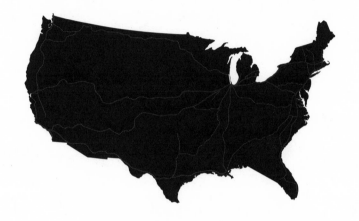

Chicago
a third-world train set

No region is more poised to bring passenger service back in a big way than the Midwest, where planning has been under way for years to create a 3,000-mile regional rail system using freight right-of-ways and emphasizing corridor service between such major cities as Chicago, Indianapolis, and Cincinnati; Milwaukee, Madison, and St. Paul; and St. Louis, Kansas City, and Omaha.

The Midwest Regional Rail System would move passengers along at between 79 and 110 mph. It would compete well against short-hop air service of 500 miles or less.

To learn more, I headed to Wisconsin and Illinois because those states, like Washington, have already put up money for infrastructure and subsidized new Amtrak service within their borders. These states believe rail should become a more important component in their transportation networks, and they are willing to fund new service and lease, or buy, train sets.

On a wet morning in early April, I waited with the Chicago-bound business commuters at the new Amtrak station adjacent to Milwaukee's Mitchell Field. Jets dropped from the low ceiling that day, roared over the tracks and touched down with vortexes of fog and mist swirling from their wingtips. In Europe, most big airports are served by train stations, but it's rare in the United States. The train doesn't quite reach the air terminal at Mitchell, but a shuttle bus comes out to pick up passengers switching to a jet.

As a commuter service, the Hiawatha has been a great success, covering the 90-mile trip in ninety minutes with an on-time performance exceeding 90 percent. In 2008, the Hiawatha carried 750,000 passengers, up 26 percent over 2007.

I arrived in Chicago right on the minute, breakfasted at Union Station, and then walked down to the Illinois DOT Bureau of Railroads on Adams Street. In a conference room across from the Sears Tower, I met with George Weber, the state's rail chief. He's a burly guy with dark, full hair, gold chain, and an open shirt. He formerly worked the Chicago yards for Amtrak and Conrail and eventually becoming a trainmaster in charge of crew operations.

Like many state rail officials, he began the conversation by lamenting the lack of federal funding for rail. Outside of some money from the Federal Railroad

Administration (FRA), Illinois had gone it alone. And it had been a struggle. In 2005 and 2006 when the Illinois legislature didn't appropriate the state's subsidy share for the Hiawatha, Wisconsin had to step in, pay the subsidy for Illinois, and keep the train running.

"We've returned to paying our historical share, and that's a good decision. That train brings a lot of business people and tourists to downtown Chicago," said Weber.

In 2008, the Hiawatha and Illinois's other state-sponsored trains carried just over one million passengers. Illinois also benefits because of Amtrak's Chicago operations. Long-distance trains arrive and depart Union Station daily, and all make some stops within the state before going on to other destinations. To a degree, these long-haul trains function as corridor trains for Illinois, but they are infrequent and don't allow daily round-trips.

In 2006, the state doubled its rail subsidies from $12 million to $24 million. These subsidies enabled Amtrak to add two trains to the 284-mile Chicago–Springfield–St. Louis corridor. The state also added more frequent service between Chicago–Quincy and Chicago–Carbondale. The Quincy route, served by the Illinois Zephyr, has been state sponsored for decades and goes back to the origins of Amtrak.

Illinois initially stepped up its support when Amtrak threatened to cut the 310-mile service to Carbondale, home of Southern Illinois University. The train passes through other college towns, too, and a grassroots movement by college presidents, chambers of commerce, and mayors urged the state to fund the service rather than see it disappear.

"Over the years the message has gotten louder. In a lot of areas, the train is one of the best forms of travel, and people see a need for service rather than more highways," said Weber.

After frequencies increased, ridership to St. Louis went up 100 percent, to Carbondale 75 percent, and to Quincy 45 percent. Frequencies make more of a difference than on-time performance, said Weber, echoing what I'd heard from others. Many riders only need to make a daily trip, so they want to be able to arrive in the morning and leave in the evening.

Overall ridership on Illinois trains had been climbing 20 percent annually, even though on-time performance has been wanting, more trains were needed, and more passenger cars, too, Weber said. Passenger trains often get delayed entering and leaving Chicago on a rail infrastructure badly in need of repair and overwhelmed by freight traffic, Weber continued. There are several sections where "slow orders" due to deferred maintenance do not allow trains to go faster than 10 mph. The Class 1 railroads, the Illinois Department of

Transportation (IDOT), and several government agencies are now cooperating on a big infrastructure project to improve train movement in and out of the city, including a separate corridor for passenger trains. The state and Amtrak are studying a new service between Chicago, Rockford, and Galena and another route from Chicago to the Quad Cities (Davenport, Moline, Rock Island, and Bettendorf). Iowa already wants to extend that train to Des Moines, while Nebraska would like more service to Omaha. The Quad Cities trains would average 50 mph, which is fairly typical on a shared-use right-of-way.

But on a portion of the Chicago–St. Louis line, passenger trains should be reaching 110 mph by late 2009 and 2010. More than $200 million has been spent by the state, the FRA, and Union Pacific in infrastructure improvements and upgrading the tracks from Class IV (79 mph) to Class VI (110). Wooden ties have been replaced with concrete ties, which are more durable and better able to hold track in place. More than 150 grade crossings have been equipped with advanced signaling systems and quadruple gates that do not allow motorists to drive around downed barriers.

People, accustomed to what's sometimes called "slow dumb freight," often misjudge the speed of an Amtrak train or an intermodal freight running 70 mph. When you get a train flying along at 110 mph—an awesome combination of speed and mass—a whole other level of safety considerations comes into play.

In Illinois the biggest delay in reaching 110 has been the lack of an approved positive-train-control (PTC) system. Using global positioning technology, PTC automatically slows or stops a train if the engineer fails to touch the controls periodically (perhaps he has fallen asleep or become unconscious), misses a signal, or is in danger of meeting or overtaking another train on the same track. Many American trains on heavy passenger and commuter lines now use cab signals, in which a radio transmits messages to the train and activates signal lights within the locomotive, which are then acted on by the engineer. And a lot of freight lines use only lineside signals controlled remotely by a dispatcher in a centralized operations center.

PTC is the latest technological manifestation of an automatic train-stop system that applies the brakes if the engineer does not comply with signals. Such systems have been around since the 1920s, when the ICC mandated that some railroads install automatic train-stop systems on lines heavy with passenger traffic. After World War II, when the ICC mandated that all trains going 80 mph or above had to be equipped with an automatic train-stop system, the railroads slowed down their trains rather than spend the money on the technology. That's why most passenger trains today do not go faster than 79 mph.

PTC is in use in parts of the Northeast Corridor, the Keystone Corridor between Philadelphia and Harrisburg, and short sections of track in Arizona and New Mexico, upstate New York, and Michigan where trains are running 90 mph and above. Its adoption elsewhere in the United States has been delayed owing to a lack of standardization in the technology and to opposition by Class 1 railroads—because the expense will run into the billions. When I spoke with Weber, it was still months before a commuter train in California crashed into a Union Pacific freight train, killing twenty-five people—an accident that would have been prevented by PTC.

Illinois and the FRA had tested a PTC prototype system a few years ago, but had been unsatisfied with the results, and pulled the plug on the project. However, by 2008 most of the disagreements and technical difficulties had been worked out. Amtrak is now spending $60 million in economic stimulus funds to install PTC on a section of track in Indiana and Michigan as well as on southern sections of the Northeast Corridor.

In Illinois, the trains will run 79 mph between Chicago and Springfield and then 110 mph for most of the 120 miles between Springfield and St. Louis. When these improvements have been made, the running time of the Chicago–St. Louis trip should be reduced from its current five and a half hours to about four hours. If the entire line were upgraded to Class VI—at the cost of $400 million—ridership is predicted to go up 300 percent, to 1.2 million passengers annually, and the travel time would be reduced to three hours.

On all its state-sponsored routes, Illinois needs more equipment. Amtrak doesn't have train sets or cars to spare. In 2009 using stimulus monies, Amtrak launched a program to refurbish nearly 100 wrecked and broken-down cars held in storage, but those won't be ready soon. New cars are, at least, three to five years off. The single-level Horizon coaches on the Hiawatha and other state-supported routes were designed for commuter service and aren't well suited for winter weather. Water and waste lines in the underbodies are exposed to the elements and subject to freezing. The car's brushed-aluminum skin hasn't aged well, either. It looks dull, mottled, and dirty.

"On the outside, they look like a third-world train set, and that is not the look we want to have," Weber said.

The state is considering rehabbing double-decker cars that ran on the Santa Fe's Super Chief route between Chicago and Los Angeles in the 1950s. Constructed of stainless steel by the Budd Company, a now-defunct passenger car manufacturer, the cars are durable and could be made to look like new, said Weber. They also hold ninety-five people, compared to the seventy-seat Horizon cars.

Illinois senator Dick Durbin has introduced a bill to shift about $400 million from the highway trust fund to help Amtrak and the states lease and buy additional equipment. Rolling stock is needed everywhere, said Weber. "We can't serve all the people who want to get on the train without the equipment. It's a big, big problem."

Back at Union Station, I went into the Great Hall to wait for Rick Harnish, the executive director of the Midwest High Speed Rail Association, a rail advocacy group based in Chicago.

While I sat reviewing notes, two workmen brought in a jitney and began removing the big heavy railroad benches. They shook a homeless man awake and shooed passengers from the benches. One worker told me, "Sir, the passenger lounge is downstairs."

When Harnish came in, he shook his head with disgust.

"What's going on?" I asked.

"Clearing it out for some event. Amtrak rents the space for charity parties, civic events. It's madness. Passengers don't matter. They just jam them into the A and B lounges."

Because the lounges were crowded with people waiting to get on long-haul trains, we found a table in the noisy food court where I shouted questions and Harnish shouted back. He grew up in Cleveland where he had watched the decline of both the railroads and the steel industry. Now, his association was arranging a trip for members and policy makers to Spain, which is investing billions in high-speed lines connecting its major cities.

Opponents of high-speed rail here often say the United States is too big for such trains, that the distances in America require air travel, but several regions, including the American Midwest, are roughly the same size as Spain with similar population density and distribution of major cities, said Harnish. The proposed Midwest Regional Rail System, which is supported by nine midwestern states, the FRA, and Amtrak, would connect cities that already have a lot of business ties and personal and tourist traffic.

"Imagine if we had a fast train between Chicago and Minneapolis. A Chicago businessperson could leave here in the morning, have a face-to-face lunch with a client, and be back by day's end," he said. On both legs of the trip, the traveler could connect to the Internet and get in a full day's work. The hassle and productivity loss of getting back and forth to Midway or O'Hare airports would be eliminated, and the train would deliver people from downtown to downtown.

Such a scenario is commonplace in Europe and on the Acela in Amtrak's Northeast Corridor, and it makes sense in the Midwest—even though a high-speed network will cost billions and take many years to complete, Harnish said.

"We've been sold this bizarre idea that automobiles and air can take care of all our needs, that the United States is somehow different than other countries. It's not true."

If the midwestern states really want a regional high-speed network whisking business people to appointments and tourists to cultural events, they shouldn't wait for the feds, Harnish argues. Illinois could link the entire state by 2015 using fast trains, intercity buses, and transit for about $1.3 billion, he said. It sounds like big money, but states already spend big money through their DOTs. It's just that the money goes to highways, not rail. Harnish again: "And why is that? Because diverting money from highways to rail goes against the policies, power structure, and the mind-set that dominates government. That's got to change. We don't need more highways; we need more rail. It's good transportation policy.

"Illinois is still moving at a snail's pace," he went on. "We can get to where we need to be a lot faster using dollars we already have, but that means making some choices."

Madison
everything has six zeros in it

At 4:00 p.m., I boarded a crowded Hiawatha train back to Milwaukee, taking a seat beside a student from the Milwaukee Institute of Art and Design. He was heading back after an interview for a summer internship in Chicago. It had gone well until he asked about salary and was told the position was unpaid. He was chagrined.

"I just assumed it was paid. Man, what a waste of time. I need experience, but I need money, too."

He illustrates and does caricatures. He pulled out his portfolio. The work was quite good, and we spent the rest of the trip looking over the pieces and chatting about careers in art and publishing. The exchange reminded me of the sociability induced by train travel. It would have seemed strange to sit together and not talk—at least a little. After detraining at the airport, I drove over to Waukesha to meet with Matt Van Hattem, a senior editor at *Trains* magazine. The magazine appeals to foamers, but its writing, photography, and journalistic credentials are excellent and professional. Most rail-fan publications take what they can get from readers and fill their magazines with amateur photographs and rambling, first-person reminiscences.

Van Hattem grew up watching trains in New Jersey and has ridden extensively on Amtrak, in Europe, and on commuter trains—logging more than 60,000 miles. He moved to the Midwest to work for *Trains*, and has charge of the "The Map of the Month" section—sort of the centerfold of the magazine.

Van Hattem said he was cautiously optimistic that Amtrak and intercity passenger service is undergoing a transformation, largely based on the success that has been happening in some states.

"You mean it is finally going to get better?" I asked.

"Maybe. The good things happening in intercity passenger rail have been driven by the states who know that unless they do something, come up with the money, it won't just happen. They aren't waiting for the feds," he said.

Outside the Northeast Corridor, Amtrak and the federal government have done very little to improve or expand services. Most routes run one train a day each way, a few routes run every other day. The corridor services connect city pairs in a region where there is a good deal of back-and-forth travel, even long-distance commuting. Seattle–Portland or Milwaukee–Chicago or L.A.–San Diego are classic examples. To work well, these corridor services need to offer frequency and relatively good time performance, and that's not what Amtrak can provide on its own. It just doesn't have the resources, which is why it's partnering with states, Van Hattem commented. "Right now, that's their niche. Amtrak sees its future with those states willing to put up money."

The Amtrak/state partnerships are working well in places like North Carolina, the Northwest, and in particular, California, which has a wonderful system of connectivity, using trains in conjunction with buses, Van Hattem went on. He hoped that other states would find these models attractive and apply them elsewhere.

"A lot of politicians may not be pro-rail when it comes to Amtrak, but may think these corridor services would be good in their districts and states. That may provide the momentum that's needed."

I mentioned that Illinois was looking to rehab old Santa Fe cars. Van Hattem wasn't surprised. The last new passenger cars in the United States were delivered in the early 1990s for the California market. The oldest single-level cars, the Amfleet, go back to the mid-1970s and the Budd Company. There are no American car manufacturers in the nation today. Foreign companies—such as Bombardier of Canada and Siemens of Germany and Kawasaki of Japan—have plants here to assemble light-rail and commuter cars, but even their components are manufactured outside the United States. "All over the system the equipment is getting old and showing its age," Van Hattem said. "And here's the scary thing—people are getting out of their cars, wanting to take trains. If we don't have nice trains to meet the demand, the opportunity will be missed."

By the end of 2008, that is exactly what happened. Trains were running full all over the system, and there were no cars to lengthen the trains. That night, in a soaking rain and wind storm that pushed my truck around on I-94, I drove seventy miles west to the state capital at Madison. In 2011, the state plans to run a train between Milwaukee and Madison. It couldn't come soon enough, I decided.

The following morning, Randy Wade, the rail chief for Wisconsin, laid out maps and studies in his cubicle at DOT and showed me how the state planned to bring passenger rail back to Wisconsin. It began in 1999, when Governor Tommy Thompson, who also was serving as chair of the Amtrak board, commissioned a blue-ribbon panel to study passenger rail in Wisconsin. The panel concluded that "high speed, inter-city rail should be part of the state's multi modal transportation system." That set the DOT and the legislature in gear. Working with Amtrak, Wisconsin three years later launched the Hiawatha

Service, and built new train stations in Sturtevant, downtown Milwaukee, and at Mitchell Field.

"We want to make it easy for people and their luggage to switch between modes. One day we would like to have seamless ticketing and baggage handling between the train and airport," Wade explained.

Intermodality is at the center of the downtown Milwaukee station, which houses Amtrak and several bus companies. Finished in 2006 at a cost of $16 million, the gleaming, all-glass building makes an architectural statement and complements the modernistic look of the neighboring art museum. Buses feed passengers onto the train and vice versa. I started two of my trips just this way, by taking the all-night bus from the Upper Peninsula, arriving in Milwaukee at dawn and then walking a few steps to get on the early morning train to Chicago.

Milwaukee will serve as the state's rail hub. Once the service to Madison is in place, it will be extended through La Crosse and up to Minneapolis and St. Paul. In about ten years, a train will run from Milwaukee through the Fox River valley and north to Green Bay. By then the Hiawatha service should be making seventeen trips a day to Chicago. The goal is to have all state residents within one hour of a train station or thirty minutes from a feeder-bus station.

What's happening in Wisconsin and Illinois dovetails with the Midwest Regional Rail System, and Wade and I spent a good deal of time talking about this proposed network of corridor trains, some running near 79 mph, others at 90 mph, and a few at 110 mph.

As now envisioned, the system would reach east to Cleveland and west to Omaha and Kansas City, from Green Bay in the north to St. Louis and Cincinnati in the south. It won't be cheap, but it holds the promise of many advantages. The system will cost an estimated $7.7 billion to build tracks and stations, install signals and gates, and buy train sets capable of 110 mph. Wisconsin's share is expected to run $1.8 billion. The Chicago–Cleveland route alone would cost $1.3 billion.

It averages out to about $2 million per mile, Wade told me. "Everything has six zeros in it. That's the nature of the transportation, but if you look at the benefits, this provides a lot of benefit for relatively low cost." Amtrak most likely would operate the trains, Wade continued, largely because of its ability to access the freight-railroad network. The states, however, would purchase or lease the train sets.

"These trains will provide a different experience than Amtrak," said Wade. "New trains, greater speed, better amenities. It will be a modern, classy experience."

The plan calls for purchase of sixty-three diesel-powered train sets costing $1.1 billion. It also calls for establishing a manufacturing center in the Midwest to build the trains. GE manufactures locomotives in Pennsylvania, but since no U.S. company makes coaches for intercity trains, here is a chance for the Midwest to diversify its manufacturing base. If America gears up for more rail transportation, it needs a domestic manufacturer and supplier, Wade believes.

The states would be responsible for building their parts of the system. The plan assumes an 80 percent federal to 20 percent state match, as is now done with highway projects.

"We want rail projects to be treated just like a highway," said Wade. "We don't think one mode should be disadvantaged over another."

The system wouldn't be entirely on line until 2025, it's anticipated. Illinois and Wisconsin are well on their way, but other states have done little. However, Wade expects a synergy will occur with each state moving to hook up to the network, not wanting to be left out.

"Rail by nature is a network, and we need to have a regional solution. We can't do this as individual states anymore," he added.

By 2025 rail and feeder buses should attract thirteen million riders, enough for the farebox to cover operating costs. Revenues can be raised further by selling advertising on trains and in stations. The trains could also carry same-day, express-delivery packages. The ridership projections aren't pie in the sky, Wade said. In the United States, he reminded me, 80 percent of all travel is less than 500 miles, and most Midwest cities are situated 100 to 500 miles apart—too close to fly and often inconvenient to drive—particularly in severe weather "That's the sweet spot for rail," Wade said. A regional system of fast trains would have the added benefit of relieving the strain on O'Hare Airport in Chicago, the second-busiest airport in the world and crucial to the national air network. Currently, one-third of all flights out of O'Hare are less than 500 miles.

"From the standpoint of pure transportation, and if you are being modality neutral, rail is the best solution," he said.

When I came to Madison, I wanted to meet with Frank Busalacchi, Wisconsin's secretary of transportation. He was in Milwaukee that day but agreed to talk via a conference call. In the coming months, our paths never crossed, but I got earfuls about the man from others who saw him as an evangelist of passenger trains.

Busalacchi chairs the States for Passenger Rail Coalition, a consortium of thirty-one states that have been advocating for more federal aid for rail. Though he didn't have much rail experience initially, his reputation as a strong promoter of a vital rail system for the country was secured when he served on the National Surface Transportation Policy and Revenue Study Commission, created in 2004 by Congress, to offer a vision, policy recommendations, and funding mechanisms that "would preserve and enhance the surface transportation system of the United States for the next 50 years."

The study was headed up by Mary Peters, then secretary of transportation in the Bush administration, who decided at the outset that the commission would not consider passenger rail as a viable form of surface transportation, reasoning there was little data to compare intercity rail against highways.

Busalacchi objected strenuously, and after being rebuffed, he formed a separate "passenger-rail working group" to gather data that would be considered by the commission. He gathered experts from around the country, held public hearings, and got some commission members to listen, even board some trains. Then he issued his own report entitled, "Vision for the Future: U.S. Intercity Passenger Rail Network through 2050." He won over some commissioners to his point of view, and a portion of the working group's recommendations was included in the committee's final report. "I was very impressed," Don Phillips, a longtime Washington journalist who writes a column for *Trains*, said of Busalacchi's work. "Either he said screw national politics, or he didn't understand national politics because he just swept the DOT aside. He essentially said, 'We're going to do our rail report. I'm not here to play your game.' And that just ran those Bush DOT people up a tree. He was an unguided missile; they couldn't control him."

The rail report, running fifty pages, recommended the country spend about $8 billion (in 2007 dollars) annually on passenger rail. That would rebuild a nationwide network, connect all major cities and population centers, and serve rural areas much as the interstate highway system does today. When the larger report, which included the chapter on rail, was released in December 2007, three members—including Mary Peters—voted against it. But nine commissioners did approve it, including "some pretty conservative Republicans," Busalacchi said.

"They got their eyes opened. We traveled around the country, visited a lot of cities, and heard from state DOTs. Those commission members came around and realized that trains and mass transit have to be part of the solution."

Remarkably, considering the commission's political makeup, the report also called for substantial increases in the federal fuel tax to help finance infrastructure investments. The commission's final report estimated the country needs to spend about $225 billion annually.

"The country is in a transportation crisis already. When we looked out twenty-five and fifty years, the needs are astronomical. That money has to come from somewhere," he said.

When Obama announced $8 billion for high-speed rail in his stimulus plan, he called it a down payment, but those monies came from borrowing, and whether that level can be maintained in the ensuing years has yet to be determined. Raising gas taxes has been a third rail of American politics. As of this writing, Obama has not touched it, although many economists say he must— not just to help finance infrastructure improvements but to create a market for fuel-efficient cars. Four-dollar gas in 2008 clearly showed that price has a profound impact on consumer behavior. Adding twenty-five cents to the gas tax would drive down annual gas consumption and channel more money into transportation projects—including mass transit, said Busalacchi.

"The numbers aren't lying. These problems are not going to go away. There has to be a shift to more mass transportation," he added.

In the coming months whether I was in Fort Worth or Oakland or Albany or New Orleans, if I picked up the local newspaper, I knew I might find a guest editorial signed by Frank Busalacchi as head of the coalition. I'm sure those were canned pieces, penned by committee and sent en masse to newspapers around the country, but when gas was four dollars a gallon the papers were publishing them.

PART 4
The Middle Atlantic

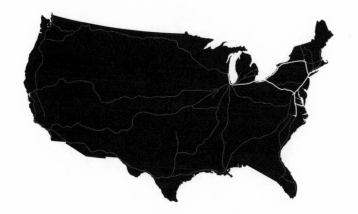

Lakeshore Limited
but i don't want a burger

Two weeks after my Madison visit, in early May, I boarded the Lake Shore Limited in Chicago, bound for New York, where I planned to pick up the Acela Express to Washington, D.C. There, I'd visit with freight and passenger railroad representatives and then make my way to North Carolina, one of the states investing in its rail network in partnership with Amtrak.

The Lake Shore follows the "water level route" of the old New York Central Railroad, avoiding the mountains that required the Pennsylvania Railroad to construct horseshoe curves near Altoona. The water level route runs across the flatlands close by Lakes Erie and Ontario, along the Erie Canal, and through the Mohawk and Hudson River valleys. Anyone who has driven Interstate 90 across upstate New York and compared it to the tortured path of Interstate 76 through Pennsylvania can attest to the differences in topography.

The Twentieth Century Limited, once called the world's greatest train, ran the water level route between New York and Chicago from 1902 to 1967. Making just three intermediate stops, it covered the 960 miles in sixteen hours. The Lake Shore with seventeen stops takes nineteen hours today.

The train left Chicago on schedule at 10:00 p.m. I took the first seat in a coach. A light over the door shone so bright I could see the blood vessels on my eyelids. The door rattled open and let in the clatter of the railbed. I moved back several rows, found two empty seats and fell asleep until Cleveland.

Ninety minutes later, we reached the little town of Conneaut, Ohio, on the Pennsylvania border. This was familiar territory: I grew up just fifteen miles away. The Lake Shore blew through town at 45 mph, but I caught a glimpse of the Pittsburgh & Conneaut Dock Company where my grandfather's locomotive had taken on water and picked up several cars of iron ore on the day of the fatal explosion. As my train passed through the fruit orchards and vegetable farms along the Lake Erie shoreline, I could see spring migration was on—the brambles flush with warblers and other songbirds staging to cross the lake. A woodchuck sat up in a field and watched us pass. The train kicked up fluffs of cottonwood seed that flew by the windows like snow.

In Erie, we were just twelve minutes behind schedule until two border patrol agents with automatic pistols and radios got on board and spent a half hour walking through the coaches asking for IDs from Asian and brown-skinned folks. If it wasn't ethnic profiling, it sure looked like it. What seemed more outrageous was the decision to hold up the entire train. Decades ago, when a train schedule was sacrosanct, you needed a good reason, but this search looked awfully routine.

Out of Erie, the train rolled through sprawling vineyards of Concord grapes, raised for jelly, juice, and jam. The woody vines were still bare; the vineyards skeletal and windswept. The field workers did their pruning in gloves, sun hats, and long-sleeved shirts. Behind them, Lake Erie stretched out for dozens of miles. It's rare to see the other shore, but from Westfield, New York I could make out Long Point, Ontario, a black finger of a peninsula jutting into the bluish water.

Near Buffalo, the train slowed through Lackawanna, the abandoned mills of Bethlehem Steel, and the weathered remains of dozens of concrete grain elevators. Steel didn't leave until the 1970s, but the elevators lost out in the 1950s when the St. Lawrence Seaway opened the interior lakes to ocean-going vessels. Until then, much of the Midwest's grain came to Buffalo (the grain elevator was invented there) and was taken by train or barge to the East Coast. In this brown field of vacant buildings and cement slabs as wide as runways, eight new wind turbines sliced the breeze along the shoreline. There's room for hundreds more.

Further along, we reached the Buffalo Central Terminal. Abandoned and forlorn, built in 1929 during the art deco heyday, the station once handled 200 trains a day. Amtrak got the building from the bankrupt Penn Central and sold it for just $75,000. The new owners sold off the clocks, ornamental stonework, and ironwork. Taggers, or graffiti artists, the homeless, and the weather moved in and did the rest.

The story is the same 250 miles west in Detroit, where Michigan Central Station still awaits rescue. In the 1980s, when I lived in metro Detroit, Amtrak boarded passengers out of a double-wide trailer surrounded by razor ribbon next to the looming hulk of the windowless old train station. It was a spooky place to catch a train.

We turned east and stopped in Rochester, Syracuse, Utica, and then Albany. I lunched with an elderly English couple on holiday and a Danish woman who has lived in New York for fifty years.

George and Gwen had spent the weekend in Chicago, and we talked election politics for a while before the conversation shifted to the food fare of trains. The Danish lady had just been on a train from Denver that had run out of food.

"There was nothing. The snack car was sold out," she complained. "I was lucky to have a candy bar in my purse."

The Lake Shore seemed little better stocked when the waiter told us only a hamburger or salad was available for lunch.

Gwen was incredulous, and dryly asked, "Do you not have the cold sandwich?"
"No."

"How about the chef's luncheon special?" She was reading the menu.

"Just the 'build your own burger' entrée or the salad, ma'am. That's all."

"Where did all the food go?" the Danish lady asked.

"They didn't give us enough in Chicago. We ran out."

Considering this was the first time lunch was served, it hardly figured.

"Can I have a yogurt?" Gwen asked.

"You can buy a yogurt in the snack car. I would have to charge you for it, too. I can't be taking foodstuffs out of his stores. What you can get, you can only order from the lunch menu."

"But you don't have anything I want on this menu."

"We do have burgers ma'am. Prime beef."

"But I don't want," she said with disdain, "to build my own burger."

Here was a first-class passenger who had spent at least $150 for her roomette, a price that included meals, and the railroad refused her a $1.50 yogurt.

She settled on the salad and the rest of us ate burgers.

Gwen said, "I don't think I will ever complain about English railways again."

Back in my coach, a Hasidic Jew had donned a tallit, a prayer shawl. He stood near his seat at the front of the car, clutching a prayer book and *shokeling*, a Yiddish word describing the swaying of the body. He bobbed and weaved like a prize fighter, fists pulled up to his chest. On subsequent trips, I watched Muslims laying down prayer rugs next to the luggage racks; Catholics signing out the cross and fingering rosary beads in their seats; families holding hands to give blessings before meals; and, in northern California, I heard the Om chant resonating from the lounge car.

As Matt Van Hattem at *Trains* magazine observed, "Trains are not like jets or buses. People have a lot of time onboard. They make themselves at home. You get to see who they are."

During the layover in Albany, the train split, and a few cars went off to Boston. We ran south along the Hudson Valley where trains never went out of style. Daily commutes of fifty to seventy-five miles into New York are only possible because of rail.

We were ninety minutes late when we passed through Yonkers and dropped into the tunnels beneath Manhattan. From Penn Station, I walked five blocks to a boutique hotel where I had a tiny room and a shared bath. After a sandwich at a bodega across the street, I showered, ironed my clothes, and set the alarm for 4:30 a.m.

The Acela Express
aboard america's fastest train

The streets smelled of rain and garbage. Delivery trucks rolled boxes onto conveyers and into the vaults beneath the sidewalks. There were enough people out that it felt safe to walk, but when I crossed Fifth Avenue, a cab came by so I got to the station early and took a seat in the waiting area for Acela passengers. My train left at 6:00 a.m.

Amtrak runs two types of train sets on the Northeast Corridor—the Acela and the Northeast Regional. Between Boston and Washington, where there is an electrified infrastructure, all Amtrak trains are powered by electric locomotives that draw power from overhead wires called a catenary. The freights and some commuter trains are powered by diesel-electric locomotives.

Acela is the faster train between New York and Washington, making the trip typically in about 2 hours 45 minutes. Riders pay a premium for the experience, $200 for a one-way ticket during peak hours. A Northeast Regional train costs half as much and makes the trip, depending on the train, in 3 hours 15 minutes to 3 hours 40 minutes. Not a huge difference, but if time is money or you're measuring the train against a shuttle flight or want more luxury, fewer stops and a smoother ride, then Acela is worth it.

Each Acela train set of two locomotives, a café, and four coaches carries 304 passengers. Amtrak bought twenty train sets for $600 million from a consortium of Bombardier in Quebec and Alstom of France. The components were manufactured abroad and assembled in Vermont and New York to create some jobs in America.

Because of Federal Railroad Administration (FRA) safety requirements, an Acela train is nearly twice as heavy as France's TGV (Train à Grande Vitesse—French for high-speed train), which is also manufactured by Alstom.

Acela's floor is reinforced to protect against debris on the tracks. Unlike Europe's high-speed corridors, the Northeast Corridor is only partially fenced; it even crosses some highways at grade. Amtrak wanted to run a push-pull configuration, but the FRA under the Clinton administration said a cab car did not meet crashworthiness standards, so another locomotive was added at the other end. The train is overpowered. Even with a single locomotive, the Acela can run at 200 mph, but FRA rules do not allow speeds above 150 mph on tracks shared with freights and slower passenger trains. Acela averages just 80-some mph, and rarely goes faster than 130 for small stretches. Its speed is limited by curves, tight confines in tunnels—especially in Baltimore—freight traffic, and other drawbacks that make true high-speed performance impossible. The high-speed corridors in Europe and Japan are straight, level, sealed from intrusion, and set aside solely for fast passenger trains. To create such a corridor in the Northeast with its dense population would cost tens of billions of dollars and require the purchase or condemnation of more land and neighborhoods.

Running with an engine at each end, the Acela is "semi permanently coupled," so adding coaches—which Amtrak does not have anyway—would be difficult and time-consuming. "That's a real shame," said Don Phillips, the transportation writer for *Trains*. "With all that extra power, those trains could pull a lot more cars and more people could be riding them."

To Phillips, Acelas are "mechanical lemons." Amtrak rarely has more than thirteen or fourteen of the twenty sets running at one time. That's a 60 percent operational capacity, and by European standards, it's pathetic, he said.

Mechanical difficulties started early. Shortly after they began running in 2000, cracks developed in key body components. In 2005, cracks were discovered in disc brakes. Still, the trains have a good safety record, and each set has run nearly a million miles. They are in constant use and usually running full. Amtrak is already talking about replacement equipment. If that happens, Phillips said, Amtrak should be allowed to buy off-the-shelf bullet trains. "FRA need not be such a hard-ass about its rules. Then we could get a TGV or something similar that is really proved out. Sure, you might have put on a different suspension and make some adjustments because the Northeast Corridor tracks are made for freight, too, but then you would have something that works."

World over, really fast trains are electric because they aren't weighed down by onboard diesel generators fed by heavy fuel tanks. Lighter trains accelerate and decelerate quicker and climb grades more easily. Traction motors create less noise, no exhaust fumes, and require less maintenance. If the power comes from a clean, no-fossil-fuel source—France, for example, produces much of its electricity from nuclear power—the trains have a small carbon footprint.

Electrifying more track in the United States will be expensive, but will be necessary to bring about so-called bullet trains. The high-speed initiative launched by the Obama administration promotes speeds up to 125 mph, which can be accomplished by diesel engines. The most likely steps would be extending the electrification of the Northeast Corridor north to Maine and south toward Florida. However, electric infrastructures are expensive to build. Early in the twentieth century, several railroads electrified their lines into New York

City and Philadelphia because the smoke of steam locomotives was a pollution and safety hazard.

In 1968, when the New York Central and Pennsylvania Railroad merged and absorbed the New York, New Haven, and Hartford Railroad, most of the Northeast Corridor came under a single owner.

But the new company, Penn Central, with its competing corporate cultures, heavy union commitments, and stifling government regulation, was doomed from the start. When it declared bankruptcy in 1970—the largest corporate failure in American history prior to Enron—Wall Street and Washington were stunned. Without government help, parts of the Northeast might be without freight service and passenger service. Like General Motors, the big banks, and AIG today, some railroads were deemed too big to fail.

To get Penn Central and the other big railroads out of the failing passenger business, the government created Amtrak. Two years later, Congress passed the Regional Rail Reorganization (Three R) Act that created Conrail (Consolidated Rail Corporation) from the remains of seven bankrupt northeastern railroads. In effect, Congress nationalized these railroads, and government planners moved aggressively to abandon lines, close facilities, and cut redundancy and waste. Thousands of railroaders lost jobs, and many towns lost their trains.

What to do with the Northeast Corridor? Its electrical infrastructure was old and in need of investment. Conrail was on government-funded life support, and the other freight railroads were into the long-haul business powered by diesel-electric locomotives.

Since the corridor was the nation's busiest passenger-rail corridor, it was decided to turn it—tracks and all—over to Amtrak, which also received rail yards and maintenance facilities, Penn Station in New York, 30th Street Station in Philadelphia, and half interest in the Union Stations in Chicago and Washington, D.C. Overnight, Amtrak's payroll doubled. Now it wasn't just operating trains, it owned a railroad, and the freights had to pay to use its tracks. Congress ponied up a billion or so for infrastructure improvements to create faster service between New York and Washington, but Northeast Corridor operations have continued to siphon off the company's limited resources for years. Amtrak struggles to maintain old bridges, tunnels, and retaining walls. It has been estimated that about $5 billion is still needed to bring the Northeast Corridor line into "a state of good repair."

About $500 million of the Obama administration's stimulus package was channeled into repair and maintenance on the corridor, including replacement of a 102-year-old drawbridge in Connecticut; reconstruction of the historic station in Wilmington, Delaware; and rehabilitation of the electrical infrastructure near Philadelphia that has been in continuous use since the 1920s. The improvements will do little to increase speeds of trains but will stem the corridor's further deterioration.

It was still dark when my train left New York, crossed under the Hudson River, and ran through the Meadowlands. In northern New Jersey, it filled rapidly with folks dressed in business attire, hefting briefcases, and breaking out laptops and Blackberries as soon as they got aboard.

The train was sleek and clean, the windows big and bright, and the ride smooth when the train got up to speed, which wasn't that often. Although Acelas can fly on a few open stretches, their passage in and out of major cities is still slow. And though the trains have tilt technology, they slow down for curves.

Some critics say up to 75 percent of Amtrak's government subsidy finds its way into the Northeast Corridor, while operations elsewhere get shortchanged. It was a complaint I heard often on the West Coast. What really burns critics is Amtrak's claim that the Acela and the corridor are moneymakers. Many Washington politicians—even some Amtrak haters who want to shut down the system—have a blind spot for the New York–Washington service. Maybe it's because some of them ride the trains to New York and enjoy the experience. And they see trains packed with riders. How could they not make money?

"The corridor is a money pit, but Amtrak covers it up with funny accounting," according to Don Phillips. Amtrak measures overall ridership and revenue rather than passenger miles traveled and passenger revenues per mile traveled, which is how airlines and other transportation companies factor costs. The billions allocated by Congress and put into the corridor infrastructure are not depreciated (amortized) as an operating cost against Acela's bottom line. Consequently, Acela's cost recovery comes out looking pretty good.

In 2009, under a new administration, Amtrak began a process of changing its accounting practices and the way it measures riders, however.

The myth of the Northeast Corridor's profitability has a long history, said Jim McClellan, who worked as a planner for FRA when Amtrak was created. Back then, some studies assumed the Northeast Corridor trains would make money for Amtrak and that those profits could offset losses on the other parts of the network. It was wishful thinking, said McClellan, but it helped support the notion that Amtrak wouldn't always need government help. And that's what the Nixon administration and some congressional members wanted to hear.

"The concept wasn't vetted well, and other assumptions were based on it being true. It was a house of cards. In our zeal to save the freight railroads and some passenger trains, we just accepted it would make money. Everyone wanted to believe it."

The Amtrak Reform Council, created by Congress in the late 1990s to help the company become self-sufficient, suggested Amtrak sell or spin off the corridor as a separate corporation, which could then sell bonds for the repairs. Amtrak would continue only as an operating company.

When I interviewed Gil Carmichael, chair of the council and the FRA administrator under George H. W. Bush, he said that the corridor actually needs $20 billion not $5 billion in improvements. "Amtrak didn't want to hear about creating a separate company because it wants its own railroad, but it would be better off without the corridor," he said. "The infrastructure company could raise the kind of money that Amtrak hasn't been able to provide."

Despite its problems, the Northeast Corridor remains Amtrak's flagship asset. More than 100 trains move 27,000 passengers along the corridor each day. Amtrak captures nearly half of the air/rail market between New York and Boston and more than 60 percent between New York and Washington, D.C. Were the Northeast Corridor to shut down, havoc would result with intercity East Coast travel.

And the Acelas do provide a glimpse of an effective high-speed corridor. We rushed through the gritty streets of Trenton, into the glassy glitter of downtown Philadelphia, and then along the blue waters of the Delaware and Chesapeake bays where egrets and sport fishermen looked up as the train passed. The train just blew by traffic on I-95.

Washington D.C.

running out of capacity

We pulled into Union Station right on schedule. This was a day to visit two rail advocacy groups that were like the flip sides of the same coin. I spent the morning at the Association of American Railroads (AAR), the mouthpiece of the freight industry, and the afternoon at the National Association of Railroad Passengers (NARP), which has advocated for riders and Amtrak for forty years.

AAR lobbies legislators, writes position papers, does research, and keeps industry statistics. Although Amtrak and some transit agencies are members, the AAR is dominated by the Class 1 freight railroads. I wasn't expecting much access to the organization. For all it knew, I was just another foamer for passenger trains. I didn't get past corporate communications, as it turned out, but that was OK. I was there to hear the official positions, the talking points.

Earlier that week, I had heard from Union Pacific, which turned me down flat for an interview. The e-mail from UP corporate relations read, ". . . we have reviewed your request and have chosen not to participate in this editorial project. As policy, we do not comment on other companies or organizations. Furthermore, your subject matter reflects more of an industry matter and not specific to Union Pacific."

That was actually the longest response I got from Omaha. Subsequent requests could be paraphrased as "Passenger trains have nothing to do with us. Go talk to AAR."

In May 2008, AAR was mainly fixated on obtaining new tax credits for capacity expansion. It also touted railroads' environmental friendliness—"One train can move a ton of freight 436 miles on one gallon of fuel—three times farther than a truck. One intermodal, double-stacked train takes 250 to 300 trucks off the road." Not a bad story. Of course, the industry also moves 65 percent of the country's coal and is heavily involved in mines, power plants, and promoting so-called clean coal. Railroads move 60 percent of the nation's grain harvest and promote ethanol for energy independence.

When it comes to long-haul shipping and moving big, heavy stuff, American railroads in terms of tonnage and efficiency do it better than anywhere else in the world. Europe has wonderful passenger trains, but only 10 percent of its goods moves by rail. What America's railroads don't do is move many people or move them speedily, and when I visited AAR, passenger trains weren't high on its agenda. Carrying people is not where the money is, and then there's that horrid history with passenger trains back in the 1950s and '60s.

I sat down with Tom White, director of editorial services, who gave me a copy of "The National Rail Freight Infrastructure Capacity and Investment Study."

There's your trouble, he said. We're running out of room on the rails. And capacity issues, I had come to know all too well, affect Amtrak and commuter railroads, too. Where there are choke points, single tracks, and congestion problems for freight trains, the on-time performance of passenger trains suffers.

By 2035, unless there is massive investment, the freight corridors will be congested. Freight traffic—on all modes—is expected to double in the next thirty to thirty-five years. Even though economic activity has slowed dramatically during the recession, America continues to add population, and those demographics alone will drive expansion, particularly in intermodal traffic.

The study estimates $148 billion is needed over the next twenty-five years to expand the system—not just maintain it. Railroads can come up with $96 billion on their own, but that leaves a shortfall of about $1.4 billion annually. And that's where tax credits come in. The railroads want a 25 percent tax credit for infrastructure projects—tunnels, ports, double-tracking, sidings, signaling, and new intermodal railway yards.

"Something has to be done," said White. "Do you want all that freight on the highways? Unless there is an expansion in capacity, that's where it's all going to end up.

"Expanding rail is good public policy."

During my travels, I heard plenty of criticisms about dumb decisions and shortsightedness by the railroads for tearing out double tracks and abandoning lines in the past—capacity they could use now—but most industry observers feel the railroads are making a sincere effort to expand the network.

In its favor, the industry isn't waiting for government. About 17 percent of railroads' annual revenues are flowing into capital expenditures that buy fixed assets or add value to an existing fixed asset. Manufacturing typically puts 2.5 to 5 percent of revenues into capital expenditures. By nature, railroads are a capital-intensive industry, constantly having to invest in their fixed assets, but their current level of investment is rather extraordinary.

Tax credits will certainly spur private investment, but the railroads are warming up to public-private partnerships, too, where they and the government would jointly participate in infrastructure projects. However, railroads feel like they are in a delicate dance with a capricious partner. They need capital but they aren't looking for a central planner.

As one freight executive told me, "We need help, but railroads should not be out there with tin cup in hand. You start taking that public money and then all the politicians think you owe them more than you do. I get very wary about taking money—because it's big money. All these projects are enormously expensive."

Railroads argue theirs is a private network. I asked White a question about this that I would later pose to government people and the freight railroads: "If more public money flows into the freight system, should the price of that aid be acceptance of more passenger trains on their lines?"

White grimaced and harrumphed, "Only if it is paid for. Passenger rail must pay its own way. Freight railroads cannot afford to cross-subsidize passenger service."

"Is that what's happening?" I asked.

"Right now Amtrak is not paying its way. It's not paying a fair share of the costs. It underpays the Class 1s by a couple hundred million per year," he said.

He was citing the "above the rail, below the rail" controversy.

By law, Amtrak pays an incremental, or above-the-rail, cost, meaning it pays a toll to run over the freight infrastructure. It does not pay below-the-rail costs, which is the price of dispatching, signaling, and all the other expense of maintaining the infrastructure. Amtrak pays about $2.20 per mile while the freights and AAR say the cost of maintaining track for those trains runs $19.90 per mile.

There are hidden costs, too, according to AAR. Because passenger trains move at higher speeds and at a higher priority than freight trains, safety requires longer spacing between trains. Freight trains may enter sidings more often when a passenger train is on the track. Freights wait while passenger trains load and unload at stations and may go into sidings when faster Amtrak trains overtake them. All of this affects time performance.

When passenger trains run on their infrastructure, railroads may maintain their tracks to a different standard. On curves, for example, the outside rail is elevated above the inside rail to bank the turn. The amount of elevation depends upon the speed of the trains. Faster passenger trains require higher elevations. All trains put more weight on the lower rail as they round a curve. Passenger trains are relatively light and put little wear on the track, but heavy freight trains going through these curves can cut in half the amount of time rail can safely be used—consequently there are higher maintenance costs.

Finally, there is the difference in revenue produced by freight and passenger trains. A freight train, of 50 some cars, produces on average about $97 of revenue per mile or about $88,000 over a 900 mile trip—say between Chicago and New York on the water level route. The Lakeshore Limited running the same route produces only about $2000 of revenue—the equivalent of 1.2 carloads of freight.

For all these reasons—which really boil down to return on investment—the freight railroads are not exactly friendly to passenger trains, particularly in a period of constrained capacity. It is fair to say that the big freight railroads, like the federal government and some state governments, subsidize passenger service. It's a cost of doing business, and that cost will rise if more passenger trains end up on the freight network.

However, the freight railroads at Amtrak's creation in 1971 agreed to the incremental cost structure for 25 years and signed on again when the agreements came up for renewal in 1996. So there's no excuses for delaying passenger trains, former FRA administrator Gil Carmichael argues.

"My argument with the freight railroads is they have forgotten the covenant made when they talked the federal government into taking over the passenger trains. They promised the American people, 'we will give you priority on our routes.' Railroads like the Union Pacific don't remember that covenant at all. It's best they did."

Months later when I chatted with a freight railroad executive speaking on background, he said, "The Class 1s and the AAR really ought to shut up and quit complaining about running a couple of passenger trains a day on these routes. The freights are making enough money now that Amtrak doesn't greatly affect their bottom lines. The whining just pisses off the public and the politicians. But, in the future, if Amtrak, the states and the federal government want to put a bunch more passenger trains out there, those costs will have to be addressed. Ramping up passenger service shouldn't happen on the backs of the freight railroads."

As White explained AAR's position, he was careful to say that Amtrak was not considered the enemy. If there is to be passenger service out there, let it be Amtrak. It's a known quantity.

"We favor Amtrak for all intercity passenger service. We don't want it opened up to Peter Pan Bus Lines or Virgin Trains," said White. "Amtrak has a dedicated force of railroad people who know the industry and understand our situation. They don't have to be taught what to do. They are railroaders."

I had lunch back at Union Station and then headed over to The National Association of Railroad Passengers in the old Railway Express Agency building. Amtrak has some of its offices on the first floor, but the other tenants are an odd mix of interest groups—the Literacy Project, the Religious Broadcasters of America, the Forage and Range Society—all there, like NARP, for close proximity to Congress.

Depending on your point of view, NARP is a foamers' club, a corrupted apologist for Amtrak, an information clearinghouse, or a dogged advocate for intercity rail and transit.

Over the months, I heard it all.

Ross Capon has been the head of NARP since 1976, so long that people would just say to me, "Have you talked to Ross yet?"

Capon is a gray-haired, balding guy who wears his glasses around his neck with a lanyard and has a tired look that seems to indicate he's been rolling a rock uphill for a long, long time.

He's encyclopedic about the legislative process, knows what bills are in consideration and which legislators are pro- or anti-rail. NARP does not lobby. It disseminates information and fact sheets and writes letters to legislators and bureaucrats. When journalists cover Amtrak and intercity rail, Capon and NARP are obligatory sources—always good for a quote. NARP's role is to function in parallel with Amtrak, to do advocacy, and take positions that Amtrak, as a quasi-government agency, cannot, Capon explained.

"Our number one goal is to get the facts to the general public and the politicians," he said. "Another part of our mission is to help Amtrak get the money it needs." He smiled. "And then we tell them what they need to do with that money. They don't always listen."

NARP's 23,000 members get a 10 percent discount on Amtrak tickets. NARP puts its brochures and position papers on trains and in stations.

"NARP doesn't exactly do Amtrak's bidding, but they have a gentlemen's agreement," one railroad historian told me. "NARP won't be too snarky about Amtrak, and Amtrak will help NARP promote itself. The two sort of need each other."

However, most people in train world believe NARP does important work. Capon was part of the Rail Working Group put together by Frank Busalacchi, and at the end of 2008, NARP joined up with AAR and other organizations to form the OneRail Coalition, which brought passenger and freight advocates together for the first time.

An issue of particular concern to passenger-rail advocates, and even the freight railroads that have to deal with Amtrak running old equipment prone to breakdown on their tracks, is Amtrak's perpetual struggle in Congress for funding.

Unlike aviation and highways, which have trust funds or earmarked monies, Amtrak receives its subsidy out of the federal government's general fund. The

Amtrak reauthorization bill, then in committee when I spoke to Capon, was looking pretty good—largely because of gas prices and record ridership. Still, he was wary.

Funding, he warned, is a two-step process. A bill authorizes a certain amount of money be spent, but it contains no money. A subsequent appropriations bill provides the actual money. Amtrak rarely receives its full authorization. The Bush administration tried to zero out the railroad in the federal budget and was only thwarted when some powerful supporters in Congress stepped in.

What rail really needs is a guaranteed source of funding, much like the Highway Trust Fund for roads, Capon said. That way, it would not have to beg for its money out of the general fund.

The Highway Trust Fund was created in 1956 to fund the interstate highway system by earmarking fuel and highway-user taxes for roads. During the build out of the interstate system, all the money went to highways, but gradually, as the system reached completion and new transportation bills were passed, some of the money was channeled to mass transit.

The Intermodal Surface Transportation Efficiency Act of 1991 (ISTEA and pronounced "ice-tea") represented a major change in legislative orientation because it began to promote a more intermodal approach to transportation. Several city transit systems got underway using hundreds of millions of ISTEA dollars. None of the transportation bills so far have provided money to Amtrak or intercity passenger rail projects, however.

"So if you are a state out there looking to invest in a public works project, do you choose rail? No," said Capon. "Highways leverage federal dollars. Rail gets no federal support. Zero. That has a huge impact on decision making." The federal government has never promoted passenger rail in a meaningful way, said Capon. Only the feds can prioritize routes, create and fund high-speed corridors, standardize equipment, and coordinate efforts between states.

Months later some of Capon's wishes came true with the election of a rail-friendly president, along with passage of 2009's American Recovery and Reinvestment Act and its billions for Amtrak and high-speed rail. In summer 2009, a draft transportation bill, passed by the House Transportation and Infrastructure Committee recommended $50 billion for intercity high-speed rail and $100 million for transit over the next six years. Highways would still receive the bulk of the dollars—about $330 billion—but the proposal to boost rail spending was remarkable. The bill called for an overall 33 percent increase in transportation spending, which would require a reexamination of the federal fuel tax. The 18.4 cent tax on a gallon of gas and 24.4 cent tax on diesel has not been raised since 1993.

The country should raise gas taxes, not just as a mechanism for funding rail and transit but to lower demand for gasoline and highway travel, Capon said. When the price of gas rises—as it did so dramatically in 2008—there is no corresponding rise in taxes collected. All the money from the inflated prices ends up with the oil companies and foreign governments. It doesn't go toward improving transportation.

"We have to move past all the politics about gas taxes . . . this so-called love affair with the car has left people with no choices. We've set up a ridiculous system for transportation. Most of us are dependent on the automobile to do anything."

Norfolk, Virginia
make those people go away

The next day was Saturday, a humid May morning portending the summer swelter of Washington. A huge man in cowboy garb sat across from me in the waiting area of Union Station, fanning his face with a white hat. He glittered with turquoise, a silver, polished belt buckle as big as a shield, black jeans with rivets, and rattlesnake boots. I had lived in Wyoming for a couple of years, and I hadn't seen anything quite so flamboyant even in the Beacon Club in Casper. It looked like a stage outfit for a singer whose name is inlaid into the fretwork of a sparkly guitar.

"Hot one out there, eh pard?" (He really did say "pard.")

"Hot one in here, too," I said, wondering if the station was this hot all summer.

Soldiers in blond desert boots, fatigues, and black berets sat down and put their feet up on their canvas duffel bags. A horde of seventh-graders and their chaperones came by wolfing down cheeseburgers and fries from McDonalds. They wore identical, iridescent T-shirts; easier to round up in a crowd, I guess.

A dog sniffed at my foot and I followed the leash up to an unsmiling Amtrak policeman. The dog went from bag to bag in the waiting area. It's the only Amtrak security I'd ever seen.

On the television, Senator Hutchison from Texas was on Fox News, saying America needs more oil refineries, more oil released from the strategic reserve, more control of speculators on Wall Street, and more drilling in America, especially in the Arctic National Wildlife Refuge.

I was glad to get on the Northeast Regional train to Newport News, the first leg of my journey to Norfolk, Virginia, to meet with an executive from Norfolk Southern. We had barely left the station, though, when the train stopped near L'Enfant Plaza for forty minutes. Track work, the conductor announced.

Just across the Potomac, in Alexandria, a man in his seventies, overweight, and wearing a knee-length raincoat waited for our train. He paced the platform, wrestled with two big suitcases, and acted a bit disoriented as he got on board.

After we left Alexandria, I was in the café car when a woman came in and gripped the conductor's arm, "You need to come. He is looking worse, and I don't think he is breathing."

A moment later, the PA crackled, "We have a passenger in medical distress. If anyone aboard has medical training, please come to the car behind the dining car."

In Fairfax the train halted and waited for the ambulance, which took about fifteen minutes. Another forty minutes went by before we were under way again. The café attendant went up to have a look; I stayed at my table. The conductor came by, "We can only hope he'll be all right. It looks like he had a stroke or heart attack."

When the conductor left, the attendant shook his head, "The guy was dead when they took him off. I saw him. He died in the chair."

The death was the talk of the café car, and later a woman who had watched the man get on the train, told me, "He fell into that chair, sweat just pouring off him. They punched his tickets and then he convulsed, took a couple of breaths, and that was it. He didn't move again."

At Quantico Creek, the train went by the Possum Point Power Station and then the Marine airfield where a fit and pumped Marine jogged next to the runway. We were in the tidewater. The Potomac stretched off to the east as wide as a lake. The track bed ran through a marshy lowland of brush, hornbeam, rhododendron, and Virginia creeper. Tent-caterpillar webs hung from the crooks of trees. Meadows resonated with yellow patches of blooming dandelion.

I thought of the Wilderness, of the armies of the Potomac and Northern Virginia blindly clashing in a confusing tangle of brush and second growth forest in early May on a day like this one—hard not to think of the Civil War as the train crossed the Rappahannock and passed Fredericksburg, Spotsylvania, and Cold Harbor. At Richmond, we veered east and onto the peninsula, entering an area famed for its colonial history—Williamsburg, Jamestown, and Yorktown.

We arrived nearly three hours late into Newport News where I boarded a greasy, beaten-up James River Trailways bus with four elderly ladies who could barely climb the stairs. This was Amtrak's feeder bus to Norfolk and Virginia Beach.

"Where you headed?" the driver asked me.

"Norfolk. I just need a taxi. Can you drop me at the bus station?"

"I'll get you close."

The bus headed onto I-64 and dipped into the tight confines of the portal tunnels beneath Hampton Roads—the wide section of the river separating Newport News from the cities of Norfolk and Portsmouth. The tunnel walls, just inches away, rushed past the windows, and when we emerged it was like being squeezed out of a tube. I looked out over the water at dozens of gantry and overhead cranes and thousands of shipping containers. There were ships in the water, ships hauled into dry docks, and Navy vessels at anchor. Lights on buoys blinked and tinged the water blue, red, and green.

The bus stopped at the Jefferson Hotel and the families of the elderly ladies helped the dear ones down from the bus. The driver pointed me down a dark street, "Bus station is over there two blocks."

I stayed in a cheap hotel that night and met Craig Lewis of Norfolk Southern (NS) for breakfast the next morning at the Norfolk Marriott Waterside, a luxury hotel in the city's historic district. Lewis works out of Philadelphia, but was in town for a board of directors meeting being held a few blocks away in NS's blue-glass office tower.

The day before he'd been in Michigan meeting with state officials who want to run a commuter train between Detroit and Ann Arbor. As vice president of passenger operations, Lewis interfaces with "passenger entities," which could be states, transit agencies, or Amtrak—any organization that wants to run passenger trains on NS infrastructure.

Unlike the Union Pacific, NS responded quickly to my request for an interview, a reflection—I later discovered—of rethinking going on within the company about passenger trains. NS isn't exactly in love with passenger trains on its routes, but it isn't hostile either, said Lewis.

Along with CSX, Norfolk Southern dominates railroading in the East and Midwest. It has 30,000 employees, owns 21,000 miles of tracks in twenty-two states, and generates $2.5 billion in annual revenues. Formed in 1982 with the merger of the Norfolk Western Railroad and the Southern Railroad, the company expanded again in the late 1990s when it and CSX divided up Conrail. If you go back to the early nineteenth century, NS represents the mergers and consolidations of nearly 350 predecessor railroads, including the Erie, Wabash, Central of Georgia, and Pennsylvania.

NS hauls large amounts of metallurgical coal, suitable for coke in steel making operations. It owns mines and has real estate interests. Its intermodal business, just-in-time delivery services, and road-railer (pulling truck trailers on trains) operations portend the future of moving all types of goods quickly on fast corridors.

Lewis was my first contact with a big freight railroad, but he didn't have the typical railroad pedigree. He had been a Pennsylvania state senator and a corporate lawyer in Philadelphia. In the late nineties, NS hired his firm to complete the purchase of Conrail, and afterward he was asked to join the company by then president David Goode, who wanted a corporate presence in Philadelphia.

Lewis recalled, "I asked David, 'Why would you want me? I don't know anything about the railroad.' David chuckled, 'I don't have anyone in this company who knows how to do business up north. We can teach you the railroad.'"

Lewis became the company's point man with the passenger entities and soon discovered the operations people at NS wanted nothing to do with passenger trains. In their minds, Lewis's job was "to make those people go away."

"You have to remember, these guys were running railroads in the seventies when passenger trains were hemorrhaging millions of dollars," Lewis recalled. "I would get up and start talking about working with these passenger folks and they would look at me like I was an alien."

But passenger trains couldn't be ignored, especially in the old Conrail territory. Amtrak runs over NS infrastructure as do commuter services in Philadelphia, Virginia, and New Jersey. NS runs over the tracks of the Northeast Corridor and pays Amtrak to do so. Transit agencies and states were looking to get access to NS's infrastructure to run more passenger trains because the costs of building their own right-of-ways are astronomical. The passenger entities were doing studies of their own, and asking for data from the railroad, including its "metrics" on average train speeds and dwell times in terminals. There was hostility on both sides. Neither trusted the other.

To Lewis, the former politician and transactional lawyer handling large corporate mergers, there were better ways to do business. NS needed to respond to these inquiries in a businesslike manner that did not unnecessarily create ill will but also clearly set out the company's terms with passenger entities.

NS sought input from other big railroads. According to Lewis, CSX had little good to say about passenger trains, Union Pacific didn't want to talk, but BNSF Railway was another matter. It had partnered with states out West and the passenger trains running on its tracks had good on-time performance. Lewis met several times with D. J. Mitchell at BNSF, while NS executives—including Jim McClellan, who headed up strategic planning—debated internally what company policy should be.

In 2004, Norfolk Southern issued a statement of principles, or business parameters, that a passenger entity would have to meet. The parameters made very clear that freight operations cannot be adversely affected by passenger trains allowed to run on NS tracks.

"The principles gave us a starting point for negotiations," he said. "Now the passenger entities have an understanding of what it takes to do business with us."

The bottom line is money, said Lewis. The infrastructure has to have the capacity to handle both freight and passenger traffic, and the capital expenditures for expansion is the responsibility of the passenger entities.

Many passenger-rail advocates don't understand the large amounts of money required for capital improvements, said Lewis. They see a track where only a few trains run by every day and think it would be easy and inexpensive to just add on a passenger train. It would take $150 to $200 million in capital expenditures to create slots for commuter trains between Ann Arbor and Detroit, he pointed out.

"When I said that to the Michigan folks, they just rolled their eyes. And I said, 'Look, you pay more than that for just one or two highway interchanges. Rail has costs, too. You can't do this on the cheap.'"

Many states would like big matching federal grants for rail—the kind that highways bring. But there are other ways to raise capital, said Lewis. Money can be obtained through tax-exempt bonding or by asking voters to add a half- or one-cent increase to the local sales tax. It's also important to factor in the increased tax value that results from the rail project, Lewis explained. When a community builds a station, puts in rail lines, and runs more frequent commuter-train service, economic development—office buildings, housing, and retail—frequently follows, said Lewis. Transit Oriented Development, or TOD, isn't just wishful thinking.

"Infrastructure is the basis of development. In that sense, rail is no different than a highway."

Some DOTs are ready to hear such a message, but others are not, said Lewis. They are addicted to highway trust funds and roads, and though they talk about rail development, that's all they do. As a case in point, he pointed to Ohio, which for years had done little to attempt to finance the 3-C Corridor, which would connect Cleveland, Columbus, and Cincinnati by rail. New York has ambitions of running high-speed trains on the Empire Corridor between Buffalo and Albany but wants the feds to pay for it.

The restaurant was full of several of the railroad's major stockholders who were leaving for the meeting. Lewis and I agreed to meet again in Philadelphia. I organized my notes on the laptop while sitting in the second-floor lobby, rich with marble, wood, and antiques. Then I went downstairs where the desk held my suitcase and took it into the bathroom. Off came the suit and on went the jeans, T-shirt, and sneakers—proper attire for the bus.

The concierge stared as I walked by.

Outside a cabby asked, "Airport sir?"

"Greyhound."

"Sir, the bus station?"

"Don't get many fares from here to Greyhound?"
He grinned, "No sir."

Because the train had already left Newport News that morning, the bus was the only public transportation back to Richmond.

Raleigh, North Carolina
a state-owned railroad

The inside of the station was blue, really blue, Greyhound blue everywhere. A blue poster on the blue wall touted "Faster Routes because we are named after a Greyhound not a sloth."

I had a relatively short trip on the bus, just ninety-two miles to Richmond, where I would catch a southbound train to North Carolina, which has been investing in rail service as a way of coping with population growth and highway congestion.

I wasn't new to the bus. Back in college, before I discovered the train, I'd taken fourteen-hour trips on Greyhound, and just recently I had started taking the all-night bus (five hours) from the Upper Peninsula to catch the train in downtown Milwaukee. During all of my research trips, I never rented a car and found I could usually catch a bus or make connections by cab.

The bus was clean, but there was little leg room and a few people yakked on their cell phones to distraction. The guy across the aisle kept calling his girlfriend in Baltimore, "Baby, baby, I'm a coming back to you. I'm almost there. Oh . . . I'm thinking about it too. You just hold on a little longer. . . ." He'd dial that phone number and turn into a piece of love-sick mush for all the world to hear, then hang up and turn back into a guy who looked like he'd rip out your liver.

I stuck in my earbuds, turned up the music, and stared out my window.

As often happens in buses, the old folks and the really large people sat up front. The young, the Goth, the punk hung in the back and struck up conversations, mostly about how people had wronged them and when it would be time to get off and have a cigarette. There were blue-hair grandmas and sweet-looking college girls who pulled out schoolbooks and did homework. And there were the poor and the carless that carried all their belonging in old duffel bags and taped-up cardboard boxes.

In Richmond, the bus station didn't connect with the train, so after a buffet meal of chicken, biscuits, grits, and greens in a diner, I caught a cab over to the depot at Staple Mills Road. There, I waited two hours for the Silver Star to take me to Raleigh.

The Star was nearly full and the attendant assigned us seats. A pert, blond college coed sat down beside me, and immediately put out her hand.

"Hi. I'm Abby."

She attended Spartanburg Methodist College in South Carolina, and her grandfather had driven down for her graduation and had some type of spell. He'd been hospitalized for a few days and she'd driven him and his car back home to Virginia. Now she was going back to Columbia.

"I've never been on a train. Do we have to stay in our seats?" she asked.

Abby was chatty about school, writing, and careers. She was one of those smart young women I teach in school whose homework is always done and whose days are all mapped out in an organizer. Abby was firstborn, motivated to succeed and, above all, saved. She'd like to be a teacher because it's a good way to serve God. She sort of fits in at her school but not entirely, "I'm not a hard-shelled Baptist. I'm sort of a mutt. I love rock music, but I love the Lord, too."

We had one of those this-is-my-life conversations that strangers stuck in airports or on trains sometimes do, although I usually don't. But I was tired and this young lady was disarmingly earnest.

The trip took four hours.

After a while I went up to the café car for a sandwich and an ice-cold beer, my voice shot from talking and from too many days of air-conditioning in hotel rooms and on the trains. The tables were empty except for the conductor counting tickets and a skinny woman who had a Budweiser, a can of kippers, and box of crackers open on the table. In between bites, she anthropomorphized about her four cats—they turned on water faucets to drink, woke her for work, and communicated their feelings about certain television shows. Who knows how long she'd been there yakking about cats and sucking down Budweisers. There are passengers who plant themselves in lounge cars and chatter for hours. When there's no one in the car, they prattle on to the attendant.

The conductor, her latest victim, retreated to another car, and I hid behind the *Richmond Times Dispatch* until I finished my beer and was ready to head back to my seat.

The towns faded into the darkness. Homes became squares of window light, and the crossing gates blocking Main Street slid by in a blur of blinking red lights. Under a streetlamp, three boys straddled their bicycles and waved at the train. Inside, the passengers read magazines, dozed, or watched movies on DVD players.

When I got off in Raleigh, there were no cabs in front of the station. Three men stood under the shadow of some trees.

"Ya'll looking for a taxi?"

I figured he was a gypsy driver and looked back for a stand.

He read my thoughts. "They don't let us park o'er here. No room. But my cab is this a way."

The driver wanted to talk and we found common ground with the price of gas. It had hit $3.76, and the city council had yet to raise cab rates.

"Don't make no sense. What they waitin' for?" the driver said. "We can't make no money this way." In the coming weeks, the lament from cabbies was the same from the Carolinas to California. "City wasn't doing a thing for taxi drivers. Too worried about raising rates and upsetting the damn tourists."

In the lobby of North Carolina's DOT building, there's a marble-tiled mosaic on the floor outlining a large graphic of the state with the word "Highways" inside. All across the country, it's the same: state DOTs adorned with emblems of bridges, overpasses, and tunnels, plastered if not on the buildings themselves then on a Web site or letterhead—nary a train because rail has always been a private enterprise and not the concern of the "highway department," which is what many DOTs were called up until the 1970s.

That should be different in North Carolina because the state owns the North Carolina Railroad Company (NCRR), a 317-mile corridor running roughly west to east from Charlotte to Morehead City on the coast. The company is privately operated, but the state is the only shareholder.

In the 1850s, the North Carolina legislature, believing it needed a farm-to-market rail link from the Piedmont to the coast, built the NCRR and also contributed to the construction of the Atlantic and North Carolina Railroad between Goldsboro and Beaufort Harbor. The railroad led to the founding of Morehead City. Both railroads were heavily damaged in the Civil War but gradually recovered. In 1896, the state leased the NCRR for ninety-nine years to Southern Railways. When the lease expired with Norfolk Southern, the state took the railroad back and merged it with the old Atlantic and North Carolina Railroad to create the corridor.

Pat Simmons, the state's rail chief, came into the transportation department's rail division in the 1990s. "I was told. We're going to buy trains, buy a railroad, and fix up stations. Would you like to come along and help?" Simmons had majored in marine biology and done survey work in the Gulf of Mexico, but didn't know much about railroads. "However," he said, "I was trained to observe facts, ask questions, and figure out solutions—and that has served me well."

Back then, the rail division had a staff of 5 and a $25 million budget. Today, Simmons oversees 50 employees with a budget of $44 million, which is still a thin slice of NCDOT's 5,000 employees and $4 billion budget.

I kidded him about that mosaic in the lobby, and he reminded me that North Carolina was known as the "good roads state."

"This department is going through a transformation to become more nimble and intermodal. The rail division has grown because we're about practical investment that increases mobility and economic development. This is not about being a gleam in the eye of the rail fan," said Simmons, a bubbly guy with longish gray hair working out of a cluttered office with train posters on the wall.

The rail division's focus is mainly on preserving and enhancing rail transportation to move people and goods within the state. The NCRR makes money by charging Norfolk Southern and CSX to run over the corridor and then reinvests the profits and dividends in the infrastructure.

For several years, Amtrak has run four long-haul trains through the state, but none made connections between the major cities of Charlotte, Winston-Salem, Greensboro, and Raleigh.

"It was happenstance if a train went near where you lived, and even if it did, it might be at odd hours," said Simmons. "We wanted to make train service more convenient, and the only way to do that was for the state to get into the market."

The state's transportation department partnered with Amtrak to launch the Piedmont and the Carolinian, state-supported trains. The Piedmont leaves Raleigh at 7:00 a.m., covering the 173 miles to Charlotte in about three hours. The return train leaves Charlotte at 5:30 p.m. The Carolinian runs between New York City and Charlotte through Washington, D.C., a distance of 700 miles. The combination and frequencies of these trains enable business travelers to spend a few hours in Raleigh or Charlotte (or stops in between) and still get home by late evening.

Although the trains are no faster than a car, they usually run full. In 2008, ridership was up 37 percent on the Carolinian, 17 percent on the Piedmont. Farebox recovery runs around 70 percent for the Carolinian. For the Piedmont, it's 34 percent, which is typical for a transit system. A third Piedmont leaving both cities at midday will be added in late 2009.

The Carolinian runs with Amtrak equipment, but North Carolina owns the Piedmont train sets. There's no mistaking these are state-supported trains. The noses of the locomotives sport a bold white star with the letters N and C, the passenger cars are painted the state colors, and volunteer train hosts staff every train and station, answering questions and handing out brochures, a popular activity for retired people and rail fans. Lack of speed is still a concern. The NCRR is predominantly a single-track railroad busy with NS and CSX freight trains.

In the last few years, the transportation department and NCRR have length-ened sidings, straightened curves, installed double track, and constructed banked turns, in which one rail is higher than the other, allowing higher speeds. By 2020, about half the corridor should be double-tracked.

The proposed Southeast High-Speed Rail corridor would run over NCRR track to create 110-mph service between Charlotte and Washington, D.C. North Carolina has received money from the Federal Railroad Administration to "seal" the corridor by closing grade crossings where possible, adding longer gate arms, putting in quadruple gates and installing highway-median separa-tors—all designed to keep people from driving around downed gates.

The corridor will get busier. Intermodal freight out of the deepwater ports of Wilmington and Morehead City is growing. There are proposals to add commuter trains in the Piedmont Triad Region around Winston-Salem and the Research Triangle near Durham. The state also plans to extend passenger service from Salisbury 139 miles to Asheville and put a train to Wilmington through Fayetteville.

North Carolina needs passenger trains because it is fast urbanizing and expected to become the nation's seventh most populous state in twenty years. The state has superb educational and medical facilities, a financial center in Charlotte, and a mild climate, but like many Sunbelt states, its growth has been underpinned by low taxes and cheap land. Urban sprawl and highways are chewing up land and degrading lifestyles.

"Go look at Charlotte. We are sprawled to the horizon. If we were doing everything so well, we wouldn't be living with all of this congestion. We are not controlling the outcomes," Simmons said. "The only alternative to more highways is rail."

The Carolinian
national train day

I had hoped to catch the Piedmont the next morning, ride it west a few stations, and get back to Raleigh in time to catch the Carolinian north to D.C. But the Piedmont was sold out for National Train Day, a creation of Amtrak's marketing department. Ticket prices had been reduced on state-sponsored trains that day to encourage family rides, and the stations were holding open houses.

When I stepped into Raleigh's station, a train host slapped a sticker on my knapsack and thrust some Amtrak pens at me. Kids got paper engineer hats and wooden whistles that sounded like locomotives.

While I waited for the train, I perused a booklet Simmons had given me: "Station Improvements in North Carolina." Since 1991, the state and local governments had spent $70 million restoring twenty historic train depots and adjacent railroad buildings—a point of pride with Simmons. In the town of Hamlet, the entire depot was picked up and moved to a new location. In other towns, stations were turned into intermodal centers for buses and trains. Several stations were reconfigured to house reception rooms and history centers. Modern platforms were added at many stops.

"If you are going to have nice trains, you also want handsome train stations because they are gateways to your towns. These stations have become anchors of downtown revitalization efforts," Simmons said.

Over thirty years of traveling by train, I've seen some pitiful stations. Amtrak doesn't have the money to repair or build stations in the five hundred or so cities and towns it serves. Sometimes, the best it could do was erect an "Amshack," a Plexiglas shelter, much like a bus stop, and leave it to local governments or citizen's groups to save the crumbling old depots or build new train stations.

In 1968, Durham's Italian Renaissance train station with its landmark sixty-five-foot tower was torn down to make way for a parking lot and the downtown loop highway. Durham got an Amshack and then moved up to a double-wide trailer. Only in 2009 did it get a decent station created from a former tobacco warehouse.

Raleigh has a pretty station, but it is much too small, especially if the city becomes a hub of more travel on the corridor. And it needs a cab stand at the front door.

As I was reading, I noticed a small, elderly black man down the bench from me. He was well dressed in a herringbone sports jacket, tie, and white shirt. His hands were folded in his lap and he looked at the frenetic goings on—the kids blowing those wooden train whistles until they were breathless—with a sedate, impassive gaze. A younger man sat beside him.

When the train came, I took a window seat at the back of a coach, and a few minutes later, the elderly man came down the aisle, struggling with his bags. He took the open seat next to me. I helped him put a suitcase in the luggage rack overhead, but he insisted on keeping one between his legs and another big satchel on his lap.

He looked around wide-eyed and concerned as the train started forward.

"This the train to Richmond?"

I nodded. We introduced ourselves. His name was Edward.

He looked about the car for a long time before he spoke.

"Last time I was on a train was 1952 during Korea. The windows were different. You could open them. The conductors wore those little flat hats," he said.

"They still do," I said.

"Do they?"

He seemed pleased, and when the conductor punched our tickets, I saw Edward staring at the hat.

"Sir, why don't we put your bags above so you are more comfortable?" asked the conductor. Edward hugged his leather satchel as if it were a bushel basket.

"I'm worried about my bags, and I don't want to lose them. My arm isn't good anymore and I wouldn't be able to get them down."

"We won't lose them," the conductor said, taking the bags. "I will tell the attendant to come back and help you off in Richmond."

He relaxed a bit and over the next two hours, we chatted. In the late 1930s, his parents would put him and five brothers and sisters on the train in Richmond to go see their grandmother in Florida. The cars were segregated and a porter would take charge of the children.

When I said I taught at a university, he lit up.

"You're a teacher?"

He had taught band and chorus in a Norfolk high school for forty-three years. He had a master's degree from Columbia University in New York and was on his way to see a brother in Newport News. He had been reluctant to go. He can't drive anymore and doesn't like to fly, so his son bought him a train ticket.

"He said, "Dad, you are going.' But since my wife passed, I just don't want to go nowhere. I try to get along, though," his voice trailed off. "We built a nice little house in Norfolk after I retired, but she didn't get to enjoy it. My son had me move down to Raleigh with them. They spoil me so. I miss them. I miss them already."

Tomorrow was Mother's Day, and he was to play the organ in his old Baptist church. "I haven't played a pipe organ for two years since I moved. But I've been practicing."

As we talked, the woods and greenery pressed close to the train, and when the locomotive picked up speed, we seemed to be rushing down a tunnel of sunlight and foliage headed deeper into the woods. At Richmond, I helped Edward off with his bags. "You'll be fine. I was here the other day, and you'll know the right train."

Union Station, Washington, D.C.
when railroads were bad to the bone

That night, I stayed at a cheap hotel at the end of the Red Line of Washington's Metro and returned to Union Station the next morning. My train back to Chicago, the Capitol Limited, wasn't scheduled to leave until 4:00 p.m., but I had arranged to meet John Hankey, the historian and for many years associated with the Baltimore & Ohio Railroad Museum. It was our first meeting. There were others.

We sat down to coffee and I mentioned my most recent trip and in particular my discussion with Edward.

"Washington was the dividing line where blacks went into one car and whites into another," Hankey observed. "When that man last rode the train, he was riding a segregated train if he was south of Washington. He wasn't just seeing a train again yesterday; he was seeing an integrated train. You two wouldn't have sat together or even been in the same car."

Months later, I found a copy of Virginia's "Jim Crow" statute regarding train travel. The law required separate cars or compartments so "no white and colored persons shall occupy contiguous seats." If a person wouldn't state his race, the conductor was "the sole and final judge of a passenger's race." After *Brown v. Board of Education*, the ICC ruled segregation in transportation illegal, but many railroads, particularly those in the Deep South, ignored the ruling.

Hankey gave me a quick tour of Union Station. He pointed out where in 1953 the runaway Federal Express from Boston crashed through the wall and slid across the concourse toward the waiting room before the floor gave way, and the locomotive and two cars fell into the basement baggage area—where the food court is today. No one was killed and the incident gave inspiration to the final scene in the movie *Silver Streak*.

Today, Union Station is a gorgeous place, a retail anchor and a vital transportation link for tourists and all the people working on the Hill and Mall. But in the 1970s, it was emblematic of rail's decline. The roof leaked, fungi grew indoors, and plywood covered holes and windows. The national park service tried to transform it for the 1976 Bicentennial into a "National Visitor Center" with a huge multimedia display set up in a kind of giant pit.

"The whole thing was terrible, an almost surreal kind of experience that some people likened to a bad acid trip," Hankey recalled.

The building was near collapse and had to be closed for several years. Finally Congress kicked in $70 million for renovation and developers added another $80 million. The station reopened in 1988 to its former glory. It's hard to imagine the city without it today.

When Hankey and I sat down to talk about the historical context of trains in America, I mentioned that a number of his e-mails had a central theme: Americans have failed to put together a rational national transportation policy.

"Yes, it goes back to our national character. We're concerned about economic and social mobility, the mobility of capital, but not so much about physical mobility. At the nation's founding, we were a country of individuals without a collective mentality or shared purpose. We felt we had a right to transportation but that it should be a highly personal process, so for a long, long time, transportation was not thought of as a public good."

He paused for a long time, as was his wont. "To really understand this you have to go back a couple of hundred years."

For the next several hours, Hankey and I moved from restaurant to restaurant, bought each other coffee and meals and talked. He sketched out a history of railroading and gave me a contextual understanding of its role in American transportation. In the early 1800s, America was an agrarian society, Hankey reminded me. People didn't travel far and if they did, they could go no more than thirty miles a day. Roads were poor or nonexistent. Canals moved substantial loads of people and goods, but at a mule's pace.

"We lived like squirrels. We had to take and eat what the world threw at us," observed Hankey. He had a number of aphorisms in his rhetorical arsenal. On a radio show a few years earlier, when an NPR commentator asked about Amtrak, Hankey had replied, "Amtrak is like a dog that walks on its hind legs. It's not so remarkable that he does it well, but he does it at all."

In the early 1800s, there was vigorous debate over the size and the role of the central government. The Democratic-Republicans (Jeffersonians) felt the government should have a direct role in planning, funding, and operating a network of roads and canals, what were then known as "internal improvements." The Federalists felt it was the role of the states and private interests to finance such improvements. These political rivalries and competition between cities, which tried to outdo one another for import traffic and control of trade routes, stymied any sort of national transportation planning.

Road building fell to the individual states, and generally Americans declined to be taxed for infrastructure. If a state had good roads and canals, it was owing to private enterprise or local government. The Erie Canal was paid for by New York, not Washington. Toll roads and private ferries were common, and, of course, they paid their way. This laissez-faire attitude toward transportation set the pattern for more than a century.

"The very same laws, policies, and cultural tendencies that worked effectively to settle the continent and create a new nation were responsible for an astonishing series of ill-informed, poorly thought through, and utterly boneheaded decisions regarding transportation." Yet, Hankey added, an infrastructure of sorts did emerge, especially as the European descendants explored the interior and clashed with native peoples. The infrastructure was created haphazardly, however, much like today's suburban sprawl.

After their introduction in the 1830s, railroads spread across the established parts of America in an astoundingly short time. Railroads overcame distance, weather, and terrain. People could traverse the Alleghenies in hours or cross the continent in days rather than months. Railroads substituted massive mechanical power for animal power.

As a technology, railroads gave mobility to people, goods, weapons, armies, and even ideas. Railroads enabled the country to communicate with itself by moving mail and delivering newspapers with a speed and over distances not previously possible. The telegraph spread with the railroad lines, building a parallel infrastructure along right-of-ways.

"Railroads changed everything. It was a paradigm shift, on an order of magnitude of the Internet and the expansion of communication services in the 1990s," Hankey said. "Without the railroads, it's hard to imagine a United States: We ought to be five different countries instead of one, and the reason we aren't is the railroad."

There was no plan or guiding hand, other than cutthroat capitalism. Post Civil War, railroad builders tended to be individuals only interested in connecting one point with another and making money for doing so. Separately owned and operated, the companies frequently didn't cooperate with one another—even to the point of standardizing track gauge. They made up their own transportation policy because the government wasn't articulating one, other than attempting some control in the waning decades of the nineteenth century in response to public pressure, Hankey pointed out. In the wake of the Civil War, the great expansion of railroads created hundreds of thousands of jobs in the drive to unite the two coasts, expand the number of places reached by rail, rid the country of buffalo and native peoples, clear the land for new settlers, and exploit its riches. The federal government enabled this expansion by giving the railroads enormous grants of land and generally turning a blind eye to their abuses. Between 1870 and 1900, American railroads laid 170,000 miles of track—nearly four times the mileage of today's interstate highway system.

Railroads were bare-knuckled, exploiting workers (especially new immigrants), buying votes and politicians, and accruing fortunes for banking magnates and robber barons. They came out of the nineteenth century with such a fearsome reputation that it damaged their ability to compete against other transportation modes in the twentieth century. It's no accident that some of the most important labor actions of the nineteenth century, such as the great railroad strike of 1877 and the Pullman strike of 1894, centered on railroads. It was the first American industry to be unionized.

For decades, politicians and citizens talked about the "railroad problem."

"Depending on who was talking—shippers or passengers or farmers—the problem was defined in different ways, but there was consensus that there was a problem," Hankey added. "It was felt that railroads had to be kept in their place, watched all the time because they were bad to the bone."

Monopoly was the biggest concern. After the network was built out—trunk lines connecting to branch lines—railroads were expected to compete against one another just like any American business. Competition would protect consumers and shippers against excessive pricing, or so the theory went. But when two different railroads ran lines next to one another, there was rarely enough business for both, and one usually failed. So the railroads—just as the steel and oil industries did—formed pools or trusts, and cooperated in rate-fixing agreements to guarantee profits.

Theodore Roosevelt and the Progressive Era came along to bust up trusts and regulate business practices. Roosevelt pushed Congress to give the fledgling Interstate Commerce Commission, created in 1887, real teeth for dealing with railroad practices. The commission had been ineffective because it did not have adequate enforcement powers. Railroads either ignored ICC edicts or fought the commission in the courts. Congress eventually extended ICC jurisdiction to other common carriers—pipelines, express agencies, water transportation, bus lines, and trucking companies.

In addition to overseeing rate changes, the ICC regulated safety and could demand the railroads install new technology. The ICC was charged with approving or denying consolidations, determining routes, and influencing labor disputes. It fought battles over accounting practices and how railroads depreciated assets. The ICC had its guiding hands, or tentacles, depending on your point of view, in all aspects of the railroad business.

During World War I, Woodrow Wilson temporarily nationalized the industry to more efficiently serve the war effort. When the railroads were reprivatized under the Transportation Act of 1920, Congress recommended that certain companies be consolidated into regional systems to eliminate redundancies and create an efficient and financially strong system. But the ICC had no authority to force mergers, so prosperous railroads just ignored the edict.

"It was a lost opportunity to bring some order and efficiencies to the system," Hankey said.

For long-distance passenger travel up to the 1930s, railroads were the only game. But with the advent of the automobile, the 1920s also saw the beginning of the age of road building. The federal government stepped up its financial aid to states to create a network of roads for cars and trucks that roughly paralleled the rail routes. Few policymakers considered how all this road building would adversely affect railroads or how the auto/road mode would fit into the nation's transportation network. Instead, attention was concentrated on how more roads could be built to more places—attention helped along by an increasingly influential road lobby that included car manufacturers, tire makers, the trucking industry, and asphalt companies.

Some railroads sought to run their own bus services as a way to create better connections to their trains. But the ICC, concerned about monopolization, barred them from owning buses or even having business relationships with bus companies. If it hadn't, the United States could have ended up with a network of interconnecting bus and train services as is common in Europe, suggested Hankey.

In the 1930s, as the road network expanded, it was relatively easy for someone to buy a truck or several trucks and get into the transportation business. When railroads complained about unfair competition and the government subsidies being poured into road building, they were largely ignored. Railroads had little political clout remaining. Roads were considered a jobs program, good government policy reflecting the will of the American people. For the average American, cars versus trains became a simple process of substitution. Henry Ford made the car affordable. Oil discoveries in California, Texas, and Oklahoma produced abundant and cheap gasoline.

By the Depression, railroads were undercapitalized and losing passenger and freight to the highways. The new dieselized Streamliner trains generated excitement with the public but did little to stem the losses. World War II put a temporary halt to this slide as all the industrial might of the nation turned toward armament production. Railroads, this time without nationalization, did a monumental job of moving raw materials, goods, and people. Millions of soldiers traveled in crowded troop trains. Gas rationing forced civilians back onto the trains and city trolleys.

At war's end, however, the ridership decline resumed, as a pent-up desire for consumer goods often took the form of car and house purchases. A house in the suburbs reached by a road in your own personal automobile was a dream for many ex-GIs.

Still, railroads in the immediate postwar years were generally optimistic about long-distance travel. Air travel wasn't commonplace and the super highway "limited access" road network was a decade or so in the future. The railroads modernized their trains, promoted cars with observation domes, and added a host of other amenities. Most people still didn't want to drive across the USA in their Chevrolet; they wanted meals and a room on board a train.

"You sometimes hear that railroads didn't try to keep their passenger business. That's a myth, they tried very hard, especially in the 1950s," said Hankey. "And some trains were quite successful."

But railroads were hampered by many forces, including organized labor, which tried to hang on to job slots being displaced by the shift from steam to diesel and other technological changes. In many states, railroads paid heavy property taxes for their private infrastructure, while the publicly owned roadways were tax-exempt. As freight continued to migrate to the highways, it became increasingly difficult for railroads to subsidize their passenger services. As one indicator, between 1946 and 1957, the ICC allowed railroads to abandon 30 percent of their passenger lines.

And then came commercial air travel, which made long-distance train travel seem old-fashioned and impractical. Who wanted to sit on a train for a day or two when you could get there in hours?

What really doomed passenger trains, however, was the four-lane "freeway." After the war, many states—beginning with Pennsylvania—built tollways. Motorists could drive from Chicago to the East Coast without having to stop except for gas and the bathroom. In 1956, the Eisenhower administration introduced the biggest public-works project in American history, the interstate highway system. The cost would run to $50 billion. The discussion was not so much should be it done as how to pay for it. Eisenhower favored toll roads; others a federal highway trust fund. The bickering in Congress went on for two years.

In *Getting There: The Epic Struggle between Road and Rail in the American Century*, Stephen Goddard wrote of the interstate highway system: "The final outcome would affect the lives of 150 million Americans dramatically, by deciding where they would live and work, whether they or their children would pay for all that concrete, how greatly the American voter could influence the process in years ahead, and whether in the American march of progress, road would finally vanquish rail."

The highway trust fund, wrote Goddard, was "the political equivalent of a perpetual motion machine." It didn't require congressional authorization. The tax monies came in and went out to the states to build freeways. And so they did.

By the late 1960s, passenger trains seemed to be passing from the scene, running with handfuls of passengers and just once a day. They were neither convenient nor that clean or pleasant. Railroads provided only the bare essentials to their passenger operations and struggled just to stay afloat with too much equipment, too much track, and not enough business. The infrastructure was in such poor shape that the industry kept statistics on standing derailments, meaning the occurrences when idle cars and locomotives derailed because the tracks failed beneath their weight.

Railroads, said Hankey, were never completely in danger of going away, but many were in a state of near collapse by the early 1970s. And even though people in most of the country weren't using trains, no one could really imagine not having them.

Congress could let the whole industry go down, or relieve it of the passenger service and hope it could pull itself together. The only other alternative for railroads was nationalization, so the Nixon administration and Congress created Amtrak in a sincere but misguided effort, said Hankey.

"Amtrak is like a platypus. It's made up of all these different parts and assumptions which together really don't make any sense. It got off to a shaky start in the seventies, and when people thought it would go away, it didn't. And for all these years, it's had the dumb luck to survive."

He paused. "And so here we are. A little better off than we were back in the early seventies with passenger service, but not much."

The Capitol Limited

america rides these trains

The last to board the Chicago-bound train, I ended up with two seats near the front of the car. I soon understood why. I was amidst a pile of kids cared for by two young Hispanic mothers, who barked at them in Spanish, smiled at me apologetically, and passed out cookies and chips. There were no infants, but the oldest weren't more than eight or nine. The young ones stood on their seats, and peered at me. I mugged and they mugged back.

I'd expected a single-level train, but the Capitol Limited, because it doesn't pass through the ancient Baltimore tunnels or into the tight, underground confines of Manhattan, operates with the taller double-decker Superliner equipment. The train runs daily between D.C. and Chicago, covering the 750 miles in about eighteen hours—if it's on time.

It never was when I rode it. The name Capitol Limited originated with the B&O's run between Pittsburgh and Washington, and Amtrak follows that old B&O right-of-way, now owned by CSX. It's a pretty path, paralleling the upper Potomac River, passing through tunnels in the West Virginia mountains and running along narrow valleys faced with sheer slopes of limestone.

The conductor punched my ticket at Rockville, and I took my laptop up to the lounge car. It was one of those cars with the old orange and blue motif—just an assault on the eyes—so I went downstairs where the café was on one side of the car and a sitting area on the other. Outside, the rain came down in a steady stream. The furrows in the fields—not yet covered by much crop growth—had liquefied, and the ditches and streams ran with mud. Outbuildings and barns, whose old boards normally had an earthy gray tone, were saturated and black as ebony. The patches of woods glistening green ran past the window like a fast film, broken with white dashes of trillium, dogwood, serviceberry, and rhododendron.

At Martinsburg, West Virginia, my car halted a few feet from a decrepit loading dock, probably the old Railway Express (REA) building. A cheap, cloth sleeping bag was unrolled on the platform next to a soggy cardboard box. Three shirts on hangers dangled from a bent nail. On the brick wall above, spray-painted graffiti warned, "Back Off Pigs. Dis my spot."

Opening in 1847, the Martinsburg depot is the oldest working train station in the United States It survived the Civil War while most of the town did not. Martinsburg was a railroad center located, like Harpers Ferry, in a no-man's-land where Union and Confederate forces waged battle throughout the war. In 1861, Stonewall Jackson and Confederate troops occupied the town, torched the locomotive shops and roundhouse, and made off with the locomotives.

After the war, the B&O rebuilt the shops and the roundhouse, which still stand preserved today. In response to a pay cut, striking railroad workers in July 1877 surrounded the roundhouse and wouldn't release any locomotives. Militia troops called in by the governor refused to fire on the workers. The Martinsburg action ignited the great railroad strike of 1877. Train traffic stopped all over the country and workers burned buildings in Pittsburgh and Philadelphia and battled federal troops. Hundreds died over a forty-five-day period that marks the beginning of the labor movement within the railroad industry.

The past wasn't far away. As the train gained speed along the river, old telegraph poles still holding dozens of wires rose out of the brush and run next to the tracks for a mile or so before falling back away into the woods. The telegraph, a technology that made communication nearly instantaneous, was as revolutionary for the country as the railroad itself. Dispatching trains by telegraph started in 1851, the same year Western Union began business.

Each small-town depot had a station agent/telegrapher who was freight and passenger agent, an agent for the Railway Express and for Western Union. He also typically handled the mail for the United States Post Office. Well into the twentieth century, even with the advent of the telephone, telegraphy still played an important role in railroad communications and the operation of track-signaling systems.

Out of Washington, the tracks had loosely followed the old Chesapeake and Ohio Canal, 180 miles long, running from Georgetown to Cumberland. Shortly after it was built in 1828, the canal was made inconsequential by the railroad. The waterway was never extended to the Ohio River. Today, it's a linear national historic park, the old towpath perfect for hiking and biking.

That night I had dinner with two young guys from Washington who were headed to Pittsburgh with bikes and gear stashed in the baggage car. After spending a night in a downtown hotel, they would use city bike paths to get on the Great Allegheny Passage, a biking trail that runs southeast through Pennsylvania's Laurel Highlands and connects up in Cumberland with the canal towpath—in total a 300-mile route free of motorized vehicles back to D.C. The Great Allegheny, which runs over abandoned railbeds and through old train tunnels, is the second longest rails-to-trails pathway in the country.

Rail abandonment has been occurring in the United States since 1916 when rail infrastructure peaked at 270,000 miles of tracks. Tracks run across private property, over federal and state lands, and across lands purchased by the railroads or given to them for building the tracks. Mainly, though, the railroads built out their networks through easements—a license that gives the holder the privilege to use land of another owner for a limited purpose. The federal government granted railroad right-of-way easements across more than ninety million acres of land—chiefly in the West.

The system was overbuilt with redundant lines, sometimes constructed just to earn profits through stock offerings. As railroads competed with one another and lost business to roads and motor traffic, they started consolidating and abandoning little-used track. Typically, ownership reverted to the adjacent landowners, which was recognized as a problem. If rail corridors fragmented, it would be nearly impossible and expensive to reassemble them again.

In the Transportation Act of 1920, Congress required railroads to get ICC permission before abandoning lines, but the law did little to stop fragmentation. In 1976, the Four R Act encouraged railroads to work with nonprofits, local governments, and state agencies to turn the beds into recreational trails. The railroads were reluctant. Although they didn't need the lines then, they didn't want to transfer away all future rights. Better to leave the corridors as they were—weedy wastelands of rusted rails and rotting ties. Meanwhile, railroads had to fight off private landowners who were filing suit, claiming the right to repossess unused tracks on their properties.

The solution was the 1983 Rails to Trails Act that allowed railroads to preserve their easements even when the railbeds became recreational trails. They could "bank" the corridor, and sell, lease, or donate it to a trail manager without reverting acreage to adjacent landowners. A later amendment also relieved the railroads from taxes and liability during the period the corridor remains a trail.

Rail banking removed the legal hurdles and gave a huge jump start to the rail-to-trails movement. It has allowed organizations and states to put together spectacular pathways, which are relatively easy to bike because the grades generally do not exceed 2 percent. All told, there are already 15,000 miles of trails established on former rail right-of-ways and another 10,000 miles in the works. But make no mistake, trains could return to these corridors, a fact that dismays some property owners who have fought the rail-banking system, calling it an unconstitutional taking of property. Most people living near these bucolic paths, however, aren't aware they reside next to a dormant railroad line.

Of course, the lines were abandoned because there was too little traffic to generate the profits railroads needed to maintain the infrastructure, and in most cases that situation won't change soon, if ever. However, transportation experts—looking decades out—expect some right-of-ways will return to rail, especially in areas of urban sprawl where light-rail or commuter-passenger service is needed. The Rails to Trails Act allows for a relatively fast process of reactivation. There is no necessity for a full-blown application or permitting process as is required to build a new line.

I wished my dinner mates good luck on their own rail-to-trail adventure. They were traveling light and planned to eat in towns along the way and stay in motels over the four to five days it would take them to reach Washington.

Back at my seat, the kids were mostly asleep, sprawled out on the floor, lying across seats hugging baby dolls and little bears. A litter of toys and potato chips lay on the floor. I had missed quite a party. One mother went around cleaning up, shifting the little bodies, tucking here and there, and stuffing toys away in backpacks.

I still had two seats to myself. I put on earbuds and music and wrapped myself in a sports coat and fell asleep. Whenever the train stopped that night—in Pittsburgh, Alliance, Cleveland, and Toledo—I sat up to look at the people getting on, preparing myself for a seatmate (who never came) and then quickly fell back asleep once the train started rolling.

Just inside the Indiana state line, I went downstairs to my suitcase, changed into fresh clothes and went off for coffee. Out the window, the fields were creamy white with a morning sun that burned bright as magnesium. A parked tractor cast a perfect shadow on a white barn. A lone mallard swam in a pond. At a table near mine, the conductor sat down, turned his hat upside down, placed his radio inside the brim, and dumped a large envelope of tickets and paperwork onto the table.

My first seatmate at breakfast that morning was a sleepy-looking woman in her forties who kept rubbing her eyes and nose saying, "I'm not a morning person." I will vouch for her on that. Thankfully the waiter brought over Ruth and Steve. Ruth was a big-boned woman over six feet tall. Her husband, Steve, wore black jeans and a T-shirt with a skull and crossbones on the front. He was missing a top front tooth, a black gap made more noticeable because he smiled broadly. We exchanged hellos, stared at our menus, ordered breakfast, and then Steve crossed his arms and sighed, "Yeah. I've been across all forty-eight states."

It was a curious remark, spoken as if in answer to a question. I looked at Ruth and when she didn't say anything I recognized it as Steve's attempt to start conversation.

"You drive a truck?" The wallet with a chain, the massive forearms, and the belly were clues.

"Yes, out of Seattle. I'm over the road."

He'd been visiting a teenage daughter in Pennsylvania from a first marriage, and now he and Ruth were on their way back west. They'd boarded the Keystone in Harrisburg and picked up the Capitol in Pittsburgh. In Chicago, they'd get the Empire Builder. Coach all the way.

"Any regular runs?"

"No. Not really. Wherever a load has to go. Mostly tin cans."

I looked confused.

"Shipping containers," he said.

Many of his runs start at the BNSF intermodal facility at the port of Seattle where he picks up forty-eight-foot containers full of consumer products. On return trips, he brings in containers packed with electronic recyclables or wastepaper—all of it bound for China.

He wanted to buy his own truck, but the company has been good to him and port business steady (this was before the deep economic decline of the fall of 2008) because he has a Transportation Worker Identity Card (TWIC) issued through the Transportation Security Administration (TSA).

"Without that TWIC card, you are out of luck. You can't get into the rail yards or the port. And a lot of guys can't get a TWIC because they have prior felonies," he said.

His company had turned to a truck-driving school to get new drivers.

"But I'm not real impressed with the folks they've been sending us," Steve said. "You have to be able to do paperwork and spell. One guy couldn't spell Washington and didn't know half of the fifty states on the map. Can you believe that?"

All through Indiana, we were held up by freights and got to Chicago two hours late. I missed the late morning train to Milwaukee and had to wait until 1:05. I bought a *New York Times*, went up to the Great Hall, and read for more than an hour until I had to shut my eyes.

I was under a patch of warm sunlight from the skylight. I zipped the bags, looped an arm and leg through the straps—so no one could pull them away—and fell asleep. I'm so tall there was no way to support my neck, so I'd sleep until my head fell forward and then I'd snap awake before dozing off again.

Down at Lounge B, the waiting line for the Hiawatha stretched clear through the lounge and out into the hall. I didn't bother getting in line; it was midday and there would be plenty of seats. I leaned against the wall and looked into the kid's playroom and the mini gym.

It was a sight to warm the heart. Pressed against the window, one of the Hispanic kids who had been in my car mugged at me through the glass. Behind her were Asian kids, black kids, white kids, and Amish kids in their country dresses, bonnets, and black pants and white shirts. There were a couple of Hasidic Jewish kids with curl locks, too—all crawling through the tubes and tumbling over one another. Their parents stood back watching.

Across the room, I saw Steve, the trucker, a pillow case over his back—I guess to hold his carry-ons. He grinned gap-toothed and waved.

On a trip a few weeks later, a woman I met in the lounge car took in the crowd around us—kids and single mothers, farmers, punkers and gangbangers, cowboys, seniors, soldiers, preppy people, tourists, and foamers. "You know who rides these trains? Look at these people. It's America."

PART 5
California

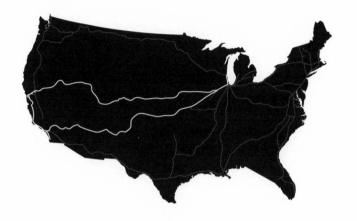

The Southwest Chief
on the transcon

The trip to California that would take me to some of the best Amtrak corridor trains now in service began on an all-night bus from the Upper Peninsula to Milwaukee and then a Hiawatha train to Chicago. As we came into Union Station, the engineer laid on the whistle and crept through a grade crossing where a taxi cab jutted into the right-of-way, its grill just feet from the train, and the crossing gate, red lights flashing, in the down position resting on the front windshield. The car door was open and the driver, a Sikh wearing a turban, stood a few feet away, hands on hips, watching us go by.

As soon as I got into my roomette aboard the Southwest Chief at 3:00 p.m., I pushed down the bed, closed the curtains, and stretched out for a nap.

The Chief runs more than half of its 2,256-mile route between Chicago and Southern California on BNSF's transcontinental line. The railroad calls the route "the transcon" because it goes from one end of the BNSF network to the other and traverses a large swath of the country.

The transcon is nearly all double-tracked and in places triple-tracked. Consequently, the movement of trains, the fluidity of traffic, tends to be pretty smooth even though some sections see 80 to 100 trains per day. The Chief arrives as scheduled in L.A. nearly 90 percent of the time, and can even be an hour early.

The train loosely follows the old Santa Fe route that was run by celebrated passenger trains—the El Capitan and the Super Chief—which operated until 1971 and the creation of Amtrak. A luxury service patronized by Hollywood entertainers, the Super Chief was the first diesel-powered, all-sleeping-car, air-conditioned, Streamliner train. Running up to 100 mph, it could cover the route in thirty-nine hours. The Southwest Chief takes three hours longer today.

An hour out of Chicago, I threw back the curtains in Princeton, one of those small towns hardly deserving of a train stop but fortunate enough to be on the main line and in a position to serve a larger geography. It's often said trains traverse the backyards of America, and it was true this May afternoon: A man, bare to the waist and laying block for a garage, mixed mortar in a wheelbarrow. At the Knights of Columbus Hall, folks arrived for a fund-raising supper. Two little girls ran out of a house toward their trampoline while their teenage

brother scribed circles with the lawnmower. A Little League coach hit ground-
ers to a line of boys between third and second base.

It resembled Grant Wood country with fields laid open by the plow and the
fresh needles of corn like an emerald brushstroke on the land. However, on
rail sidings and between the fields sat tanks of anhydrous ammonia and, out
on the land, farmers in humongous tractors shot out mists of fertilizers to feed
a monoculture of corn that devours nitrogen like sugar. Natural fertility isn't
adequate. It wasn't so much spring as the season of inputs.

In my roomette, I thumbed through local newspapers that were delirious
with ethanol fever. Once American grain farmers fed the world, now they were
to fuel the United States. By the end of 2008, the whole notion had lost its
allure: investment dollars had dried up, flex-fuel vehicles didn't save the auto
industry, and the press discovered that industrial farming with diesel and oil-
based chemicals requires more energy than it produces.

We crossed the Mississippi River at Fort Madison, cut through a corner of
Iowa, and started across Missouri to Kansas City. That night I had dinner with
David Wurfel, a film producer and brand marketer for Capital One, who was
behind the "What's in Your Wallet" commercials. An athletic-looking guy with
a mustache and a friendly, nervous manner, he had moved from Virginia to
New Mexico and was on his way home. He has traveled much in his career for
on-location filming but boards an Amtrak train whenever possible.

"Oh, I'm a bit of train nut. A friend of mine who is an engineer for CSX
once let me park a locomotive," he said.

The glasses of wine during dinner and the lingering fatigue of my bus journey put me right to sleep that night.

At daylight, we changed crews in Dodge City, Kansas, still as much a cattle
town as the 1880s when Texas cowboys drove herds to the railhead for shipping to Chicago. I stepped off the train into a bright, cool day where a strong
odor of cattle, hay, and manure wafted over from the feedlots and holding pens
supplying 6,000 head a day to the Cargill Meat Solutions plant (a wonderful
business-platform euphemism for a slaughterhouse) that turns out 4.5 million
pounds of beef as well as byproducts—tallow, hides, and "case-ready offal."

Now on the southern Great Plains, we sped by thousands of steers and cows
grazing with their calves on fresh spring grasses. The youngest, unaccustomed
to the world, turned and skittered away from the tracks as the train roared past.
It was the same with colts and lambs. By fall they would be as stoic as the rest,
barely lifting their heads at our passing.

After Garden City, Kansas, the Rockies appeared on the horizon and the flat
plains broke into buttes, mesas, and arroyos. Pronghorn antelope and mule deer

mixed with the cattle herds. At breakfast a black-hatted cowboy ate his eggs while keeping his lid on throughout the meal. Across the aisle, four bareheaded Amish men, well up in their years, closed their eyes and prayed.

I ate with Ben, a sixty-five-year-old electrical engineer from Louisville who was headed to the Grand Canyon to hike by himself and then to Utah for a Sierra Club outing. He was sinewy, hard-muscled for his age. He said, "I decided to take the train to lower my carbon footprint, but lord, what a hassle."

His wife drove him to St. Louis where he took the Missouri River Runner across the state, which has only a 70 percent on-time performance owing to freight congestion. It got in late, so he sat in Kansas City for twelve hours to wait for the Chief. Once aboard, he had hoped to upgrade to a sleeper but no luck.

"Still, it was a pretty good seat in the coach for sleeping," he said.

At Trinidad, Colorado, the Chief went over the Continental Divide at Raton Pass, a relatively low Rocky Mountain pass at 7,800 feet, but still a steep 4 percent grade for a railroad. Heavy freights need a helper engine to make the climb, so BNSF takes another way around and sold the line from Raton to Las Vegas, just north of Albuquerque, to the state of New Mexico for $71 million.

In 2003, the New Mexico DOT and a regional council of governments got into railroading when they launched the Rail Runner Express, a commuter service through the Albuquerque–Santa Fe corridor, where 50 percent of the population resides. The purchase of the Raton line anticipates the day there will be corridor trains running between Albuquerque and Denver as a complement to I-25.

In Albuquerque we had a long layover, and artisans and Native American traders set up booths on the platform to sell silver, turquoise, and rugs to passengers. I stood next to the sleeping car and chatted with Sharon, the attendant, who had been professional, polite, and utterly competent throughout the trip.

In her late fifties, Sharon had been with Amtrak just three years, having worked at Vons, a grocery-store chain in California. After her husband died, she retired, but was bored so she went to a job fair and was recruited by Amtrak. It's been a good adventure, a great second career, she said.

"I like the tips on the train, but what I really like are the letters and the drawings I get from the kids—things I can put up on the fridge back home."

Sharon was exactly the type of employee Amtrak looks for—customer-service experience, maturity, self-confidence, and a willingness, or lifestyle, to spend days away from home. Her biggest problem this trip was the toilets. At higher elevations and in the thinner air, the vacuum pumps to remove the waste jam up. Toilets have long been a problem on the Superliner cars. The only way to get the pumps working is to turn them off and then on again—and usually after one flush, they lock up until the train returns to a lower altitude.

"You need bathrooms that work," she said. "I'm really here for my passengers. They are number one, not Amtrak."

Out of Albuquerque, we met fast intermodal trains, several loaded with UPS priority containers and piggyback trailers rushing east at 70 mph. Nicknamed Z trains, these are BNSF's highest-priority trains because they carry time sensitive freight. The company has 50 to 100 Z trains out on the transcon at any one time. Other railroads have similar services—harbingers of a future when fast trains will whisk freight between cities and along corridors. In the meantime, the railroads are gaining back market share once lost to the trucking industry, which is now using rail to ship trailers long distance.

Night came west of Gallup and I went to bed early because, if I wanted breakfast, Sharon would wake us at 5:00 a.m. The train was due into L.A. at 8:15 a.m., but it looked like we would be early.

Pacific Surfliner
on board the california car

Sharon knocked on my door in Victorville, and I sat down for breakfast as the train pulled into San Bernardino. Afterwards, I showered and shaved, put on my business clothes, and got ready to go to work. I was to meet Jack Wilson, Amtrak's assistant superintendent for road operations in Los Angeles.

As the train crossed over freeways and ran through the sprawl of the Inland Empire, I took out my California research folder filled with printouts and executive summaries of rail studies.

California may be synonymous with the automobile, congested freeways, and sprawling car-dependent suburbs, but California has more passenger trains than any other state outside the Northeast Corridor. And those intercity trains oper-ated by Amtrak California, a partnership between Amtrak and the California Department of Transportation (Caltrans), generally run frequently and have good on-time performance.

Of the 28.7 million people who rode Amtrak in 2008—a record-break-ing year with ridership up 11 percent—about one-fifth boarded a train in California.

Amtrak runs four long-haul trains in and out of state. The Coast Starlight between L.A. and Seattle, the California Zephyr between Chicago and Emeryville (San Francisco), and the Southwest Chief are dailies. Three days a week, the Sunset Limited runs between L.A. and New Orleans. But these don't account for the bulk of the ridership—that occurs on the state-supported corridor services: the Pacific Surfliner between San Diego and L.A., the Capitol Corridor between San Jose and Sacramento, and the San Joaquin between Bakersfield, Sacramento, and Oakland.

California not only subsidizes the trains, it owns most of them. It also contracts with Amtrak and bus companies to provide connecting feeder buses to many of the stations. As a result, about 80 percent of California's population has easy access to a train or a bus that feeds in and out of the rail lines. Several bus routes are testing new markets, establishing ridership, and paving the way for future trains.

It's not perfect—and for a state its size the rail-bus network isn't adequate and certainly doesn't replace the automobile and freeways—but California has accomplished a level of connectivity and intermodality in intercity public transportation unmatched anywhere else in the United States. And it has plans for much more. Many rail experts told me that California—not the Northeast Corridor—is the model for an expanded nationwide network of intercity trains, because it operates not just in dense corridors but across less populated areas connecting major cities.

Rail and connectivity hasn't come cheap. Since 1976, California has invested nearly $2 billion, all of it unmatched by the federal government. Much of the money came from two voter initiatives: Proposition 108, the Clean Air Bond Act, and Proposition 116, the Clean Air and Transportation Improvement Act. Caltrans created a rail division in 1992 to disburse those funds to local governments for station improvements, train sets, and infrastructure investment. In 2008, voters approved a $9-billion bond issue to begin construction on a bullet train between Anaheim and San Francisco. For all these reasons, I'd come to California.

We arrived forty-five minutes early in Los Angeles and that's because the Chief often "runs hot" coming in from San Bernardino. Triple-tracking and BNSF dispatching keeps all other trains out of the way, said Jack Wilson when he met me on the platform.

"As compared to UP they are a delight to work with, but they nickel-and-dime us for every bit of incentive. Yet, they do deliver these trains on time," Wilson said.

He wore a Panama hat, had a Blackberry on his hip, and smoked a long, dark cigarette. He led me down a tunnel into the long hall that runs into the Union Station's main lobby and then up to his office. Wilson started with Amtrak in 1974 in food service and worked his way through different departments from Shelby, Montana, to El Paso to Chicago. He came out to California in 1993 and has charge of eight field managers responsible for train crews, customer service, and rules compliance. They oversee the Coast Starlight, the Sunset Limited, and thirteen Surfliner trains.

Each train has its own ridership personality, Wilson said. The Sunset Limited is dominated by retirees. Some Surfliners are mostly commuter trains; others are filled with pleasure travelers.

"Did you see Amish on your train?" he asked.

"Yes."

"Probably headed to San Diego and then over the border to Mexico."

"Why?"

"Health care. They see doctors down there and buy cheap drugs. A lot of them don't have health insurance and self-pay."

"They must stick out like sore thumbs in San Diego."

"We see them on the Sunset, too, headed to El Paso and then across the border."

He was proud of Amtrak's West Coast operation, and I sensed—as I did from others on the Pacific coast—that the Northeast Corridor and the East, in their opinion, get way more attention than they deserve. The nation's next two busiest corridors are in California. "We have our own little world out here," he said, "and we kick out a lot of trains with not a lot of people. Everyone has to pitch in to get it done."

And it was busy that summer. The Surfliners have a walk-on policy, and some of the commuter-oriented trains—early morning and late afternoon—were standing room only.

As I heard everywhere in the United States, there wasn't any more equipment to be had, and it was desperately needed. "We're victims of our own success," Wilson remarked. "We're seeing a lot of new riders who had no idea these trains are as nice as they are. We want to keep them as customers, but it isn't good to have standees."

Wilson left me in the lobby, where I spent an hour walking about the terminal. Built in 1939, L.A.'s Union Station has been called the "last great train station." Not as large as the landmark stations in the East, it is charming and uniquely Californian with outdoor courtyards, archways, a pastel color scheme, art deco detailing, and scores of wooden chairs with brown leather cushions. There are none of those hard railroad benches. It looks and feels like an old movie set and has been featured in several films. Functionally, it's a busy transportation hub with Amtrak and Metrolink trains, bus service, L.A. light rail, and "Flyaway" bus service to LAX.

I caught an early afternoon Surfliner to San Diego to meet with George Chilson, the chairman of the National Association of Railroad Passengers (NARP).

The Pacific Surfliner corridor between L.A. and San Diego is the second busiest in the country. Initially Amtrak ran a three-frequency, daily train called the San Diegan, but in 1976, California began subsidizing more service. Today there are eleven daily round-trips, including five that continue through L.A. to Santa Barbara, and two that terminate at San Luis Obispo. Caltrans designed and bought railcars for the corridor and created slots for more by purchasing miles of track and investing in more capacity with the freights on the shared right-of-way.

On board the Surfliner, I got my first look at what has become known as the "California car" that was developed to match up to double-decker Superliners for commuter and intercity service. The cars are painted ocean blue outside; inside, they are bright and airy with big windows and pleasant blue-gray color schemes. The seats are cushy with front trays low enough for typing on a laptop. Surfliners have bike racks, automatic wheelchair lifts, and multiple doors on both sides. A straight rather than a winding stairway connects the lower and upper decks.

Bill Bronte, Caltrans rail chief, told me, "Huge battles were fought just over the seats—how they reclined, the footrests, and the seat back. We wanted to improve the Superliner concept and produce something special."

Everyone I met—including Amtrak personnel—loves the California car, and sees it as a model for the future.

Although San Diego is 129 miles to the south of L.A., the train takes two hours and forty-four minutes averaging just 47 mph. In southern California, however, even that beats traffic. When more infrastructure improvements are in place, the time could be reduced to two hours. Still, the ride is smooth, the Amtrak people running the trains are professional, and the price is affordable. A ticket between L.A and San Diego costs $29.

As the Surfliner headed out of Union Station, we ran a gauntlet of ware-houses, factories, and storage yards. Tourists may come for the glitz and showbiz, but L.A. works. Manufacturing is central to the economy. You see it from the train—the machine shops, sheet-metal fabricators, parts manufacturers, found-ries, acres of wire cable, pipes, and shipping containers—all of it surrounded by block walls and cyclone fences fifteen feet high.

Spray-painted graffiti, the tagging, the declarations of territory and supremacy, unwound alongside the train like a ribbon of color, words and symbols scrawled across buildings, fences, retaining walls, underpasses and overpasses, and storm-water canals. Except where it's scrubbed away with solvent or painted over, the script—much of it ugly and incomprehensible—runs unbroken for miles.

In Anaheim next to the stadium, we stopped alongside a Metrolink train. The coaches looked blue and white to me, but its Web site says periwinkle. Each car can carry 300 people.

The first time most Americans heard of Metrolink was September 2008, when news video shot from helicopters showed a shredded derailed coach with firemen climbing up ladders and passing down the dead and injured passengers. Nearby, a yellow Union Pacific locomotive lay on its side, mostly intact after a head-on collision that killed 25 and injured 135. It was the nation's worst train accident in twenty-seven years.

Metrolink is a relatively new service created in 1991 to carry long-distance commuters around suburban Los Angeles on existing freight lines. The state bought up nearly 450 miles of infrastructure from the freight railroads, but Metrolink, the Surfliners, and the freights still share the right-of-way. Metrolink is mostly a weekday service, and when we passed through the Irvine station, the parking lots there held thousands of cars of commuters.

After San Juan Capistrano, the train took to the beaches. It's easy to see how the service got its name: The track runs right next to the Pacific with sunbathers, and, yes, surfers out on the rolling blue waters.

Eventually, we climbed a bluff and ran past the San Onofre nuclear power plant and then into the undeveloped lands of Camp Pendleton—a miniature of the southern California coast before settlement. After Oceanside, we began meeting Coaster trains, a commuter service running to points north of San Diego. Sprinter, a smaller light-rail system, runs east to west connecting with buses. As we neared San Diego, the hillsides shown green from winter rain, the creeks ran full, and the harbors and beaches lent a beauty to what was otherwise a congested sprawl of city and suburb.

It's hard to believe that San Diego's train station was nearly torn down in the 1970s. It's a gem of mission architecture with white brick walls, spires, and a red-tiled roof. It looks like it belongs in a California landscape much more so than the downtown office towers.

Although officially designated Union Station, it's really the Santa Fe Depot. A huge sign on the roof proclaims this fact, and inside the railroad's "blue cross" emblem is worked into the ceramic-tiled walls and the ironwork of the chandeliers. The full name of the railroad was the Atchison, Topeka and Santa Fe Railway—but everyone called it the Santa Fe. It merged with the Burlington Northern in 1996 to become BNSF, a much less romantic moniker.

But the station remains a grand public space with redwood beams soaring over the waiting room and natural light coming in through big windows on the gabled ends. That day, all the doors were open and a breeze wafted through the station. Birds hopped about, picking up crumbs. Coaster trains and San Diego's light-rail trains also come into the station, and a few steps away, city buses pulled in and out of a transportation center. All this connectivity made me wish I'd gotten a hotel close to a rail line rather than a cab ride away.

At the height of rush hour, George Chilson drove over to meet me at the hotel. Chilson wrote his thesis on the economics of American passenger trains when he was at Princeton in 1963. He earned an MBA from Stanford and went to General Mills where he helped develop the marketing for the granola bar. In California, he worked in the vitamin and natural-food industry, retired, and went into real estate and property management. He's been chairman of the National Association of Railroad Passengers since 1998.

Like many Americans, he said, southern Californians chose where to live based on $1.50 gas. A story in that day's *San Diego Tribune* tried to show the real costs of moving out of the city to places like Escondido and Temecula on I-15 where homes are bigger and cheaper, but the commute is sixty to eighty miles. That extra 500 square feet of living space in the suburbs becomes mighty expensive when gas is $3 or $4, said Chilson.

"It's a different story for people who live in San Bernardino, Riverside, and Oceanside, which are served by Metrolink, Coaster, or a Surfliner. Those people have a choice to take the train, but those poor suckers out in Temecula have to drive. If you don't have any choices, how can you express a preference between a car or a train?" he went on. "We have been bamboozled to believe that automobiles could take care of our transportation needs, so we built no choices into the system. And now when we need options, there aren't any."

Over the past twenty years, rail transit in California has expanded through voter referendums and local governments that have come together to form authorities. Local governments have responded quicker than the feds because they are closer to the people, Chilson believes. Highway congestion, urban sprawl, the loss of open land, and a degradation of quality of life have made many people—and local politicians—realize that reliance on the automobile is not sustainable.

"It's just getting too expensive to build and maintain this highway infrastructure. Costs are going to drive this move to rail more than anything else," he said.

What type of rail should the country invest in? I asked. Something like the proposed bullet train between L.A. and San Francisco or more Amtrak trains running on the existing rail network?

Both, said Chilson. Passenger-dedicated, high-speed rail owned by the public has to become a bigger part of the intercity transportation network, but the private railroads also need to expand their systems for shared access with more conventional-speed passenger trains.

"The Class 1s don't call themselves railroads—they call themselves freight railroads. And that nuance has a purpose—it's an attempt to say we are not in the business of moving passengers and have no obligation to do so. We are private businesses responsible only to our customers and shareholders," he said. "Now I don't blame them for trying, but it's really an ill-conceived construct for what is a unique industry."

Railroads are not like Wal-Mart, Ford, Intel, or any other private business, he pointed out. They control a significant national transportation infrastructure vital to the economy, the security of the country, and the mobility of the people. The nation's rail network cannot be used just to move goods. It must move people again, and in vast numbers, he said.

Expanding that network requires public investment, and, in Chilton's view, Amtrak should not be in charge of the investment decisions. Rather, the U.S. Department of Transportation should create a division to develop the national network for both passenger rail and freight movement. The Amtrak reauthorization act passed a few weeks after our conversation requires DOT to come up with a national rail plan.

"Amtrak has been beaten down for a long, long time. Its main goal is to survive, not thrive. And in most places that's all it's done."

Consider, for example, he suggests, the Sunset Limited service that runs just three times a week between L.A. and New Orleans. Prior to Hurricane Katrina, it once went clear to Miami, but Amtrak cut off service between Florida and Louisiana owing to storm damage and has never resumed service. Granted, the Sunset had severe on-time performance issues, said Chilson, but it passed through Sunbelt states with booming populations, the country's fastest growing cities, and places starved for train service. The corridor deserves attention, and it hasn't gotten it from Amtrak.

"Amtrak works well as a partner with the states that are already making investments, such as California. But we shouldn't look for Amtrak to lead. It's not a place where you get a lot of new thinking."

The Coast Starlight
a california train inside and out

The next morning, I caught a Surfliner back to L.A. and then switched to the Coast Starlight for the 464-mile trip north to Oakland. The Starlight runs this segment in about eleven hours. Fifty years ago, the Southern Pacific did it in nine and a half hours.

There are pretty train rides all over America, but it's hard to imagine any landscape more sublime than the California coast north of Santa Barbara and the mountains of central California. Nor does any other train exude such a regional flavor. Whether I was looking out the window or interacting with other passengers, I knew I was in California.

Out of Ventura, the train followed the Pacific coast for 100 miles. Near Oxnard, sea lions bobbed in the waves. We cut through Vandenberg Air Force base where we could see the rocket-launch facilities. There were state parks with Airstream trailers whose canopies flapped in the wind. We ran through fog banks where the Pacific rolled heavy with waves, capped with white and tinged greenish blue from below by the forests of kelp. Like the young calves in Kansas, waves of gulls fled from the train.

I lunched with Jenny, a feminist and radio commentator for Pacifica radio—a listener-supported, commercial-free network of community stations. Jenny wore a peasant dress that showed a good deal of bodice, and she just bubbled: in her fifties, she was going back to college to study theater arts and literature. She's white but plans to attend a predominantly black college. The California sun has given her skin cancer; she had four white spots removed. See right here. She bought some organic vegetables that day outside of a V.A. hospital where residents care for the garden. "But the prices, man. The prices. They were Brentwood prices."

In the lounge car, two filmmakers from L.A. watched out the windows and scouted locations to shoot a music video for a major band. They wouldn't say which one. They snapped stills with an expensive digital camera, made notations in a notebook, and marked locations on a California road map. They chatted with a woman sitting cross-legged in the lounge reading *The Engaged Spiritual Life*. She was headed to a meditation retreat.

At San Luis Obispo, an autistic man stalked along the tracks with a handheld scanner and time schedule—a trainspotter with an obsession. He wrung his hands, swayed from side to side and muttered, "Hurry up, you're late. Come on, come on, you're late."

If he craved predictability, I pitied him if all he had was this train. We were only twenty-five minutes off schedule, but the Coast Starlight has a reputation as the Coast *Starlate*, and at its endpoints can be hours behind schedule.

Leaving the coast behind, we passed the California Men's Colony, a rather ominous looking prison, and immediately negotiated two horseshoe curves and several tunnels to gain altitude for the Cuesta Pass, where we got spectacular views of the Los Osos Valley. The mountains were classic California coast, humps of golden grass, gentle and rolling, mottled with copses of cypress and eucalyptus trees with vineyards, cattle, and crops. It is a landscape where with a little water you can grow just about anything.

I had an early dinner with a retired engineer and his wife from Orange County. He once worked on the Redstone Mercury project, and they moved out to California from Chicago in 1961 for the aerospace industry.

They had a sleeper but had emerged to "slum it." It was said with tongue in cheek. On the Starlight, first-class passengers have their own parlor car, with a bar, food-serving area, and a movie theater downstairs. There's wine tasting and a breakfast buffet, too. Parlor cars run nowhere else on Amtrak's system. The engineer, a self-described Orange County Republican, cocked his thumb in the direction of the sleepers, "It's like a whole other world back there. I wonder how much money Amtrak is losing on that."

North of King City in the Salinas Valley, the hills muscled up into mountains and the produce fields sprouted purple cabbage, spinach, and lettuce. Silver irrigation pipe ran between the rows and sprayed out jets of water. Rainbows formed in the mists over the rows. Somewhere along this stretch, someone pelted the train with tomatoes, and the splattered remains on the lounge-car windows refracted the light like reddish sunbursts.

"Far out," said a filmmaker and snapped a picture.

As the evening came on, the train reached San Jose and then ran along the east side of San Francisco Bay to Oakland. As yet, there's no direct train service between Los Angeles and San Francisco. Caltrains, a commuter service out of San Jose, goes up the peninsula to San Francisco on the bay's west side through the Santa Cruz Mountains. California has plans to subsidize another train it will call the Coast Daylight, which will make a direct run to San Francisco.

We reached Oakland at 10:30 p.m., about an hour late.

I knew my hotel was close by, but the neighborhood away from the platform looked funky. I went back inside, got a phone book from the ticket agent and called a cab.

A woman in early fifties came out of the restroom taking a cigarette and a lighter from her purse to smoke outside. Right then, the Starlight pulled out of the station.

"Hey, hey! That's my train. Where is it going? Where is it going?"

We all looked at her.

"Where is that train going? Is it coming back? Oh my God."

The ticket agent said, "Ma'am, you were told to stay train side."

"But they said ten minutes. Ten minutes. It hasn't been ten minutes. All my things . . ." she suddenly grasped her purse as if it were about to leave too. Her lips quivered.

"Ma'am, if you can get a cab to Emeryville, you may be able to catch up with it there." Getting stranded happens. I was aboard the Lake Shore Limited, riding home from college and drinking beer in the lounge car with a bunch of guys I had met on the train. During a stop in Utica or Syracuse, someone spied a bar across the street and decided to make a dash for a couple of six packs.

"Don't do it, man," we warned, though a couple guys shoved money at him. He was just emerging from the bar with a bag of beer when we pulled away. When a conductor says stay train side, you do. And though the engineer usually gives two blasts of the whistle before pulling out, don't count on it.

The woman came out to the curb wiping away tears and clutching a piece of paper that said Emeryville. She had been headed to Portland. I gave her my cab, but she probably wasn't going to make it anyway. The next cab unfortunately didn't show up for forty-five minutes. As I waited, I walked around the concrete patio examining the life-sized statue of C. L. Dellums, a founder and president of the American Brotherhood of Sleeping Car Porters. He died in Oakland in 1999. A couple of homeless people lay on two nearby benches. The air smelled of the sea. It was damp and foggy and not hard to conjure up Jack London stories on this dark night.

A young woman who had just gotten off the last Capitol Corridor train joined me at the cab stop. She saw the folks asleep on the bench and gave me a nervous look.

"What to share the next cab?" I said. "I'm not going far."

"Thank you."

The cab took two turns and stopped in front of my hotel.

After checking in, I stepped onto Embarcadero Street where two sets of tracks divided the street in half. I ran my eyes along the rails to the platform and the skywalk over the tracks just a block or two away. I had been that close the whole time.

Capitol Corridor
trains in the streets of oakland

I'd seen photographs of trains chugging down the middle of Jack London Square in Oakland. The first train came through at 4:30 a.m. and blew its whistle right beneath my second-floor window. I went back to sleep and perhaps forty minutes later it happened again. This time, I threw back the curtain and saw the end of the train entering the station. Tree branches touched the window, and from within those branches two foot-tall birds stared back at me. The trees held a colony of nesting black-crowned night herons, which after apparently fishing on the bay, had returned to regurgitate for their babies. So I made coffee and sat in a chair and watched the birds eat and waited for the next Capitol Corridor train. It came right down the street between cars and pedestrians, and just beneath my window it let loose with a blast.

Gene Skoropowski, the executive director for the authority that runs the Capitol Corridor trains, had suggested we meet on the westbound that leaves Jack London Square Station at 9:03. Five minutes before the train was due and he hadn't arrived, I called his secretary. Look for a smartly dressed man with big head of white hair. The train pulled in, and such a man emerged from the coach and started looking around the platform. I didn't realize he'd be coming by train.

"I may ride back with you unless I have to give testimony at the legislature in Sac today," he said.

Sac is short for Sacramento. The coaches of the Capitol Corridor, second-generation "California cars," are a bit different but just as inviting as those of the Surfliners. The café is on the upper level with several seats with tables for workspaces. We got a coffee and a cinnamon roll from the café and went upstairs where Skoropowski had laid out maps and performance charts on a table.

I'd been hearing about the Capitol Corridor service from passenger-rail advo-cates who see it as a prototype for the kind of corridor service that could be replicated elsewhere. Skoropowski had gotten high praise, too. George Chilson told me, "Gene's one of those entrepreneurial managers. He has thought of things, and done things that the Amtrak people who run the Surfliners haven't even dreamed about."

Skoropowski didn't start out running a railroad. In 1970, he was an architect in Melrose, Massachusetts, riding the commuter train into Boston. The service, the equipment, was awful. On rainy days, the cars leaked and riders sat under their umbrellas. However, when he heard the train would be discontinued, Skoropowski complained to his mayor, who suggested he represent the town on the transit board.

Skoropowski was on a committee that hired David Gunn to run the Boston train system. When the state bought 200 miles of track from the Boston and Maine Railroad and turned it into a publicly owned commuter-rail operation, Gunn hired Skoropowski to become his operational planning manager.

"I was always telling David what they ought to be doing about the trains, so when they bought the Boston and Maine, he called me up and said, 'I'm going to hire you and put your big mouth to work.'"

Skoropowski took to railroading. When Gunn went to Philadelphia to run SEPTA (the Southeastern Pennsylvania Transportation Authority), Skoropowski followed to become assistant general manager. Gunn went on to run the Washington Metro system and later became president of Amtrak. Skoropowski joined the Fluor Corporation, a multinational construction firm. As director of rail transportation, he headed up projects in Southern California, Montreal, London, Paris, and Amsterdam. He also did work on the proposed Florida bullet train, which was cancelled by the Jeb Bush administration.

When I interviewed Gunn in 2009 after the stimulus package set aside $8 billion for high-speed rail and another billion for Amtrak, he worried there weren't a lot of people who can put the money to good use and who know how to make a passenger-rail system work.

"You need people who can pull this off, and Gene is one of the people. What's happened with the Capitol Corridor is really admirable. He has a good relationship with the freight railroad, and he's ready to spend money and get results," he said.

Skoropowski unfolded a route map. "This is the best job I've had in my life. For the first time, all my attention is focused on one line, on one route. This is the world."

The Capitol Corridor mainly runs 133 miles between San Jose and Sacramento (although one train reaches east to Auburn), serving sixteen stations, including Silicon Valley, the Bay Area cities of Santa Clara, Berkeley, Oakland, and Fremont, and the Delta cities of Martinez and Richmond. A model of connectivity, it intersects with BART (Bay Area Rapid Transit), Sacramento's light-rail system, Caltrans buses, San Jose commuter trains, and Amtrak long-haul trains.

When Amtrak and Caltrans began the service in 1991, there were just three round-trips. Ridership was low, about 400,000 annually; farebox recovery just 30 percent. The state had bought new locomotives and plenty of California cars. Their equipment was first class, but the problem was frequency, Skoropowski said; there just wasn't enough service to build a market.

In 1998, a joint-powers board made up of sixteen elected officials from regional planning and transit agencies took over the operations. Caltrans owns the trains, and Amtrak provides operating crews, station staff, and maintenance facilities. The board operates, manages, and markets the service, overseeing details down to the café-car menu. It hired Skoropowski as the Capitol Corridor's chief executive in 1999.

"My role was to get this stuff moving," he said. "We had millions of dollars of investment sitting there not collecting money. We needed to turn these trains and build ridership."

By 2001, the Capitol Corridor expanded to nine round-trips using the same number of train sets. Today, it runs sixteen round-trips on weekdays and twelve on weekends, which translates into a train about every hour starting before dawn and lasting until late evening. It moves 1.5 million riders annually and runs on time 85 to 90 percent of the time—equal to the Northeast Corridor performance. The service costs $50 million to operate. About $27 million comes through the farebox; the remainder in state subsidy. Ridership went up 16 percent in 2008 and an additional 9 percent in early 2009. Demand is substantial, and if cars were available, at least two more coaches could be added to good effect, Skoropowski told me.

The trains average 50 mph or 1 hour 48 minutes between Sac and Oakland and 43 mph or 63 minutes between Oakland and San Jose. The route, which runs along the east side of San Francisco Bay and then west across the Sacramento River Delta, parallels I-80, I-680, and I-880—all highly congested freeways. Once the train hit its eighth and ninth frequency per day, it became a viable alternative to driving, said Skoropowski. People don't worry about catching the train. If they work late or quit early, there's always one available.

The route runs almost entirely on Union Pacific tracks, a busy stretch of railroad through the oil-refinery towns of Richmond and Martinez, heavy with container traffic to and from the port of Oakland.

Since 1991, California has spent $750 million on the Capitol Corridor, purchasing train sets, building and upgrading stations, but mostly putting money into double-tracking, sidings, and maintaining the infrastructure to Class-IV to Class-V standards, which allows passenger trains to run 79 mph and freights 70 mph. In 2003, California paid $24 million to double-track sections of the Yolo Causeway across a managed floodplain on the Sacramento River delta. Union Pacific put up $1million and managed the project, which cut ten minutes running time for the Capitol Corridor, but also benefited the freight service, too. What's ironic is the causeway once had a double track when it was owed by Southern Pacific, but the rails had been torn out for scrap or to be used elsewhere on the system.

"What makes this work is capital, capital, and capital. It's the money that goes to the freight railroad for physical improvements. It took me about three years to get inside the heads of the railroad and find out what they needed," he said. "It's fluidity—they don't want their trains held up by ours—and we've put up money to make sure that doesn't happen."

From Martinez to Sac, the right-of-way is wide enough for two, even four tracks, which means a dedicated passenger line could be put in some day, but between Richmond and Martinez it's very tight, and any solution will be extremely expensive.

"As long as we're running on shared-use right-of-way, this has to be a partnership. The freight railroads look at it from a business perspective and passenger railroads need to as well," he said. "I think the folks on the freight side are surprised how well it has worked out."

A lot of people are surprised since Union Pacific doesn't have the best reputation for cooperation, but Skoropowski worked to separate Capitol Corridor incentive payments from the rest of the Amtrak system. The Capitol Corridor, he argued, is an intrastate, state-supported service that shouldn't be penalized for UP's performance outside of California. If the Capitol Corridor runs on time, the railroad gets incentive money. The authority also funds a dedicated track crew to do regular maintenance overnight—when passenger trains aren't running—which reduces slow orders, requirements to slow trains because of track conditions or when track gangs are out working.

"This is a mutual relationship. Would they like us to go away? Of course, that would make their life easier, but then we take away some of the public benefits, too," he said.

Out of Oakland the train ran along the bay where we could look across and see the San Francisco skyline. At Emeryville, warehouses were being turned into condos and office parks. Transit-oriented development, Skoropowski remarked. After the 1989 Loma Prieta earthquake damaged the 16th Street Depot in Oakland, Amtrak moved its operations to Emeryville, and once the station got hourly Capitol Corridor service, developers saw opportunities.

I remembered George Chilson saying two nights earlier, "I don't think any city has ever put up a bus stop and seen major development. But put up a train station or build a new transit stop and the developers are flocking to build." Here was an example of that.

North of Martinez our train crossed the Carquinez Strait on a rail bridge built in 1929 by Southern Pacific Railroad. To the east I could see the highway truss bridge put up in 1962 to carry Interstate 680 over the bay. Its three lanes were no longer sufficient for the traffic, so in 2007, California put up the George Miller Memorial Bridge at a staggering cost of $1.3 billion.

As we passed under the bridge, its 100-foot pillars were so high up I couldn't even see the cars and trucks. Skoropowski noted that trains complement the highway system, not compete with it.

"People in California like their cars. They like them on the weekend and they like them when they get to the train station to drive home. But they don't want to drive them into the city every day," he said. "Our best marketing tools are the interstates. They are hopelessly congested and they parallel our routes. People can look over and see this train."

The train turned east toward Sacramento, running through countryside dotted with cattle. Skoropowski recalled bringing a bunch of politicians on the train and having one of them look out and ask, "Where are all your riders coming from? There's nothing out here."

Rail doesn't necessarily need densely populated corridors. It's not always about where people live but where they travel from and to, said Skoropowski. The Capitol Corridor runs through sparsely populated lands, but it connects some big population areas, including the University of California at Davis with 30,000-some students.

In Sacramento, we stepped off the train and went over to a coffee shop in the former REA Building. Thirty minutes later we headed back to Oakland. At the Davis station, hundreds of bicycles were parked under sheds, in racks, and chained to trees and fences. Many students ride the train home on weekends or to visit the Bay Area.

Throughout the trip, Skoropowski chatted with the conductors, attendants, and engineers. He knew many by name, and has a reputation for riding the trains. He even holds the public meetings and hearings, required by law, on the trains. "Why hold meetings where just a couple of rail fans show up? Our customers are out here on these trains, so we brought the meetings to them," he said.

Public notices are posted on the trains several days in advance, and then during meeting night everyone who wants to attend crowds into a rear car where Skoropowski speaks through a small bullhorn.

"It works. We get so much more input," he said.

When I was in North Carolina, the rail chief there, Pat Simmons, called Skoropowski a "national treasure." I could see why. He's a smart, passionate, and an aggressive problem solver.

We talked about Amtrak. Although the company's future may lie with more partnerships with states willing to subsidize corridor services, Amtrak also needs four or five more long-distance trains to better connect those corridors, he said. The Sunset should run every day. Corridor trains should be established between L.A. and Phoenix and Las Vegas, and then on to Albuquerque, to El Paso, and so on. All of these cities fall into that 100- to 500-mile corridor range, and they all have big, growing populations.

"It isn't like there's a market for corridor trains but not long distance. You can't have one without the other. Why did we build Interstate 80 across Wyoming? It wasn't because of traffic jams in Wyoming. It was all about connectivity. And if you want the political support nationally, you have to serve the nation with a nationwide system."

Besides, he said, long-distance trains also function as corridor trains. A train is not like an airplane going point to point. People get on and get off at stops along the way.

On my Southwest Chief trip, we'd left Chicago with 203 people and got to L.A. with 171, but at one time we had as many 247 passengers. There were thirty-two stops on the way and large exchanges of passengers occurred at Kansas City; Albuquerque; Galesburg, Illinois; Topeka; Lamy (Santa Fe); and Flagstaff. Only a majority of the 50 or so sleeping-car passengers went the entire distance—and they paid a premium.

The Amtrak critics usually focus on its failure to make a profit, but some claim America is just too big for trains or that Americans just won't ride trains. They prefer to drive or fly.

Such comments burn Skoropowski. It's nonsense, he said.

"I'll slap down my statistics in front of everyone. Don't tell me people won't ride trains. I live in the car-culture capital of the planet and people want trains. They need trains."

Back in Oakland, we walked over to Jack London Square along Embarcadero Street and I remarked how unusual it was to see a train coming down a street with no fencing or grade crossing to keep pedestrians and cars away. The train runs on the street about two and half blocks to the station before it reenters the railroad right-of-way.

"It's dangerous," Skoropowski agreed. "We came up with a solution that would have provided more protection and left some of the ambience in place, but the city didn't want to hear about it. The trains are part of the tradition of the square."

We bid good-bye and I walked down to waterfront where I had a dinner of sole and scallops and watched containers being lifted off a ship and placed on trains. Then I got on a Capitol Corridor train headed back to Sacramento.

Caltrans, Sacramento
a billion dollars ready to go

Reading the *Sacramento Bee* at breakfast the next morning, I learned oil had hit $133 a barrel, and Goldman Sachs, the investment bank, was predicting $6 a gallon gas by year's end. Across the street from the train station, a gas station sign read $3.99. The bank was wrong. Gas would go up a few cents more, but by year's end, the world economic slowdown drove down demand and prices with it.

It was windy when I walked over to the California Department of Transportation on N Street. Women held down their skirt fronts and men tucked their ties inside their shirts. Palm fronds lay on top of cars where they landed after being blown off the big trees near the capitol. Bill Bronte, chief of Caltrans' division of rail, often rides his bike to work, but it was too windy this day. A big barrel-chested man in his forties, Bronte came into the rail division as a budget and bond manager during the procurement phase of the California car. Morrison-Knudsen, a large construction firm with a rail-transit-car division, had designed the cars and started production, but then went into bankruptcy.

Bronte worked with the bondholders and courts to create Amerail, a shell firm, to finish the car order in Hornell, New York, which has locomotive/car facilities that go back decades to the Erie Railroad. Eventually sixty-six cars were built at $1.5 million per unit.

Amtrak bought an additional fifty coaches for the Pacific Surfliner corridor. California "tied on" to the order for another twenty-two to beef up its fleet. California owns all coaches and locomotives on the Capitol and San Joaquin corridors. Amtrak had invested very little in terms of capital and equipment in California, Bronte explained, so the state had to step in if it wanted more services and greater frequencies

Caltrans is in the market again—this time for thirty-six cars. When we spoke, the department was in talks with Illinois, Oregon, and other states to come up with a common design, tie in with other orders, and create some economies of scale, said Bronte. The car builders—all foreign—have never had enough steady business to keep an assembly plant open in America.

"It's a real problem. The transit and rail-car industry is one of boom and bust.

If we want to keep the industry going, we need to space out these orders," he said.

New equipment won't be on line until 2011 or 2012. The Surfliners are running mixed consists of good-looking California cars and beat-up Superliner cars it is leasing from Amtrak.

"We are getting to the point of standing room on some of these trains. When we look out a couple of years, I worry we'll be like a third-world railway with people hanging from the sides of the cars," he said.

Equipment aside, most of California's money has gone into the purchase of railroad lines that the freights no longer wanted or projects that increase capacity of existing freight lines. When I asked Bronte what he would do if the federal government ever came through with more money, he didn't hesitate.

"I have a billion dollars worth of projects ready to go or very close. If the money comes, California can invest it, and we also have a track record to match anything they give us." California would triple-track L.A. to Fullerton and double-track the BNSF line through the Central Valley where the San Joaquin service runs between Sacramento and Bakersfield. As well, the Capitol Corridor has all that expensive work to be done between Martinez and Richmond.

Months later, a federal funding match was established in the new Amtrak bill and then reinforced with billions more in the stimulus package. When I last spoke to Bronte in 2009, he said California is in a good position to get some of those dollars because of its shovel-ready projects.

The ability to bring money to the table has given California real clout with BNSF and Union Pacific, too, said Bronte. If California wants new routes or frequencies, it does not go through Amtrak but negotiates directly with the freights. It's a delicate dance, and there is wariness on both sides. The freights like to say the state is simply replacing capacity it is stealing for passenger trains.

"And when they say that, we smile, nod our heads, and then move on from there," Bronte said. "Neither railroad wants passenger trains, but BNSF is willing to engage early, get ahead of the curve, and make it work. UP won't even talk to you unless you have the money committed."

Typically, the state presents the freights with the number of frequencies it wants to add and lets the railroad model the track improvements and determine costs. "And then we have our people look at it, to make sure they aren't asking too much or if it's enough to do the job," he said. "So far, we've been able to work things out."

Our conversation shifted to the Capitol Corridor. Bronte pointed out that the money for those infrastructure improvements comes from the state: "Gene has done a lot of good things, and it's really commendable the relationship he has created with UP, but we've funded them," he said. Then he pointed across the street toward the capitol building and the California legislature. "And we fight a lot of battles over there for the Capitol Corridor and the other services."

Such public-private partnerships in California aren't limited to passenger rail. Under a 2006 bond issue, there's $2 billion available to improve goods movement in California. BNSF and UP will get big infrastructure benefits, said Bronte. The tunnels over Donner Pass in the Sierras will be enlarged, and the tops of other tunnels in Tehachapi Pass will be taken off entirely to allow the passage of double-stacked container trains. The state's also helping to move rail facilities closer to the docks in Long Beach. Now the containers come off the ships, are put on trucks, moved up the 710 freeway, and then placed on trains for the run east. It's inefficient, contributes to poor air quality in the L.A. basin, and congests highways.

As I was leaving, I asked about the Amtrak ticketing machine I'd seen in the building. Employees are told to take the train if they have departmental business that does not require a state vehicle. And though it may be one of the more rail-friendly DOTs in the nation, Caltrans is still highway-centric.

Bronte said, "When I give talks, I joke that the 45 people in rail division get a lot of assistance from the 26,000 highway people in the department."

High Speed Rail Authority, Sacramento
building another hoover dam

After my conversation with Bill Bronte, I got a sandwich down the street and then walked into the capitol building and stood outside the governor's office guarded by two policeman. The name Schwarzenegger over the door still seemed incongruous to me, but this was California—eccentric, reeling financially, and perhaps even ungovernable but also bold, progressive, and willing to take chances with a governor and, perhaps, with a bullet train.

Schwarzenegger twice put California's proposed high-speed train on hold, but later endorsed the project as did the legislature, and in November 2008—a few months after my visit—voters approved Proposition 1A, a $9.95-billion bond issue to begin construction. Some of the 2009 stimulus monies for high-speed rail should end up in the California project and more may be coming.

If so, the United States may see its first bullet train within fifteen years running 200 mph between Anaheim and San Francisco. California would run steel-on-steel technology, based on the TGV in France and the Shinkansen, the bullet train in Japan. The California project may, in turn, spur Texas and Florida, which have some level of planning under way, to build their own bullet trains.

California has big transportation problems: it contains three of the nation's most congested urban areas, transportation accounts for 40 percent of its air-quality problems, congestion costs $20 billion a year in fuel consumption and lost productivity, and the state may add another twenty million people over the next twenty years, reaching fifty million. These statistics have staggering implications. If the train system is not built, studies show government will have to build 3,000 additional miles of freeways and expand all major airports at a cost of $82 billion.

When I visited the California High Speed Rail Authority a few blocks from the capitol, I spoke with the group's executive director, Mehdi Morshed. "People think this is a project whose time has come," he said. "The World War II generation built just about every important component of California's infrastructure, and now they are gradually crumbling and over capacity. Our transportation problems aren't going to go away; they are just going to get bigger unless we do something." Separate from Caltrans, the authority was created by the California legislature to do the planning, design, and environmental studies for the bullet train.

Morshed has been involved with the high-speed train concept for more than ten years. He's a civil engineer who designed bridges for the DOT and then worked as a transportation-policy consultant to the state senate for more than twenty years.

The California high-speed train system will be completely separate from the freight railroads and Amtrak. The public will own the right-of-way. The slower passenger trains will work as a feeder system and dovetail with the bullet train.

"If we want efficient modern railway transportation, we need our own tracks, our own facilities. It will be safer, more frequent and much, much faster than anything that can be done on the shared right-of-way," Morshed explained. "We're not going to get bogged down in this tug-of-war between the freights and Amtrak that's been going on for decades."

Still, the partnership between Amtrak and California has been a smart way to go for the short term. "The incremental approach on a shared right-of-way holds you over until you can take the next leap," he said. "You don't want to hit a brick wall and then be fifteen years away from a solution."

He could have been referring to Florida, which has focused past efforts on building a bullet train and has not pursued a corridor strategy with Amtrak. Today, it has no corridor service, no bullet train, and spotty Amtrak service.

The first phase of California's high-speed network will be construction of a spine running from Anaheim through L.A. to San Francisco; later extensions will reach Sacramento, San Diego, and some airports. Routes have been selected, engineering work is under way, and the state is determining how it will acquire a 50- to 100-foot-wide right-of-way. Some land will be purchased. Easements will be used when possible and condemnation when necessary. The tracks may run next to freeways and freight railroad tracks.

When built out by 2030, the system would run 800 miles from San Diego through Anaheim to L.A. and then north across the flatlands of the Central Valley to San Francisco and Sacramento. A high-speed line requires level track, and in California's mountainous topography it will require 30 to 40 miles of tunnels. The right-of-way will be fenced and grade separated—meaning the tracks will go either over or under highways.

About 100 train sets will be in use, able to reach speeds up to 220 mph. Estimated times between stations would be: Los Angeles to San Francisco, 2 hours 30 minutes; San Diego to L.A.'s Union Station, 1 hour 18 minutes; Bakersfield to L.A., 54 minutes; Union Station to Palmdale Airport or Ontario Airport, 25 minutes.

Electrical power will come from an overhead catenary. The project will require 0.5 percent of the power coming from the grid. California has an ambitious goal to get 33 percent of its electricity from renewable resources by 2030 (it's currently 11 percent). With the eighth-largest economy in the world, the state is the twelfth-largest source of greenhouse gases, with about 41 percent of those emissions coming from transportation. Remarkably, even without new renewable energy sources, the train, by moving people from cars and airports, is expected to reduce the state carbon footprint by 7 percent. Add in renewables and that percentage goes up dramatically. By 2030, the trains are expected to carry one hundred million people in California annually and remove seventy million passenger trips from the highways.

Building the high-speed rail system will create 160,000 construction jobs and 450,000 permanent jobs—through direct employment and economic development spin-off. Extensive commercial and residential development will cluster around the stations, said Morshed. Most surprising, he said the system would generate $1 to $3 billion in annual operating surpluses.

"Profit?" I said.

Morshed shook his head, "Wrong word. It's not a profit, but a surplus that will pay off the bonds, reward investors, and be reinvested into the system."

"Is that optimistic?"

"No. The analysis is based off the Japanese and European experience. There will be an operating surplus of $1 billion if we capture 7 percent of the market now traveling by airplane and automobile. That's doable," he said.

The entire project will cost $40 billion over a fifteen- to twenty-year period, and the first train could be running in ten years. The bond issue raised $9.95 billion. About $10 to $12 billion will be required in federal support and an additional $8 to $10 billion should come in from private investors. Building the spine will cost $30 billion, and then the operating surplus should leverage the rest in bonding and investment.

The sheer size, technical complexity, and mega-dollars required can seem overwhelming, Morshed concedes. Some critics, who still oppose the project, simply can't conceptualize it. Governor Schwarzenegger, at first, shied away from the project but has embraced it as part of his green initiative.

Morshed, who spent a good deal of his professional life dealing with legislatures, said some politicians—especially term-limited politicians—don't have the time horizon for transportation policy. In California a person can serve six years in the assembly, eight years in the senate.

"I thought term limits free politicians to think and act more boldly knowing they can't stay in office for decades," I said.

Morshed gave me a look that bordered on condescension.

"It doesn't work that way. Instead, term limits shorten a politician's time horizon. They think, 'What's in it for me? I might be at the groundbreaking but I won't be around to ride the trains,'" he said.

"To do this kind of project you need a different mind-set. We're like eighty-year-old farmers planting fruit trees for our kids and grandkids. We ourselves may never see the fruit the trees will bear. This is a project as big as Hoover Dam. Is our generation capable of looking that far ahead and doing something for our children?"

What about some of the critics who say that private business ought to be doing this—that if there really was a market for a high-speed train, private business would undertake it?

Morshed just rolled his eyes. The private sector will not risk $30 billion. The time horizon is too long; most investors want quicker paybacks. The environmental permitting, public hearings, and other hurdles are too complicated to overcome without government help, he said. And private capital would be competing against highways and airports—and those modes already are heavily subsidized by government.

Big transportation projects have to be undertaken by the public sector, which puts up the seed money and then invites in private capital with long-term time horizons such as pension funds, international banks, insurance companies, and wealthy private investors.

Public transportation always polls well in California, Morshed continued, because it's just no fun out there on the highways and at the airports. Just look at the bond issues that had helped create Amtrak California and the other commuter services. People voted to ante up billions.

"Bond issues have worked in California because people know they are buying something. If you ask people 'Do you want higher taxes?' They say, 'No.' But if you ask, 'Would you like better transportation or cleaner air? They say, 'Yes.' So Prop 1A is asking, 'Do you want to buy this train system? Are you ready to make this investment?'"

In November 2008, voters answered in the affirmative.

California Railroad Museum, Sacramento
railroads become road kill

The next day, I had an early-morning interview with Kyle Wyatt, curator of History and Technology at the California State Railroad Museum in Old Sacramento, a state park recreated to resemble the city in the 1800s. Wyatt's office is on the second floor of the "Big Four Building," a facsimile of the mercantile store where Leland Stanford and three other Sacramento merchants formed the Central Pacific Railroad, which then worked from the west to lay track over the Sierras as part of a transcontinental railway.

As with California's proposed bullet train, private capital would not finance on its own such an audacious endeavor as the transcontinental railroad, so the federal government gave the railroads every other section of land (640 acres) for twenty miles on either side of the tracks. Within Nevada alone the land grant amounted to 5 million acres. Over time, land swaps and sales consolidated the holdings, but a property map along the original route still resembles a checkerboard of public and private lands. Plenty of financial shenanigans went on, too, enriching the Big Four and other financiers, but the road got built, and California and the West came fully into the Union.

Wyatt, a slim man with long hair and a flannel shirt, sat me down at a table in the library's reading room where historians peruse its extensive collection of photographs and documents. American railroad history runs recent in Sacramento. Months after my visit, an original section of the transcontinental railroad was uncovered just a few yards from the museum.

I asked Wyatt, "Do the freight railroads owe America because the land grants enabled them to build powerful organizations with control over critical transportation corridors?"

There are two ways to look at that argument, he said. In the nineteenth century, railroads benefited greatly from land grants and laws that gave them the right of eminent domain. In the twentieth century, however, they suffered a backlash when the government invested more in roads and airport construction.

"Were the railroads overregulated?"

He shrugged, "Regulations are what they are. They were designed when railroads were the sole transportation mode for people and goods. If we give you a monopoly, we have to limit the amount you can charge your customers, but also allow you and your investors a reasonable rate of return."

But then railroads had to compete against largely unregulated interests—trucks and airlines, which could cut rates and provide more flexible service. Railroads were required to go through elaborate hearings to change rates and service. When they asked for relief from the government, it was slow in coming, partly because railroads had been proclaiming themselves—as they do now—as private businesses.

Wyatt extended his arms, "Railroads were playing both sides of the street, and a big truck came along and ran them over. They were road kill. In an earlier era, railroads did it to the stagecoaches and the canals."

Passenger trains generally were profitable until the 1920s when roads and autos started to take away passengers. But some trains—including the Santa Fe's Super Chief and El Capitan as well as the California Zephyr, operated jointly by the Western Pacific Railroad, the Chicago, Burlington and Quincy Railroad, and the Denver and Rio Grande Western Railroad—were profitable well into the 1950s.

The Zephyr had Vista Dome cars that offered 360-degree views of the landscape, and a cadre of car hostesses, the Zephyrettes, who acted as tour guides and babysitters to lure families and mothers aboard. The Santa Fe looked to economy to lure passengers with the El Capitan, a chair-car-only train. The distinction is lost today, but in a coach the seats did not recline, while seats in chair cars reclined quite comfortably for sleeping. Santa Fe charged an additional $5 for its "Ride Master" chair cars—well below the cost of a sleeper. Like other railroads, it also introduced cheaper food service as an alternative to the full-service dining car.

But what held off the demise of the passenger train through the 1950s was the money received for hauling express packages, newspapers, and the like. It was known as the "head-end revenue" because the baggage and Railway Express Agency cars ran just behind the locomotive at the "head end."

In its heyday, the REA, much like UPS or FedEx now, was the quickest way to move personal and business packages from town to town. REA functioned as a separate company, moving freight on fast, reliable, high-priority passenger trains. The railroads hauled REA cars and provided terminal space. REA divided its profit among the railroads in proportion to its traffic on each line.

Railway post-office operations generated significant revenue, too. From the late nineteenth century, many passenger trains carried mail on post-office cars where clerks sorted and delivered mail en route. The Railway Post Office reached its peak in the 1920s and gradually declined as the government switched to trucks, airmail, and central sorting centers. The remaining post office routes were largely abandoned by 1967, and by then, too, the REA had lost out to trucks and air freight.

"The loss of those revenues led to the transition to Amtrak. There was nothing left for passenger trains. Any profit was gone, and the railroads wanted out," said Wyatt.

The Southern Pacific was notorious for its attempts to discourage passengers. It offered vouchers for bus service and instructed its own employees not to take the trains.

In these circumstances, even the ICC regulators were less than sympathetic. Railroads were sometimes ordered to improve their services. A few railroads took pride in their streamlined passenger trains even after the creation of Amtrak on May 1, 1971. The Santa Fe, for example, tried hard to keep Amtrak from using the name *chief* on its Southwest route, while the Denver Rio Grande & Western Railroad refused to come into the Amtrak fold and kept running its trains for several more years. But about half of the nation's passenger service disappeared with Amtrak's creation. Of the routes selected for Amtrak, some made sense and others were selected to mollify important politicians whose votes were needed to pass the bill.

"What you have with Amtrak was a typical political compromise," Wyatt said. "It is neither fish nor fowl, but mostly it is just foul."

Yet, said Wyatt, Amtrak has managed to maintain a skeleton national network, which can now serve as an "armature" on which to hang the corridor trains, the regional networks, the commuter trains, the light rail, and perhaps a bullet train someday. Also, Amtrak is of value for its human capital, people who have expertise in passenger operations.

"Amtrak is what we have right now. As long as it exists, it can be upgraded and reinvented. It can evolve," he said.

Amtrak Western Division, Oakland
freight that talks

The station was a short walk away. I had planned to ride the San Joaquin south to Bakersfield, stay overnight and come back the next day before heading home, but if I returned to Oakland, I could talk with Don Saunders, Amtrak's assistant vice president of strategic partnerships. He had just relocated to California to work with the western states willing to make investments for Amtrak service. He also sits on the board of directors of the Association of American Railroads, which is dominated by the big freight railroads. I boarded a Capitol Corridor and headed to Oakland and Amtrak's Western Division office in Jack London Square. Saunders had a corner office that overlooked the intermodal terminal at the port of Oakland, the fourth-busiest port in the nation. Down below, gantry cranes lifted forty-foot containers off a ship whose homeport, or, at least flag, was the poor landlocked African country of Malawi. The waters of San Francisco Bay glittered in the afternoon light, and occasionally the moan of a train whistle broke through our conversation.

In his late fifties, Saunders is a railroad guy who came up through the ranks. In 1973, much to his father's dismay, he quit college and went to work for the Gulf, Mobile and Ohio Railroad. His dad, grandfather, and two uncles were railroaders, too. He became a locomotive engineer and pulled container and coal trains and sometimes an Amtrak train. At that time, the host railroads supplied the locomotive crews to Amtrak, but in the late 1980s Amtrak began crewing its own trains, and Saunders came over as engineer. Then he went into management, first as a road foreman. He has moved seven times in his career and spent much of it in Chicago and California, where in the 1990s he managed Caltrains, the commuter service between San Jose and San Francisco.

Saunders immediately struck me as a straight shooter. He was neither sensitive nor apologetic about the company's problems.

So I asked him: Why were Amtrak service personnel so inconsistent in the way they treated passengers.

Two reasons, he said. First, Amtrak inherited employees from the freight railroads and the operations it took over during the 1980s. Conductors who formerly worked freight trains found themselves with cars full of passengers instead of coal—and didn't want to deal with freight that talked. A few had worked railroads prior to Amtrak that were trying to discourage passenger travel, and come out of that culture.

"Those folks were not customer-centric, and fortunately most have retired or have been moved into other positions," Saunders said. "We've been making an effort to change some of that culture."

He spoke about "block training" wherein regional employees come to a central location for a few days of role playing real situations that have occurred on trains. They're taught how to avoid arguing with a passenger, ways to apologize, and instructed when to "comp" a meal or even a hotel room.

I mentioned the dining-car attendant on the Lake Shore Limited who was reluctant to give a $1.50 yogurt to a sleeping-car passenger.

"There are a lot of inconsistencies out there, I admit," he said. "Our employees on the trains are largely unsupervised, so the company tries to give them a 'tool box' of skills and techniques to defuse a situation. We could do a better job."

What has improved, he said, is hiring. Amtrak does more screening and testing and turns away people it believes are unsuited. It used to be a lot less selective. Now it looks for people with customer-service backgrounds in the hotel, food service, and retail industries. These folks already have experience working with the public.

I told him about Sharon, my sleeping-car attendant who had worked at Vons.

"You're seeing more people like her on our trains. But they aren't easy to find and keep," Saunders explained. "You're also seeing more young people and women, and they are going to change this industry. Unlike you or me, whose fathers and grandfathers worked for the railroad, they don't have that family connection."

The entire industry is concerned about finding the next generation of railroaders in all job classifications. A wave of retirements is coming. And though the industry pays relatively well, the hours are odd and the work can be hard. A lot of time is spent away from home, and the tolerance for drug use is zero. It is a 24–7 industry.

We moved to the on-time performance problem, which has been Amtrak's curse since its birth.

"You know the best thing we've done, Jim? It's to keep people informed. We tell our people to get on the PA system and tell passengers what is happening—that there's a freight train up ahead or a derailment or a problem with the weather. Don't leave people in the dark," he said. "You tell people what's going on and you apologize."

What if the PA system doesn't work?—a problem I encountered several times.

He gave me a wry smile, "Want to talk about equipment? Want to talk about running the wheels off the equipment? That's exactly what we were doing."

We did talk about it—and it came down to Amtrak desperately needing more rolling stock—which won't be coming for three to five years.

"Ridership is going through the roof and we're not in the best position to handle it. On the Capitol Corridor out here, Gene is running thirty-two trips a day with eight consists. There's not a lot of downtime to keep that equipment in good repair."

Almost on cue, a train whistle sounded from the square as it came down the street and into the station. When he had moved back to California a few months earlier, Saunders located in Fairfield so he could ride the Capitol Corridor to work every day just as he had ridden Metra in Chicago.

His new duties include promoting and facilitating "strategic partnerships" in the western region. I'd been told by a couple of freight executives that Amtrak is out there marketing itself to states. And certainly guys like Saunders are telling states what Amtrak can do for them, which is a lot because it has a lock on intercity passenger service. No other passenger entity can access the freight-rail network, offer nationwide ticketing, or provide the insurance liability.

Amtrak was once a company of long-distance trains with a few corridors, but now corridor trains supported through state partnerships is where the growth is, said Saunders. Amtrak has fourteen state partners and another fourteen states who want to talk.

"I think our company and board have woken up to that fact. These corridors are the future. We're not going to walk away from long distance, but we can really grow these 500- to 700-mile services," said Saunders. "For that kind of service, the stars are really starting to line up for passenger rail."

We moved on to talk about the contentious relationship between passenger and freight interests over allocated costs, problems with capacity, and the costs to Amtrak of late trains. Corridor trains in Michigan and Missouri have 40 to 60 percent on-time performance. The Sunset Limited has zero percent on-time performance, the Zephyr in 2008 about 20 percent. Yet, the host railroads— some of them—are trying harder, he said.

He rubbed his temples and said, "It gives me a headache just to talk about it."

All of this needs to be worked out if the country is going to move ahead with passenger rail, said Saunders. What has happened in California and a few other states shows what can be done—that even with railroads like Union Pacific, accommodations can be reached, said Saunders.

"What the country has to decide is how robust a passenger system it wants, and if it is willing to pay for it. If it is and if it gives Amtrak a clear mission of what it should become, I think we can become that."

He sighed, "I've been at this twenty years. Amtrak is a roller coaster."

I had heard from plenty of Amtrak critics that the company's biggest problem was a lack of vision, not money, but I had to agree with Saunders, too: If the country doesn't know what you are supposed to be—even why it created you—how are you able to figure that out on your own?

I'd been reading the company's corporate history. It couldn't be screwier. When I looked back at all the machinations, near bankruptcies, reorganizations, last-minute rescues, reform boards, hostile relations with the freight railroads, broken-down equipment, demands to be profitable, mandates for new services, board members ignorant of railroading and politicians who micromanage from the sidelines—to the point of worrying about the price of beer in the dining car—it's a wonder Amtrak is still here.

California Zephyr

a stunning long way to go

†††††††††

My train back to the Midwest, the California Zephyr, left from Emeryville the next morning, but I decided to stay in Oakland that night and run up to Sacramento on an early Capitol Corridor train.

I boarded the Zephyr at Sacramento at 11:30 a.m., settled into my roomette, glad the frenetic week was over. My only regret was not having ridden the San Joaquin. Rain droplets pattered against the window. In the consist, we were the third car behind the locomotive after the baggage and crew-sleeping cars, close enough to hear every blast of the whistle for the next two days. But after all my recent miles on the rails, it wasn't a bother.

The engine gave two blasts and we were out of Sacramento and soon traveling through the Roseville Yards, a six-mile maze of tracks and switches where Union Pacific sorts thousands of cars. It's the largest railroad yard west of the Rocky Mountains. Southern Pacific built Roseville in 1902 at the intersection of the transcontinental main line and a line coming north from the San Joaquin Valley, where cheap irrigation water combined with flat topography and plentiful sunshine turned semiarid desert into America's fresh-produce basket. In 1927, the Pacific Fruit Express constructed the largest ice-manufacturing plant in the world to pack fruits and vegetables for shipping east. The ice house operated until 1974 when SP's reefer cars became self-refrigerating. By then, however, much of the business had migrated to trucks on Interstate 80.

Leaving the Sacramento River delta, we ran through dun-colored grasslands where startled black-tailed jackrabbits ran from burrows tunneled into the ballast. Kids in hooded sweatshirts and baggy jeans stopped along a dirt road to watch the train pass.

In the Sierra foothills, we picked up the American River where a year earlier, Kelly and I had driven up to Sutter's Mill and panned for gold. American history runs thick in this part of California. The discovery of gold, the tens of thousands of settlers coming west in Conestoga wagons, and the connecting of the country coast to coast with the transcontinental railway—it was pretty significant stuff, and some crew member got on the PA every few minutes to read from a prepared script, doing a poor job of pronunciation and not deviating at all from the script despite circumstances, "If you'll look out the left side of the train and across the valley, you will see . . ."

We couldn't see a thing. The more altitude we gained, the more it rained. We ran a ridge between the American and Yuba rivers, and mist rose from the valleys like an insidious gas engulfing the train. The woods were wet and rich with redwood and western cedar, and the occasional big-toothed aspen leafed out in brilliant green. I was just able to make out barren hillsides stripped away by nineteenth-century hydraulic mining. Miners used the elevation of the mountains to channel water into pipes that gradually were reduced in diameter to increase pressure. By the time the jet of water shot into the hillside, it was powerful enough to put a hole right through a man. The miners washed large amounts of gravel, but tore up the mountains, dirtied the rivers, and buried farmland down on the delta under layers of silt and mud.

At Colfax, the train rumbled through one of the dozen or so tunnels blasted out by Chinese laborers. The diesel engines resonated off the close-in walls, but when the vibrations ceased, I knew the engine had reached the other side. Progress was slow, just twenty miles an hour. At Blue Canyon, the steepest part of the grade, we gained 2.24 feet for every 100 feet forward. The tracks snaked left and then right to lessen the grade, and by pressing my face against the window, I could see two vintage railroad cars at the rear of the train. Amtrak stores private cars in L.A. and earns extra money by hooking them on for a hefty fee.

Higher into the mountains, the trees and brush were still bare from winter. The rain morphed into sleet and then into snow. Several inches already covered the forest floor. Hundreds of feet below, cars and big rigs ran over Interstate 80, its two wide swaths of concrete a peculiar sight after many so many miles of forest and rock and rivers. A railroad right-of-way has no standard width. Usually it's 50 feet wide and sometimes up to 100 feet, but that's thin compared to the 300-foot swipe of an interstate highway.

Ironically, the train went over Donner Pass and past Donner Lake just as I was munching on the Southwest chicken salad in the dining car. Over the intercom, that unsteady voice—like a sixth-grader forced to stand and read aloud—related a few facts about the Donner Party and cannibalism. To be fair, Amtrak often has skilled docents riding the trains and announcing historical footnotes and sights, and when it is done well, this mobile historical lecture is one of the great aspects of train travel.

On the descent to Reno, the locomotive shook off the confines of the mountains and gained speed. The food I'd eaten and the sway of the carriages made me sleepy. I put down the bed in the roomette, and napped all the way to Winnemucca, Nevada.

Dinner that night was a delight. I befriended a couple, Anne and Dennis from England, who I ended up chatting with over the next two days.

Dennis was a compact, bald-headed man wearing a polo shirt with the word "Bentley" monogrammed onto one sleeve. He brokers used Bentleys to "guys who can afford to drive them" but owns one himself for a chauffeuring and wedding business. A banty rooster of a man, Dennis was having a delightful time. He joked with the waiter, laughed, and winked. He'd been a school-teacher for thirty years until the government offered early retirement.

He and Anne had sailed to New York on the QE2, and then flew to California so Dennis could see a Union Pacific Big Boy on display, a gargantuan million-pound steam locomotive built in the early 1940s to pull heavy freights across the high plains.

"Do you know the term foamer?" I asked.

He didn't but loved it. Anne thought it fit.

Dennis said, "When we got to the bloody museum, it wasn't open but they let me in when I told them how far I'd come."

Now they were headed to Chicago where they would get a flight home. As we ate, the train crossed the Humboldt Sink and then followed the river toward its source. For Dennis and Anne, the dusty-ochre emptiness of the Great Basin was a marvel, a terrible beauty. Anne said, "I looked at the map. It's 2,500 miles, a stunning long way, to Chicago."

And the Rockies were to come.

Colorado River
yak-yak on the radio

‡‡‡‡‡‡‡

I woke outside Spanish Fork, Utah, as the train climbed onto the Colorado River plateau. It was still dark, but coffee was ready and I took a cup back to the lounge where I could look out both sides of the train. The red and green signal lights along the tracks shone like the eyes of animals. Headlights of a car several miles off dipped and rose, disappeared and appeared again as it weaved its way between folds in the land.

As the light grew, I could see a line of hills—the Book Cliffs—off to the north. The red light of dawn lit up their summits and then spread down and out across a range land of sagebrush and bunch grasses. The train rumbled over dry washes and flushed waves of swallows nesting beneath the bridges and trestles. Mule deer foraged in the greasewood along the washes, and in the creases of the hills there were occasional aspen stands.

Pronghorn antelope darted from the train, running into the distance, mouths open as if drinking in all that space. This rail route had belonged to the Denver and Rio Grande Western Railroad, whose motto was "through the Rockies not around them." The D&RGW was one of the few railroads that continued to operate its own passenger trains and didn't allow Amtrak access to its infrastructure. Until 1983, the Rio Grande Zephyr ran three times a week between Salt Lake City and Denver.

Amtrak ran its cross-country trains through southern Wyoming on the Overland Route, which skirts the mountains between Ogden and Cheyenne. The homesteaders and the transcontinental railroad went that way for the same reason, but it's not as scenic, so when D&RGW stopped running trains and later merged with Southern Pacific, Amtrak established the California Zephyr over the Colorado Rockies, which we were now approaching from the west.

We followed the Book Cliffs, made up of buttes and mesas, for nearly 100 miles and entered the San Rafael Desert. After breakfast, the skies darkened, and I went to the sightseer lounge car to watch the coming rainstorm. The Amish men, who had ridden on my train to L.A. the week before, were in the lounge passing a big bag of potato chips back and forth, pouring drinks from a two-liter coke bottle and chatting in German.

They had a route guide and road atlas propped up against the window.

"Looks like it's going to be a soaker," I said.

"Yah. We could use that back home in Indiana. It's been dry."

His name was Levi, and one of the men was his brother, who needed to come to California, so the rest decided to keep him company. They'd gone from the Chief to a Surfliner and south to San Diego. They stayed a couple of days there, enough time to cross into Mexico, I surmised. Then, they'd come north on the San Joaquin to Merced and over to Yosemite National Park on one of Amtrak's motor coaches. These were not young men, but they were a lively group and having a glorious time, taking it all in.

When I first sat down, the sky was bright and backlit, so the rain appeared as gauzy grayish curtains dragging over the desert. But as the storm and train closed distance, a gloomy darkness filled the lounge car and a minute later we hit a black wall of thunderstorm. The wind rocked the coach and sheets of water ran down the windows so thick the desert was just a smear of color. Minutes later when we could see again, the sagebrush trembled in the wind and greasy ooze had replaced the formerly hard matrix of soil. It was if the bare ground had melted.

I tapped Levi on the elbow, "Gumbo."

"Gumbo?" he said. They all looked puzzled.

"Not the food," I said, pointing to the slick, waxy ground. "Liquefied soil."

Also known as expansive soil, gumbo has a heavy clay content that absorbs water. In Wyoming and probably here, too, the key ingredient is bentonite, which swells and expands exponentially. Dirt roads as hard as concrete turn gelatinous in minutes. Step from the truck and six inches of muck sticks to your boots. In North Texas, BNSF frequently has to reset track after a hard rain because of gumbo when the roadbed slumps and shifts.

We crossed the Green River roiling with mud and looking dangerous. In 1869, John Wesley Powell passed by this spot on his way to the confluence of the Colorado and the Grand Canyon, about as daring an adventure as ever undertaken, especially for a man that had lost an arm at Shiloh, only had wooden boats, and no idea of what lay ahead.

At the edge of the town of Green River, a gaunt, grizzled man in cowboy boots and hat, flannel shirt, and leather gloves tended a bonfire in the front yard of his trailer home. He sat on a lawn chair next to an American flag flying on a flagpole made by peeling a skinny lodgepole pine. A yellow ribbon, tattered and dirty, hung just below the flag. He looked up and waved forlornly.

As we descended to the Colorado River, the land broke into canyons and arroyos. At Grand Junction, during a long smoke stop, Dennis and I walked around the old shuttered station, which had a For Sale sign on it.

Like a lot of folks do during long stops, I walked the length of the train for exercise. The platform extended well beyond the last coach so I kept going until I saw three passengers—all young people—standing by a stack of railroad ties passing a pipe. I was making them nervous, so I spun about, but the smell of pot grew even stronger. Beneath the windows of the last coach, a woman, probably in her forties, sucked hard at the last bit of a joint. She looked up at me and took another hard toke. She didn't seem to care who saw her.

Back in my sleeping car, I saw an elderly man sitting in his roomette with a handheld radio, a schedule, and a notebook full of notations. His door was open and I said, "You a rail fan?"

He grinned, "Now, how did you guess that?"

Rich Lewis, from Erie, Pennsylvania, had been on the rails nearly ten days. He'd taken the Builder to Seattle and then come south to California on the Starlight and now was on his way home. A retired electrician, he had never worked on a railroad but had train-spotted for decades. "What have you been hearing on the radio?" I asked.

Last night around midnight, he told me, the train nearly hit a tractor trailer at an unguarded crossing. The truck was pulling two stock trailers, probably filled with cattle or sheep.

"I was listening to the yak-yak on the radio," Rich said. "I heard the whistle and the engineer was really pulling on it. Then the air brakes engaged. I stuck my face against the window, and when we went through that crossing, the back lights of the second trailer were just a couple of feet away. The engineer got back on the radio and said, 'Man that was close.'"

The dining-car attendant came through taking reservations. Rich and I agreed to have dinner together.

Just before the Continental Divide, we entered the tunnel district, passing through twenty-eight tunnels in about thirty minutes and then into the Moffat Tunnel, 6.2 miles long and 9,239 feet above sea level, for several minutes of pitch blackness. A water tunnel runs in parallel bringing western-slope water to Denver. When completed in 1928, the Moffat cut the distance between Denver and the West Coast by 176 miles; previously trains out of Denver first had to go south and then west along the Arkansas River valley.

After the divide, the train followed Boulder Creek down into foothills lush with little bluestem, grama grasses, and clumps of sagebrush, tipped with fresh sprigs of growth. The scalloped-shaped mountains of the Front Range ran off to the north and south. To the east, the Great Plains sprawled away, flat as a table and mottled by great cloud shadows. Denver itself lay under a brown haze of pollution.

Denver
waiting for those freighters

The train had a two-hour-long delay in the city due to equipment problems. When I went to dinner, Rich was seated across from a Japanese couple. Sanzo Yahagi taught nineteenth-century American literature at Gakushin University in Tokyo where most members of the Imperial Family, including the emperor, were graduates or students.

"Melville is my line of study," he said. "You know *Moby-Dick*?"

"That was a good movie," said Rich.

"Yes, yes. Gregory Peck," He turned to his wife. "Gregory Peck is her favorite actor." She nodded in the affirmative.

"She thinks I sort of look like him. Don't I?"

We couldn't tell if he was making a joke, so Rich and I maintained a neutral expression.

Yahagi was on his way to Boston to spend several weeks studying archival material at the Boston Public Library. He planned to go to Walden Pond and to visit Ralph Waldo Emerson's grave.

As we waited for our food, the head-end power shut down, knocking out the air conditioning and lights, too. It was dusk and the low light seemed appropriate for dinner. Rich offered a toast and we clinked glasses.

Yahagi said, "We find you Americans so different. We Japanese don't say too much about ourselves, and if we meet somebody we . . ." He held up his palms as if to push off an intruder, "But you Americans. We sit here and talk like friends. We like that. It is very different for us."

Eventually, the conversation turned to trains in Japan and the Shinkansen, the bullet train. "If the train is just a minute late people are very mad. The train is run very differently than Amtrak."

"You mean much better," said Rich.

Yahagi was diplomatic, "We are very proud of our trains."

The food wasn't ready, the head-end power had not come back on, and the car was getting uncomfortably hot. Dennis and Anne were at a nearby table. He hit me on the shoulder, "We're going out for some air." I followed.

We watched the lights coming on in the downtown high-rises. Dennis had his hands in his pockets, rocking on the balls of his feet.

"So Jim, why are we just sitting in the station with no electric?"

"You think I know?"

"Well I was hoping. I'm getting this feeling about your American railroads. They are really for freight aren't they? I mean they don't go very fast, and we have to wait for all those freighters to pass by. It's their track."

When I got back on the train, Yahagi and Rich were wiping their sweaty brows. Just as the food arrived, the air-conditioning mercifully came back on.

As I read in bed that night, the California Zephyr followed the South Platte River through Sterling and Fort Morgan and into the darkness of the high plains. That night I dreamed of trains, and whenever I woke, I'd cup my hands against the window and look for the name of a town, attached to a hardware store or a bank sign or painted on a grain elevator, but Nebraska at night was largely big and black and absent of towns.

In Omaha, I sat up in bed, pulled the curtain back, and let in the daylight. If UP had been willing to talk, I would have spent the day here doing interviews.

It would have been good to hear the company line as a contrast, because at breakfast I got an earful from Tom Landolt, a locomotive engineer who had retired from UP a few months earlier.

I was eating with a young couple when the waiter brought Tom over to our table. He wore tight, western-cut blue jeans, cowboy boots, a western shirt, and a down vest. His corduroy ball cap said "Brotherhood of Locomotive Engineers."

Conversationally we all felt around a bit until the whistle let out a blast, and one of our tablemates asked, "Why do they have to blow that horn so much? It's hard to sleep."

"Grade crossings," Tom said. "Gotta do it."

Some American communities, especially suburbs that have grown up around railroad tracks that were previously surrounded by farmland, have been working to create quiet "whistle-free" zones. A Federal Railroad Administration study found collisions increased significantly when whistle bans were instituted, and supplemental safety measures had not been added to the crossing. Today, a community has to meet fairly strict FRA standards to upgrade their crossings before a whistle ban can be approved. Sometimes, the easiest way is to just close the crossing if it isn't a significant artery.

We were in western Iowa, running through cornfields and the backsides of farms. The state highway was a half mile distant running parallel to the tracks. We were crossing driveways and farm roads, and the horn had been particularly incessant.

"Man, a lot of these crossings don't carry any traffic," I said.

"Until they do," Tom said. "And then people might try to beat the train, so you lay on that horn."

Tom had been a range conservationist for nearly twenty years, working the national grasslands in the Nebraska Sand Hills before he joined Union Pacific. Ranchers pay grazing fees to the forest service to run cattle on public lands, and guys like Tom drive pickups and ride horses over the range making sure ranchers adhered to their grazing allotments.

"So it was your job to determine the AUMs," I said.

His eyes widened, "You know about AUMs?"

My first reporting job was for a small paper in Wyoming, and I wrote plenty of stories about grazing permits. An AUM (animal unit month) is the amount of forage needed to sustain one cow and her calf, one horse, or five sheep or goats for a month.

"Yup. That was me," he said. "For twenty years I rode a horse and counted cattle and listened to ranchers complain, 'You're trying to cut my AUMs.' I got tired of that and went to work for the railroad."

Tom was in his fifties when he hired on with Southern Pacific, which was taken over by UP in 1996. When I said I was surprised he could switch careers at that age, he snorted.

"After the merger, they were taking anybody. They took a car salesman who had three heart attacks and a bad back."

The merger, he said, was hell, and the entire system almost immediately broke down. Experts called it the nation's worst railroad logjam in at least twenty-five years. The blame fell on the administrators of the Union Pacific Railroad, who had too few locomotives, engineers, freight cars, administrators, computers, and more out on the system. Omaha had closed yards and other facilities that SP people said would be needed in a crisis. Cargo was stranded all over the country. Crews got into idling locomotives with attached freight cars ready to go and never moved for an entire shift. Locomotives ran out of fuel. Freight that had taken three or four days to reach a destination took a month. Billions of dollars were lost by shippers.

Tom recalled, "I never saw so many people angry in all my life, and mostly because Omaha wouldn't listen to anyone in the field. Omaha knew best. Problem was, they didn't know what to do."

I told him about my book and said the company had refused an interview.

He said, "Let me tell you a story. I was running a freight train in New Mexico on a real cold night, and the Sunset Limited was coming up behind us. Now, I had a real heavy train, and we had to go up a grade, so I talked with the dispatcher and said I would pull over and let the Amtrak go by. And he said,

'No sir. We don't pull over for them. They can just slow down.' And I started up that hill and broke down. Now, the Amtrak had to back up more than ten miles and wasted hours. Now there was no reason for that to happen, but that's the attitude. They do not give a damn."

He'd been visiting friends in Nebraska and was on his way home to Lordsburg, New Mexico. To get there, the skeletal nature of America's passenger-rail system being what it is, he had to take a train to Chicago, then to New Orleans, and finally catch the Sunset to New Mexico. We chatted going into Chicago, and the last time I saw him, he was boarding the City of New Orleans.

"You know, Jim. I only wanted to be two things in my life—a cowboy and a locomotive engineer and I got do them both. You can't beat that."

PART 6

Texas

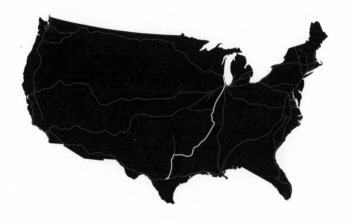

The Texas Eagle
diner lite

In June, I took my sons to visit my sister in Houston on the Texas Eagle, the train with Amtrak's worst on-time performance but one fiercely protected by politicians and citizens along the route between Chicago and San Antonio.

Before we boarded in Chicago, the boys and I walked over to the Sears Tower and went up to the observation deck. South of downtown lay a great swath of rail yards most people never see or think much about.

In the late 1800s, when ranchers and cattle replaced Indians and bison on the Great Plains, the railroads effectively centralized the meat industry in Chicago. Several railroads purchased land for the Union Stock Yards and Transit Company. The animals were butchered and packed into tin cans and later ice-filled railroad cars.

In 1920, the Chicago stockyards supplied 80 percent of the nation's meat and employed 40,000 people. By the 1970s, availability of long-haul trucks and the interstates had led to the decentralization of the meatpacking plants, but looking down from the observation deck I could still make out the yard's outlines.

We boarded the train at 1:30 p.m. for an 864-mile trip to Longview in east Texas where I had an interview the next morning. The following day, we'd catch the Amtrak bus into Houston.

And therein lies one of the strangest disconnects in Amtrak's network. It's impossible to take a direct train between America's third-largest city, Chicago, and its fourth largest, Houston. There hasn't been a connection since the Lone Star succumbed to the Amtrak Reorganization Act of 1979 that, with several subsequent acts, canceled a number of established intercity rail services. If Amtrak had had its way, the Texas Eagle would have died, too. But that didn't happen, thanks to some remarkable Texas activists.

I'd reserved two roomettes for the trip home but we were riding coach south. Colin, ten, and Patrick, eight, had never been on a train, and Kelly, fourteen, was there to show them the ropes. An hour out of Chicago, they were bumming money for snacks from the café. They'd made friends in the lounge car where they played cards and reveled in the freights rushing by the opposite way.

It was a pretty day as we crossed the flat farm country through Joliet, Normal, and Springfield. But by 8:30 that evening when the Eagle neared St. Louis, it already was an hour late. Summer solstice was just a week away, so daylight was running long, and as the train paralleled the Mississippi River on the Illinois side, we could look across where the sun had just dropped behind the St. Louis skyline and turned the reflective glass on the skyscrapers red and orange. The arch soared above it all shimmering silver. People pulled out cameras and cell phones and started shooting. The train traveled up an elevated track and then turned westward across the river on the MacArthur Bridge.

The kids plastered themselves against the windows, gawking at the waters swirling against the caissons. A gambling boat lay at berth at a downtown pier; tugboats pushed grain barges upriver, the ripples trailing back and out in great Vs.

Past Busch Stadium, the train stopped beneath a tangle of highway over-passes. Although people have referred to the train station as an "Amshack," it isn't technically—but it was pathetically small and tucked away in an ugly part of town. Months after our trip, the city opened the Gateway Transportation Center, a new $26.4-million multimodal transportation hub.

When the train finally left the city, it was near dark. We had a cooler full of sandwiches to eat in our seats. Afterwards, we took out blankets and went to sleep.

The Ozarks passed in the night. The sun rose north of Little Rock, and the land unfolded in great rectangles of cotton and rice fields interspersed with catfish farms. We went up to the dining car for breakfast but had to wait in the lounge car for forty-five minutes before seats were available. Once we got inside the dining car, I saw why.

The Cross Country Café is Amtrak's latest dining car. Critics call it "diner lite." Two-thirds of the car is set aside as the restaurant with ten tables that seat about twenty-eight people. (A typical dining car seats between fifty to sixty people). The other third of the car consists of a snack counter and four tables, where that morning conductors were doing paperwork and car attendants sat drinking coffee and gossiping.

Veteran passengers and Amtrak employees aren't pleased with its purpose, which is to combine the café and diner in one car and eliminate the sightseer lounge. That's happened on the City of New Orleans, but the Texas Eagle has managed to hang on to its lounge car. It's all about cost cutting. Congressional critics mandated Amtrak reduce losses on food service and labor, so the company introduced the "simplified dining car" concept, which eliminated an onboard service-staff member, leaving three servers and one chef. The staff reductions eliminated one hundred positions across the system.

In the past, Amtrak officials have complained that some of the railroad's financial problems stem from the large number of unions that represent its workforce of 19,000. It has tried to streamline work rules and "combine crafts" so its employees can perform more tasks. Amtrak has also wanted to contract out some functions now done by organized labor—such as food service.

Not surprisingly, all of these moves were met with resistance from the unions. But the central issue was wages. For the eight years between 2000 and 2008, the company and its employees were unable to negotiate a contract. During this period, the employees were prevented from striking by requirements of the National Railway Act and, in lieu of a contract, received only cost-of-living increases.

It was a poisonous atmosphere, one of the darkest periods of labor-management relations in Amtrak's history, according to Edward Wytkind, president of the Transportation Trades Department of the AFL-CIO. The TTD represents millions of workers in aviation, mass transit, and rail-related industries.

Though management blamed much of its financial problem on the high cost of labor, he said, statistics show that Amtrak employees generally earn lower salaries and benefits than transit workers. Management also said its hands were tied because Amtrak was receiving inadequate funding and its finances were in poor shape.

"For years, they just refused to bargain on any important issue," Wytkind told me in a telephone interview. "They sent people to the negotiating table who couldn't make decisions or wouldn't part from their previous positions. It created the highest level of acrimony I'd ever seen at Amtrak. Workers felt like they were being scapegoated for the company's financial problems. Morale was bad."

At the same time, the George W. Bush administration was trying to zero out Amtrak in its budget.

"It was the old trick of starving the beast, and when it doesn't perform well declare it a failure and try to get rid of it," said Wytkind. "They had no intention of funding Amtrak so it could meet its obligations to the employees. And Amtrak's management wasn't willing to step up and say this is what we need for our people."

That the Bush administration wanted to get rid of Amtrak, privatize it, or break it into pieces was no mystery. After Bush came into office, Amtrak's board was packed with people who were openly hostile to the whole idea of government-supported passenger service.

Former Amtrak president David Gunn, who was fired by the board largely for his candor and refusal to run the railroad on a shoestring, told me in an interview that some of the board members "didn't know the front from the back of a locomotive."

"They were loyal Bushies and were there to croak Amtrak. That's what it was all about. And the way some of them behaved in terms of their policies was just vicious. They were awful," he said.

Wytkind agreed with Gunn's assessment of the board and gave him high marks for trying to make the company's finances more transparent to Congress. However, he also said Gunn never addressed the labor-management issues at the bargaining table. There was no serious effort to resolve the deadlock, and by this time, the workers wanted back pay for their years without a contract as well.

After Alex Kummant was named Amtrak's president, George Bush in 2007 signed an executive order establishing a presidential emergency board to revive the stalled negotiations. The board mediated the dispute and, ironically, sided with the unions, ruling that Amtrak owed its workers $200 million in back wages.

At that point under the Railway Act, Amtrak could either accept the recommendations or the employees would have the right to strike within thirty days. They threatened to do so, which would have caused havoc on the East Coast. Several powerful senators and representatives put pressure on Amtrak to come to the table, and in January 2008, it signed a contract to pay wage increases that average 35.2 percent over the period of 2001 to 2009. A typical worker received $12,800 in back pay. Labor relations improved under Kummant, who left the company in 2008, and current president Joe Boardman has made an effort to reach out to the unions. The Bush appointees are gradually being replaced, and the new Amtrak bill, passed in late 2008, called for an expanded board with one seat to be filled by labor.

The long wait we had for breakfast was an indication that the Cross Country Café doesn't work well in summer when the trains are packed with passengers. For my part, I couldn't imagine a long-distance train without a lounge car. The train would feel a lot more confining. There would be no place to linger, meet people, play cards, or have a chat. The big sightseer windows, which wrap into the ceiling, provide a better view than in the coaches.

My boys loved the lounge, and I let them wander between it and our seats. Just past Texarkana, I went looking for them and met David Gascho of Lafayette, Indiana, who was riding down to Texas with his grandchildren and children. He'd been playing cards with all the kids in the lounge.

"Hey, you have real nice boys," he said. "They told us everything about you."

I laughed, "Everything? I haven't told them everything."

"Well, we know you're writing a book about trains."

As we spoke, the conductor came on the PA with a folksy drawl, "Ladies and gentlemen, girls and boys, we have congestion up ahead with the Union Pacific. We'll have to pull our signals manually, and go a bit slower. Ya'll sit back and we'll get moving soon."

We had reached northeast Texas where the Texas Eagle loses a lot of time. The twenty-three miles of single track between Marshall and Longview carries some of the nation's heaviest railroad traffic. Trains come through this stretch twenty-four hours a day. And unlike the Texas Eagle's consist of one locomotive and seven cars, the freights are long, double-stacked intermodals, what some railroaders have come to call "Wal-Mart Chinese Doodad Trains." We didn't get into Longview until 1:00 p.m., four hours behind schedule.

Longview, Texas
don't you get it? we don't care

Longview is Amtrak's second busiest station in Texas—the reason being all those passengers heading to and from Houston on the motor coach, which was idling in the parking lot when we arrived. A wiry guy with curly hair and glasses bantered familiarly with the conductor and kept a sharp eye on the passengers getting off the train. He was looking for me.

Griff Hubbard is a thirty-four-year employee of Amtrak, a fifth-generation railroader who helps "revenue manage" the Texas Eagle—meaning he books the train and sets prices and discounts. The only revenue-management operation outside of corporate Amtrak, it's overseen by the Texas Eagle Marketing and Promotion Organization (TEMPO), a rail advocacy group of small-town politicians, business leaders, rail fans, and other folks who helped save the train.

Hubbard gave us a ride to a hotel frequented by overnighting Union Pacific railroad crews. I got the boys fed and settled in front of the television, and took a cab back to the station.

Hubbard's second-floor office looks down on the tracks. On one wall is a copy of the first paycheck he earned as a track laborer for the Texas and Pacific Railway (T&P). Hubbard was Amtrak's first station agent in Texarkana and came over to Longview as station agent before transitioning to revenue management.

An intermodal entered the yards and rumbled by the station, shaking the windows and vibrating the floor.

"Does it always do that?" I asked.

"Yes sir, the UP railroad is a five-gallon bucket with ten gallons going into it. There are fifty-four movements a day through here. That's a train about every twenty minutes."

Hubbard was a folksy, articulate man with a habit of calling everyone sir, sometimes to both begin and end a sentence. When I asked about the Texas Eagle's on-time performance, he said, "Sir, you just personally experienced what is the norm, not the aberration, yes sir."

The Eagle's poor on-time performance makes it difficult to maintain ridership—although, Hubbard conceded, when gas was $4 a gallon, ridership went up 27 percent, revenues 25 percent.

Still, the Eagle had never been a great performer, either in being on time or in recovering costs, so Amtrak put the train on a hit list with three other trains in 1996 when the railroad was running a deficit of $100 million and about to go into Chapter 11.

It was an ill-timed move, said Celia Scott Boswell, the then mayor of Mineola, a town of 5,600 people west of Longview. Mineola had lobbied Amtrak for a stop, and because the town is near Tyler with 100,000 people and colleges, Amtrak agreed it was a good idea. In April 1996 with Amtrak bigwigs in attendance, Mineola held a "Welcome Amtrak" ceremony and agreed to repair the old T&P station. Then five months later, Amtrak tried to kill the train.

Boswell was livid. During a phone interview she told me, "I didn't like it all. We had this big to-do at the station—and either they knew then the train was going to be cut or they were going to do this to us despite everything we had just done. It just wasn't acceptable."

Boswell teamed up with the mayors—all of them women—of Longview and Marshall, and they enlisted the help of Senator Kay Bailey Hutchison.

"Amtrak messed with the wrong people," said Hubbard. "It messed with the East Texas ladies auxiliary."

It was a cryptic pop-culture reference.

"You've watched *The Andy Griffith Show*, right? Well, Sheriff Andy is walking Barney around Mayberry, giving him advice. Andy tells Barney, 'You don't arrest Otis the town drunk. When he's had too much to drink, Otis comes to the jail on his own.' Then Andy points to Aunt Bea as she was getting out of a car parked illegally, and he warns Barney."

At this point in the story, Hubbard did a ringing imitation of Andy-speak, "But Barney, now that there's Aunt Bea, and she's a member of the ladies auxiliary, and you don't ever, never, ever, never want to mess with the ladies auxiliary. That's trouble you don't need."

Hubbard grinned and spread his arms wide to frame the punch line, "Now that's what happened with Amtrak."

The mayors formed the "East Texas Mayors Commission to Save the Texas Eagle"; they argued that losing the Eagle would leave Dallas–Fort Worth, the fifth-largest urban area in the country, without train service and would set back any effort to make rail part of the transportation mix in Texas.

"Our goal was to keep the train going. If we lost it, we'd never get it back," Boswell said.

Hutchison secured some federal funding, but Amtrak needed about $6 million to keep the train going for another two years. Hutchison suggested the mayors ask the state legislature and Governor George Bush for a bridge loan that would give the railroad time to build up ridership.

It was a tough sell. Legislators stood on the statehouse floor and declared the money was being stolen from the highway fund and dumped into a railroad with no future or ability to pay it back. Members of the governor's staff advised Bush to steer clear.

Hubbard recalled a phone call he got from Boswell, "She asked me, 'Do we know who Karl Rove is and why he is telling Gov. Bush not to sign our loan?' Well, back then, no one knew who Karl Rove was."

Newspapers in Texas editorialized in support of the loan, and there was a groundswell to save the Texas Eagle. Eventually Bush let it be known he wouldn't veto the loan.

In July 1997, the legislature approved a $5.6 million loan. Amtrak put up as collateral twenty old railcars parked on a siding in Elk Grove, Illinois. The East Texas cities along the route also agreed they would help pay the loan back if Amtrak defaulted.

Amtrak actually paid the loan back early. During a ceremony held in the state capitol in Austin with Hutchison and Bush in attendance, then Amtrak president George Warrington presented Texas with an oversized check. Bush, standing next to Boswell, turned to her with a surprised look and whispered, "This is great. Gee, I didn't think they would pay it back."

It's ironic. As president, Bush tried to kill Amtrak, but as governor, he helped save the Texas Eagle. Since that time, Texas hasn't provided any money for the Eagle. There is no state subsidy, and the Texas Department of Transportation doesn't have a rail division.

TEMPO replaced the mayor's commission and expanded its membership to other states served by the Eagle. It encourages communities to rehabilitate their train stations. It has a program of volunteer hosts to greet passengers. It maintains a marketing Web site for the train. And in cooperation with Amtrak, TEMPO has taken over revenue management. Bill Pollard, the group's president and a Little Rock dentist, Hubbard in Longview, and Jesse Padilla, an Amtrak product-line agent in San Antonio, work as a team.

Pollard rides the train every few weeks. Hubbard meets every train in Longview, and Padilla meets all the trains in San Antonio. Being close to the action, talking with the crews and passengers, the men understand travel trends and passenger wants and needs, said Hubbard.

"We don't have to wait thirty days to get a survey to know what passengers think. If you're out there, they'll tell you," Hubbard explained. "And if I overbook a train and there are standees, the conductor will step off and say, 'What the hell have you done today?' . . .

"Now, the reason I'm good at setting prices is because I know the passengers.

I know why Aunt Mary takes the train, how often she does, and what she is willing to pay. No Web site or ticket agent on a telephone knows Aunt Mary like I do . . . in my opinion, sir."

"What have passengers been telling you about the Cross Country Café?" I asked.

He grimaced, not wanting to offer an opinion.

I gave him mine. It was too small, and inadequate for a whole train. The lounge/café part of the car seemed like a hangout for the crew, which discourages passengers from sitting there.

"Sir, let me just say that TEMPO has made a strong move to hang on to its Sightseer Lounge Car. You know one of the gracious parts of the train is the lounge car and dining car experience. If we get away from that too far, ridership and revenue will suffer," he said.

"In my opinion, sir, we have to ask ourselves, do we want to have a bus line on rails—meaning basic minimal seats in an aluminum car body on flanged wheels—and pretty much little else? Or, do we want a train with all of its amenities?"

Can anything be done about the Eagle's poor on-time performance? I asked.

He again cited the ten gallons going into the five-gallon bucket metaphor, but recalled a period in 1978 when Amtrak—in a rare bit of gumption—sued the Missouri Pacific Railroad (MoPAC) for delaying the Inter-American, which ran between Chicago and Laredo. Hard feelings got even harder, but the train ran on time.

"You could set your watch by it," said Hubbard.

Missouri Pacific merged into Union Pacific in 1982, and MoPac's chief officers eventually came to run UP. MoPac was known as a take-no-prisoners, hard-assed railroad. I heard that from historians and a freight executive who said, "Those MoPac guys were tough bastards. It was drilled into them."

And Hubbard had a telling anecdote about a UP executive who had started his career in MoPac, had been in Longview recently, and stopped by the station to chew the fat. During the conversation, Hubbard said something about how the railroad and Amtrak might cooperate to improve the Eagle's on-time performance.

According to Hubbard, the executive snorted, "You know, Griff, you just don't get it. Amtrak doesn't get it. And maybe you guys will never get it, but we just don't care—that attitude is instilled in the people running this railroad. It will take a full generation to run it out, and it may just pass on to the next generation.

"You need to understand this . . . if you're right to the minute on time and an ass in every seat, we don't care. If you are nine hours late, and nobody is on the train, we don't care. If you have engine failure and are stuck, we don't care. If you bring a few million to the table in incentives, we don't care. We're a $3-billion company, it means nothing to us.

"So no matter what Amtrak does. No matter what you do, we don't care. WE DON'T CARE."

Hubbard leaned back in his chair, "After that, I think I got it. I also sensed he didn't think their attitude should change, no sir."

It was late afternoon and Texas-hot outside. Passengers jammed the tiny waiting room, which is built into the corner of a much bigger and empty depot, still owned by Union Pacific. The city of Longview would like to take it over and rehab the station, but hasn't been able to come to an agreement with the railroad.

Having run out of chairs, the passengers plopped on suitcases, fingered their tickets and looked glum. Outside, away from the air-conditioning, more people stood in the shade of the building, smoking cigarettes and fanning themselves with newspapers. Wal-Mart Chinese Doodad trains rumbled by.

Hubbard and I got into his SUV and we watched as a woman in a silky white pantsuit and gold high heels unfolded a paper bag, placed it against her bottom and sat down on a dusty curb.

He shook his head, "We are not a third-world country. We should not be treating passengers this way; yet it happens nearly every day. It's like I'm still back in the 1970s and nothing has changed."

Houston

a pitiful harvest by bus

The next day, we were to catch the Amtrak connecting bus to Houston, but the Texas Eagle was again running three to four hours late, and the bus was likewise delayed. The kids swam at the hotel's outdoor pool while every thirty minutes or so, I dialed 800-USA-RAIL and heard, "Hi, I'm Julie. Amtrak's Automated Agent. To check if a particular train is running on time say 'Train Status.'" On board a train, where nearly everyone these days has a cell phone, Julie is as good a source of information as a conductor.

It was pleasantly hot—at least at poolside—and the kids were having fun. White cargo vans came and went with locomotive crews coming off the road or getting ready to take a train out. The guys paced around the lobby, ID cards dangling from their necks, and talked railroad.

Finally, it was time to get a cab. Inside the train station, we found a college student whose friends had dropped her off at 8:30 a.m. because the train was scheduled in at nine. Newbie, I thought. She didn't know about Julie.

There were no more seats inside, so we went trackside where a metal storage shed cast shade on some lawn chairs. The agent came by with a stack of newspapers, walked down the platform and dropped them where the sleeper cars would halt. I was taking a picture of Colin and Patrick near the tracks, and my elbow crossed the imaginary plane extending vertically from a bold yellow line painted onto the platform, warning passengers back from the tracks.

The agent barked, "Sir, you do not go past that yellow line. It is there for a reason."

"A please step back" might have sufficed, but then railroad platforms are dangerous as hell. Had the station been larger, it could have kept passengers inside until the train came in. But Longview was a shoebox and I'm sure this guy had seen people do every stupid thing imaginable on the platform, so his tolerance level was very low. Really, zero.

Minutes later, the Texas Eagle arrived and we scooted over to the waiting motor coach. Passengers coming off the train put their bags into the belly of the bus and we set off to Houston. It was a pitiful harvest. That day, the national passenger-rail service delivered all of forty people to the nation's fourth-largest city—and it did it by bus.

Amtrak runs or contracts out thousands of miles of bus connections, made necessary not just to connect two big cities like Chicago and Houston, but to make connections to other parts of its bare-bones national network—to cover routes that used to have trains. My kids were excited to see television monitors above the seats, and the driver cued up the *Alvin and the Chipmunks* movie before pulling out. We made good time on Route 59 running through the piney woods of Nacogdoches and Lufkin, and past sprawling sugar-beet fields, pastures of big-humped Brahman cattle, and hardware stores emblazoned with signs still extolling last fall's football team. About halfway there, we stopped at a 7-Eleven, and everyone got off to buy pizzas and subs. It wasn't a bad trip. The bus was clean, and the driver kept movies going the whole way.

Because the train had been late, however, we reached the city at rush hour, and because of Houston's labyrinthine highway network under endless construction and reconstruction, it took ninety minutes from the urban edge to reach downtown.

In the 1970s, my sister was one of the Yankees who fled places like Youngstown and Lansing for Texas. Rust-Belters and migrants crossing from Mexico flowed into Houston in staggering numbers. The city added a million people in ten years during the oil and construction boom, a time when the word "Michigander" was as nasty a slur as wetback, and bumper stickers declared "Let the Yankee Bastards Freeze in the Dark."

I have been to Houston many times in the past thirty years—for work and family—and watched the city balloon out another 20 miles in a breathtaking sprawl of freeways, feeder roads, malls, and housing developments, all of it resembling a big-box, retail strip of highway gone berserk. Today, the urban area covers 500 square miles. And Texas's population will likely double over the next fifty years with profound implications for surface transportation. Houston has the beginnings of a light-rail system. Dallas is further along with both a light-rail system and a commuter railroad running into the western suburbs to Fort Worth. Amtrak service in Houston is dismal. The Sunset Limited between New Orleans, Houston, El Paso, and L.A. runs just three times a week, and it's usually late.

There may be no better symbol of rail's current irrelevance and the highway's supremacy in Texas than Houston's Amtrak station, a squat, sixties-era, stucco-type building near a dirty overpass of I-45. It looks like it once housed an automotive repair shop or perhaps a plasma-for-pay center.

Although my sister had picked me up here in the past, she couldn't find the exit off the freeway. I stood in the parking lot with the cell phone and tried to give her a landmark.

"I'm looking across the street and there is a big fenced-in area of transform-
ers, power units, and electrical stuff. There's a parking lot here full of holes,
we're at the back of that. "

Just beyond us lay the glass and glitz of downtown Houston. Union Station,
built in 1911, was swallowed up and incorporated into Minute Maid Park,
home to the Astros. Over left center field, there's a steam engine celebrating the
nostalgia of trains. The former passenger waiting area, beautifully restored, can
be rented out for meetings and galas.

Dallas
a texas t-bone bullet train

Elise, my wife, flew down from Michigan, and my brother came from Pennsylvania, and we spent a few days fishing and visiting down on the Gulf. I left the boys with Elise, who would drive them to San Antonio where they'd join me for the trip back north while she flew home. I headed to Dallas–Fort Worth, catching a Southwest Airline shuttle flight out of Houston's Hobby Airport. Southwest operates planes between the two cities every fifty minutes. No waiting, open seating, just a big bus in the sky.

In the 1990s, Texas made a run at building a bullet train in a triangle configuration between Dallas–Fort Worth, Houston, and San Antonio. The legislature created an authority that in 1991 signed a franchise deal with a consortium, Texas TGV, to privately fund and build a 200-mph train.

It was a fight from the beginning. A rival German consortium that did not win the franchise filed suit. As planning got under way, the airlines, chiefly Southwest, supplied money and lawyers to the opposition, packed the scoping meetings, and roused the property-rights interests to oppose the train. Small towns saw it as a project for the big cities. Farmers and ranchers worried the electrical catenary would make their cows sterile.

In those days, Southwest was mainly a regional airline, dependent on its shuttle flights. Herb Kelleher, its chairman, threatened to pull his headquarters from Dallas and his planes out of San Antonio if the cities supported the project. High-speed trains, he said, were "a somersault backward into the 19th century."

The interests vested in the other transportation modes were powerful as well. The state legislature waffled; the politicians weren't correcting bad information. And the financing deal didn't work out. The whole effort bogged down and collapsed in 1994 when the Texas legislature withdrew the franchise.

I'd taken the air shuttle several times. The plane was packed, and I ended up in a middle seat between two big guys. There were moments in the flight when I had to fight off claustrophobia—perhaps because I'd lately spent so much time on roomier trains.

The *Houston Chronicle* that day had a story about airlines and menu pricing. Most were already charging for checked bags, but not Southwest. And it was still handing out free peanuts and a soft drink. If it had been charging, I would have had to elbow the guy next to me in the throat just to get my wallet out of my back pocket.

Truth be told, I took perverse pleasure in what was happening to the air industry. The façade of superiority had faded. Their planes were dirty, the airport unfriendly, the system treats passengers like cattle, and their service can be as crappy as bus lines and Amtrak. But their biggest crime is the way they deny people physical space and comfort.

When we landed at Love Field in Dallas, I headed to Dean International, a public-policy consulting firm near the Park Lane train station. First, I had to take a bus to Hampton Station downtown where I could get on the Red Line.

The bus driver was a friendly guy who resembled Ralph Kramden, that is, if Ralph had been black, wore an earring, and spoke in a quiet tone of voice.

When I asked if the bus went to the DART Station, he said, "You got it, buddy. Stick close, and I'll let you know. Ya'll ridin' the train instead of driving?"

"Yeah, I want to try out DART."

DART (Dallas Area Rapid Transit) was created in the early 1980s when fourteen cities and Dallas County voted for a regional transportation system. In the 1990s, the authority began acquiring rail lines and building stations, using more than $100 million from the Federal Transit Administration. The first light-rail trains rolled in 1996, and ridership immediately exceeded expectations. People in north Texas have taken to trains, and the system has big expansion plans.

"Now I'm just me, driving my bus down here, but I can see it," the driver said as he weaved effortlessly through the traffic. "Trains just make sense. You could move hundreds of people from the suburbs on a train, and then you get them down here and they can get on a bus or a DART train.

"Now you *could* do that if this city was organized that way, but it's not—not yet anyway. The people who built all of this were just thinking cars and trucks. Do you realize how many parking lots are down here just to make room for all these cars?"

He was talking intermodal, interconnectivity, but we didn't have time to finish the conversation. We'd come to my stop and he pointed where to find the train.

At Park Lane station, the neighborhood was under massive reconstruction. Run-down buildings were being razed for hotels, apartments, and retail stores in a $700 million, thirty-three-acre example of transit-oriented development. The rail line has been luring developers who already are jockeying for real estate on lines yet to be built.

At Dean International, I walked into a roomful of people just concluding a meeting. Most were consultants, there to meet with—as I was—Robert Eckels, the former county judge of Harris County (Houston). He chairs the Texas High Speed Rail and Transportation Corporation (THSRTC), a group trying to resurrect the idea of a bullet train in Texas. Made up of transportation officials, business people, and leaders of counties, towns, colleges, and cities along the route, the group is mainly a promoter of the train. It is not an authority, and receives no state money.

"What we do represent is interest in the train, which is bubbling up from communities and organizations," he said. "What role this group will play in the future is unclear. Our goal now is to get this thing moving again."

A trim, gray-haired Republican, Eckels is a power player in Texas politics. He'd been on the campaign trail in Houston the day before with John McCain. As county judge in Texas, he oversaw the executive, legislative, and judicial functions of the third-largest county in the country. Eckels also headed up the effort to resettle Hurricane Katrina victims in Texas and coordinated the evacuation for Hurricane Rita.

We sat down at a conference table and he pulled out a map of Texas and began sketching out the proposed new route of a Texas bullet train. The Texas TGV back in the 1990s would have run an 1,100-mile triangle between Houston, Dallas–Fort Worth, and San Antonio. The new proposal calls for a 900-mile T. The bottom of the stem begins at Houston, runs to Killeen and is crossed by a line between San Antonio and Dallas–Fort Worth. It's been nicknamed the Texas T-Bone, and it would provide service to the major airports, DART and the Transit Agency in Houston.

. "Continental and American are members of our group. They said we'll support you if you service the airports. Southwest, this time, has said it will remain neutral," Eckels explained. "That's a big hurdle we've overcome."

These days, Southwest is more a national than regional airline and less afraid of local competition from the train. American and Continental see the train as a way to bring more customers to their long-haul flights.

The train would parallel the highly congested I-35 corridor between San Antonio and Dallas–Fort Worth. The T formation picks up Fort Hood near Killeen as well as College Station. And though the route doesn't have a straight-line connection between Dallas and Houston, the speed of the train will make rail travel between the two cities competitive with air shuttles and highway traffic. The train would reach one million college students and 70 percent of the state's population. The train would connect Houston to Dallas in ninety minutes and Dallas to Austin in sixty minutes.

A bullet train could shrink Texas and turn what are now independent major cities and college communities into what Eckels called the "Texas Metroplex." A college student in Houston might commute daily to College Station. Research, educational, and medical facilities could be tied together, synergies created. Major airports would concentrate on long domestic and international flights rather than short hops. Eckels was talking mega-region where fast, convenient rail transportation opens up new economic opportunities.

"We aren't set on this route. It's just the one that seems to make sense from political and marketing points of view," Eckels said.

The right-of-way would mostly parallel current rail corridors and existing highways. Still there would have to be substantial acquisition, easement, and condemnation. Long sections, particularly in urban areas, would have to be elevated.

Would that rile the property-rights interests again? I asked.

"There's going to be some taking of land. There's no way around that. And there'll be opposition to this, but I think less than before," he said.

The bullet train may have an easier time coming in the wake of the Trans Texas Corridor, a proposal to create a 1,200-foot-wide corridor between Brownsville and the Oklahoma border to move goods across the state to and from Mexico. The governor and the Texas DOT had proposed putting toll roads, pipelines, power lines, and railways all into one mega-corridor, sometimes called the NAFTA Superhighway. It generated enormous opposition—from anti-immigration groups to environmentalists. In early 2009, TXDOT declared the whole idea dead.

Although the Texas TGV and Trans Texas Corridor failed, they show a need for Texas to address transportation in a big way. And that's why the interest in high-speed trains has bubbled back up, said Eckels. "The train makes even more sense today than it did fifteen years ago. The resistance has really gone down because the world has changed. I think people are seeing what an opportunity this represents."

In a state as big as Texas, though, the train must be fast. The group is "technology neutral" between a steel-on-steel and a magnetic levitation train.

Like many high-speed proponents I had met, Eckels was a bit dismissive of the shared right-of-way, incremental approach of Amtrak and the freight railroads. A train going 80, even 100 mph is not going to lure Texans off the highways, but a bullet train will, and it should capture a good share of the air shuttle market—currently about 14,000 people per day between Dallas and Houston.

"I want people in traffic on a toll road looking up at an elevated right-of-way when a train goes by at 200 mph and say to themselves, 'Hey I want to be on that,'" he said.

The state's relatively flat topography will entail significantly lower costs per mile for high-speed trains compared to California with its mountains and tunneling requirements. Estimates for the Texas train runs from $11 billion to $22 billion, depending on the choice of technology.

There's been no thought of raising taxes, tapping the state's general fund, or taking a portion of the gas tax to create seed money for the train, he said. The aim is to finance the project as a public-private partnership leveraging private funds with tax-exempt bonds.

The THRTSC could turn itself into a local government corporation. The involved cities and counties could write memorandums of understanding among themselves and then issue tax-exempt bonds. The local governments would have no liability or taxing authority to pay off the bonds. Those would be paid off by the riders of the system through operating surpluses. That there will be operating surpluses is a given, said Eckels. Texas, like California, has analyzed the financials of other bullet trains around the world.

The big hurdle is getting the capital up front needed to build the system, before surpluses can begin flowing back to the investors. A private entity—say, a consortium of TGV, Alstom, or Bombardier—could invest as a partner or come in as an investor/operator. A build-operate-transfer agreement could be arranged, he said.

"The first guy who walks in here with $2 billion could own this system," Eckels said. "As a local government corporation, we could become the financing mechanism and reduce their costs of borrowing by 1 or 2 percent through tax-exempt bonding."

One reason Eckels heads up the THRTSC is his track record for putting together big, complicated deals. He negotiated the construction of three sports stadiums in Houston, including Minute Maid Park. He built toll roads in Harris County without increasing property taxes. He is now a lawyer with the international law firm Fulbright & Jaworski, which has a national public finance practice.

So who would invest in such a train? I asked.

"Patient money," he said.

The long time horizon would produce steady if modest returns for pension plans, large banks, and wealthy families. What's needed now is an investment-grade market study that clearly shows investors the economics of the project.

Would Texas accept federal funds? I asked.

"Well, sure. Perhaps, the feds could supply block grants, and maybe TXDOT could do the grade separations to keep roads separate from the train tracks. And if the state and TXDOT want to come in and build this train that would be OK, too. There are a lot of ways this could happen."

He did note that TXDOT and the legislature probably didn't have the appetite considering what happened with the Corridor and the Texas TGV. However, by summer 2009, the Texas legislature was reconsidering the idea of creating a high-speed rail authority, which it will need to have any hope of snagging rail funds from the federal stimulus package and perhaps the next transportation bill out of Congress.

From the conference room, we could look out to the nearby construction zone where the steelworkers were "hanging iron"—shinning up vertical I-beams and bolting in cross pieces.

"There's a hundred million dollars worth of development around this DART station that is the result of tracks being here. We should be capturing some of that value in taxes and revenue that we are creating by building the tracks—and that money can funnel into the system."

It's complicated, but it has been done, and may be the only way in a conservative, tax-shy place like Texas, he said. "We've built toll roads and stadiums this way, but it has not been done for a rail system. I want this train but I'm still a Republican, and I want to do it without new taxes."

My next stop was Fort Worth to interview executives at the Burlington Northern Santa Fe Railway. I caught the DART downtown to Union Station and boarded the Trinity Railway Express, a commuter train running the thirty miles between Fort Worth and Dallas, stopping near the DFW airport in Irving and Richland Hills. Badged in blue, white, and red with a white lone star, the trains were hard to miss. The Trinity trains are a joint project of DART and the Fort Worth Transportation Authority.

My seatmate, a sports-information director at a Dallas college, had begun taking the train when gas hit $3. A woman who heard us talking chimed in, "I own a Chevy TrailBlazer, which I am no longer driving because that sucker costs me a $150 a week." She's considering retirement because the highways are congested, and though the train was pleasant, it takes a long time. "I'm just tired of this poop. It's just hard to get to work every day." That month Trinity had its highest ridership ever, up 19.8 percent. DART was up 14.2 percent.

Coming into Fort Worth, the train rolled by a consist of vintage railcars—dome cars, Pullman sleepers, and chair cars—hooked up to a BNSF locomotive. Perhaps there was a railroad museum nearby? I wanted to get a cab to my hotel, but wasn't sure where to get off. When the train stopped at the Fort Worth Intermodal Transportation Center, all I saw were city buses, so I rode to the end of the line: T&P Station. Texas and Pacific. A train station, right?

Detraining, I followed a big hallway into the building and turned where I saw a mammoth space ahead. It was the passenger terminal, but no one was there. There were no furnishings, just marble floors and a soaring ceiling with chandeliers and inlaid panels of chevrons and zigzag designs that I recognized as art deco. What a stunning space. The sound of my clicking heels and rolling suitcase echoed off the walls. I walked straight on through and outside into an empty parking lot. I didn't get it until I looked up on the building, which went up ten stories, where a huge a sign advertised, The Texas and Pacific Lots: Condos for Sale. I later learned the passenger terminal, like the one in Houston, is only used for events and galas. I took the address off the building and called a cab from my cell phone.

BNSF Headquarters, Fort Worth
we care. we really do

BNSF's headquarters lie north of downtown Fort Worth where the city sprawl falls away, the sky opens up, and you sense the nearness of the Great Plains.

BNSF is a behemoth railroad, and along with its rival, Union Pacific, they cover not only the Plains, but the Rocky Mountains and the West Coast, too. It operates in twenty-eight states over 32,000 miles of track. It has more than 6,000 locomotives and an annual fuel bill of $2.1 billion. It's the nation's largest grain shipper with more than 1,500 elevators along its tracks. It hauls millions of tons of coal out of northwest Wyoming. It has the shortest intermodal route from the Pacific Rim to Chicago.

BNSF is the product of more than 300 predecessor railroads including such iconic names as the Northern Pacific; Chicago, Burlington and Quincy; Great Northern; and St. Louis–San Francisco Railway. It has 38,000 employees and earns about $1.1 billion annually. Being a big corporation, BNSF had me submit written questions, and I worked through Pat Hiatte, general director of media relations, who walked me from the visitor's center to see D. J. Mitchell, the assistant vice president of passenger operations.

Hiatte stuck around for a time, but Mitchell didn't need a handler, and Hiatte had tours to give that morning to rail fans in town for the National Railway Historical Society Convention. That explained the line of vintage railcars I'd seen as my train had pulled into Fort Worth. Some were owned by various historical-society chapters who had filled them with members and travelled to Texas on the end of Amtrak trains.

D. J. Mitchell was a thin whip of a man in his late fifties, fast talking, down to business. He grew up in Ypsilanti, Michigan, and worked for the Burlington Northern before the merger. BN's culture, he said, was intellectually oriented but to the point of "paralysis by analysis." Santa Fe on the other hand, was more willing to take chances. The merger, he said, brought together their strong points, and most industry watchers view BNSF as a well-managed and forward-looking railroad.

It certainly has a good reputation with passenger entities, who sing its praises but also say that BNSF—and Mitchell, too—don't do anything out of charity. It's a business arrangement. When Amtrak, Metra in Chicago, Sounder in

Seattle, and Metrolink in L.A run on BNSF infrastructure, they have an on-time performance over 90 percent.

Mitchell looked down at a printout of my submitted questions, "You ask what makes us different. Why do passenger trains on our tracks have such good time performance?"

He looked up, "OK, here's the simple answer: 'We Care.'"

"You care?" I said.

"We do. We really do."

I was remembering Hubbard's "We don't care" anecdote.

"Well, why? What's in it for you guys?"

"Because we believe that Amtrak and the commuter services that run on our network are customers. And like all of our customers—coal, grain, or industry—we believe they deserve good treatment."

Gee, he even sounded sincere.

"Have you seen our corporate values?" He went over to his computer and pulled up a document. Having worked in corporate communications myself, I realize the importance of everyone "walking the talk" and "singing from the same song sheet." I used to write that stuff in speeches for executives. But, I'd seen people trot out corporate tenets rather than answering questions.

Maybe Mitchell sensed my doubts.

"I am not blowing smoke . . . this is like real stuff. It's not a bumper sticker. It's how we manage the whole corporation. We are flat-out different than the other guy."

The other guy was Union Pacific, and I remembered what Kyle Wyatt, the historian at the California Railroad Museum, had told me: "BNSF knows it's in the transportation business. That's what it does. The UP can forget it's a railroad."

OK. BNSF cares. How does it put that into action?

That, Mitchell said, is the complex part.

First the railroad participates in building the timetables with the passenger services. It analyzes dwell time spent in terminals, run time, the speed of the train, traffic patterns, the condition of track, and the recovery time, or cushion, built into the schedule to account for delays. There's computer analysis and modeling. It talks to its field people and runs the proposed schedules by its dispatchers.

"There's a science and art to doing this, and we think we're pretty good at it. If the schedule is too tight, we'll say so. We don't want an on-time performance of 60 percent or 70 percent. We want these trains to be successful," he said.

There's a financial motive, too. BNSF earns incentives for on-time performance. If it is consistently losing a train—"lose" meaning it's not earning incentives—BNSF goes through a detailed analysis, including having its own people ride the passenger trains.

"We will get to the root cause. And if it's our fault, we do something about it. I've told our people, 'Hey we have to do a better job with these trains. The state has spent money on infrastructure and we've got to come through.'"

But sometimes, in Mitchell's words, "it gets to be a mess out there."

In Texas, for example, the ports of Houston and Galveston can get so congested that grain trains back up all the way to Oklahoma City because it's a single-track railroad. The Temple to Fort Worth section has terrible on-time performance. The ground dries out in the summer and the ballast sinks. In winter, the soil turns to gumbo, the ballast slumps, and the rails become "bumpy." In both instances, slow orders have to be put on until repairs are made.

"When trains are late it's not because we're being mean or spiteful. The problems are usually short-term and episodic and we work through them," he said.

The railroad has a twenty-four-hour passenger-operations desk in its Fort Worth dispatching center, mission control for its trains, all tracked by GPS. The desk acts as liaison with the dispatchers and Amtrak's operations. Crews on passenger trains can call the desk at any time and get an update on conditions or relay information regarding their train status.

"It's a direct line between this company and the entire Amtrak structure," he said. "Information flows both ways."

In Washington and California, I'd been told that BNSF had been a good partner in infrastructure projects but a hard bargainer, too. Out of the $300 million spent in improving tracks around the King Street Station in Seattle, BNSF put in just $8 million because the benefits were almost entirely for Amtrak Cascades and Sounder.

"There has to be a commercial reason for our investments. Now if there is a nexus where our interests and that of the passenger organizations intersect, we'll be there," he said. "But to do otherwise would put our franchise at risk."

The most obvious places for capital investment are rail yards, ports, terminals, and the conjunction of tracks coming in and out of cities—the typical choke points, he said. I mentioned the capacity study commissioned by the Association of American Railroads and asked if the freight railroads are going to need public money in the future to meet their infrastructure needs.

That brought an uneasy smile from Mitchell. BNSF is not asking for public funds. It invests $2 billion in capital expenditures annually. Where those investments are being done, how quickly they are put in place, is driven by the railroad's business needs. If the public entities want it to go faster, they need to bring money to the table, he said.

"If there is a public need, we're ready to engage but we're not looking for public money. We have a commercial reason to exist and should generate enough business to keep us going. Start taking public money and you're a couple steps away from nationalization. I don't think anyone wants that."

Still, the railroad expects there will be more demand from passenger entities to access its network, though Amtrak historically with its "incremental cost" structure doesn't contribute much to keeping up the infrastructure. The Hi-Line across the northern tier of states, he said, is some of the best railroad track in the country, kept up to high standards for the grain and the intermodal business.

"And Amtrak—the Empire Builder—rides on that for free," he said, immediately holding up his hand. "Now that's not a complaint. That's what the law says we need to do, and we know our responsibilities. But if they just had to pay their share of rails, ties, and ballast, it would be an awful lot of money."

What about the incentive money earned from Amtrak for running its trains on time? BNSF can earn up to $32 million annually from that. Mitchell shrugged. The incentives are important to his budget in passenger operations, but for the entire company they are insignificant. Incentives don't change the fundamental business model.

OK, if it's not just about the money is there some pride, too? I asked. The visitor's center displays a lot of passenger-train memorabilia—dining car china, time schedules, and advertising posters. The Santa Fe ran the Super Chief, the Great Northern the Empire Builder, and CB&Q the Black Hawk.

Sure there is pride, he said. The railroad understands that communities in North Dakota and Montana along the Hi-Line depend on Amtrak. Many BNSF employees and their families ride the Empire Builder. "We are really proud of it. Passengers know when they are running on our tracks."

I said, "Do you really think passengers know whose railroad they are on?"

He smiled. "I think so. Because if it's not us, it's the UP, and the difference is significant. When I'm on an Amtrak train and they learn I'm from BNSF, I get thanked by the crews all the time—passengers, too."

Back in the visitor's center, it was easy to tell the railroad guys and the vendors from the rail fans in their shorts, train T-shirts, and ball caps weighed down with buttons. They carried plastic ditty bags with BNSF stuff. A nerdy-looking fellow (there's no other way to say it) in a red vest—a *Classic Trains* magazine logo on the back—herded the group where Pat Hiatte stood on the stairs.

Hiatte said, "OK. We need to be quiet when we go upstairs. You'll be seeing several valuable artifacts including actual land grants signed by Ulysses Grant and Abraham Lincoln."

As they went upstairs, a couple of railroad guys came down with two men from India dressed in blue suits. They all bid goodbye, and when the Indian guys were outside out of earshot, one turned to the other, "How many times do you hear about building a railroad and have to worry about your employees being eaten by tigers?"

I was in no hurry. My train to San Antonio didn't leave until afternoon. The place was like a museum with Frederic Remington statues and large oil paintings. A century ago, the Great Northern commissioned artists to paint sublime scenes of Glacier National Park to lure rail tourists to hotels owned by the railroads. Glass cases held vintage rusty rails, surveying chains, railroad watches, and signal lights. It was a foamer's delight.

Texas Eagle
no mac and cheese

At the Amtrak ticket counter in Fort Worth, I met Bob Murray, a retired cop from Chicago.

"How's the train running?"

"Two hours late."

"Where are you going?" I asked.

"Chicago."

"Going the wrong way aren't you?"

"Taking the long way." He was going to San Antonio to catch the Sunset Limited to New Orleans and then up to Chicago.

Murray had been in town for the rail convention. His father had worked for Railway Express Agency on the Rock Island Line from Chicago to Omaha. Sometimes, he would take his son, and they would throw bundles of the *Chicago Tribune* and *Sun Times* off the train, stay in a dormitory, and come home the following day.

It was nearly 4:00 p.m. when I took the last seat in the last coach, so I could stand at the rear window and watch the tracks running away from beneath the train. I was at one end of the T of the Texas T Bone, running south through Cleburne, McGregor, Temple, Austin, San Marcos, and finally San Antonio. Amtrak does the route in about eight hours; a bullet train would take about ninety minutes.

Lunch was BBQ pit-smoked beef brisket with garlicky potatoes—one of the Eagle's regional menu items. As I ate, I chatted with Chris Worley, sixty, the lead service attendant who has been with Amtrak for thirty years. A round-faced man with a melodious voice and big smile, he seemed well fitted for his job.

"I love the Texas Eagle. I just hope they don't screw it up," he said.

He pointed to the pretty blue decor of the Cross Country Café and the stylized lamps on each table.

"Sure, this car is nice, but it doesn't have enough capacity. We have to provide people service. And if the train is late—and this one is a lot—we need to be able to satisfy them in another way with good meals."

He also worried about having just one cook down below—the result of the crew cutbacks.

"What if he gets sick or passes out. How are we going to handle that?" he said. "There's no margin for error."

Although it was just June, fields of brownish feed corn and drooping sunflowers stood ready for picking. Fresh-cut hay lay drying in windrows, and where it had been raked and stacked it resembled cubes of shredded wheat. Red shorthorn cattle grazed the pasturelands. We ran down the west side of I-35 through small towns where the water towers boasted the image of the high school's mascot—the Holland Hornets, the Bartlett Bull Dogs.

In the lounge car, Bob Murray told me about the historical convention, which had held its banquet in that gorgeously restored T&P station.

"The main speaker told us all about the station and the history of Texas railroads. He was real knowledgeable, problem was he didn't know when to quit," he said.

A railroad historian told me rail fans have a share of obsessive-compulsive personalities who find comfort in all the nomenclature, the numbers, and the pedigrees of different railroads.

Bob smiled knowingly, "Yeah there were some people at the convention who were really unique individuals."

Bob had retired from Cook County Sheriff's Department, and said he didn't get too far down his "to do during retirement" list before he got bored. He went one day to a railway society meeting where he heard a guy speak about Trails and Rails, a partnership between Amtrak and the National Park Service to do historical interpretation on board trains in summer. Now he rides the Empire Builder from Chicago to Winona, Minnesota, and the Texas Eagle from Chicago to Quincy, talking about the towns and history along the way.

"It's part of what makes the experience different. Most people want to hear about the history. Although sometimes we get some cranks who just want us to be quiet."

While we talked, the conductor kept coming on the PA, telling us about freight-train congestion and apologizing for the delays. Some of the convention participants, Bob said, had come down on the Texas Eagle a few days earlier with their vintage railcars hooked on to the back of the train. Near Edgewood, not far from Dallas, the train pulled into a siding to let a freight by, and both of its locomotives quit, and neither would restart.

With the head-end power gone, there was no air-conditioning. It was nearly 100 degrees outside. Emergency officials sent out school buses and firemen to help unload the passengers and their luggage, and everyone was taken to a school gym until Amtrak could arrange motor coaches and bring everyone to Dallas.

It wasn't the first time I'd heard this type of story. Trains have broken down in southern Illinois and Florida. An executive of CSX said the company supports more money for Amtrak just so it can run better equipment that doesn't fail and jam up the tracks. During one of the Florida incidents, the conductors wouldn't let passengers off the train, and people called the local police complaining they were being held hostage.

"Sounds like one of those stuck-on-the-runway, waiting-to-take-off stories," I said.

Bob sighed, "You know they've had thirty years to figure this out, and this stuff still happens. I heard that Amtrak isn't even ready to get new cars, haven't designed them."

"I heard the same thing."

As we came south, bunches of prickly pear cacti and mesquite stippled the grasslands. Rocky ridgelines and outcroppings sharpened the topography of the Hill Country. At dusk, the live oaks against the right-of-way turned black in silhouette, and the fractal geometry of their branches flickered the light inside the car. Out the back of the train, the polished tops of the rails caught the last light and ran off behind the train to a vanishing point.

The train was nearly empty and I went off to the dining car to ask Chris Morley about it. He was at a dining table with piles of cash and receipts, doing his reconciliations.

"We are past our major points—Longview and Dallas–Fort Worth," he said. "You watch as we come north tomorrow, the train will fill up."

Morley and his crew stepped off at Austin rather than riding to the end of the line—another way Amtrak tries to save money. I would see the problem with that the next morning.

That night, the train didn't make San Antonio until 12:45 a.m. I took a cab to the hotel where Elise and the boys waited, slept four hours, and got up for the return trip.

From San Antonio, we had to ride coach until Longview where we would get our sleepers. As we pulled out at 7:00 a.m., the car attendant handed each passenger a white paper bag with a muffin and a six-ounce container of warm orange juice. Fortunately, Elise had repacked the cooler, and we had more supplies. The dining car and café were closed until we got to Austin at 11:00 a.m. and picked up Chris Worley and his crew.

At Temple, two chubby young women in their early twenties came down the aisle holding unlit cigarettes, waiting to get off for a smoke. They wore gobs of makeup, tight hip-hugger jeans, and low-cut shirts that showed their virtues as well as their deficits. One's shirt said, "What Happens in Your

Mouth Stays in Your Mouth." Fortunately, the kids didn't ask me what that meant.

These classy ladies attracted the attention of two guys behind us who had been chatting in Spanish for the last three hours. The younger one had a shaved head, wore a sleeveless shirt, and displayed tattoos from fingertips to shoulders. The older one, whom he kept calling Tio (Uncle), had a pockmarked face and black ponytail flecked with gray. Tio, who hadn't stopped talking since he'd gotten on, elbowed the nephew and off they went. I watched out the window and as the girls lifted their cigarettes to their mouths, Tio snapped open his Zippo, and started talking and talking. The girls covered their mouths in mock embarrassment. The nephew just pulled on his cigarette and smirked.

I could see it coming. Lounge lizards. Kindred spirits. They all got back on the train, went to the lounge, and pounded beers all afternoon. Matt Van Hattem at *Trains* magazine told me he rode the Texas Eagle once and said it was like being on a train with Jerry Springer, his guests, and the audience.

In the midday light, the Hill Country looked dry and hot. Turkey vultures turned and soared on the updrafts rising from the ochre-colored ridges and bluffs of the Edwards Plateau— limestone bedrock that stretches for hundreds of miles across central Texas. There's not much soil for farming, and mostly we passed shorthorn cattle grazing in the open spaces between copses of live oak and mesquite.

In Fort Worth, the train had to go past the station and then back in to its platform, taking a good fifteen minutes. There was a crew change, a half-hour layover. I sent Kelly running into the station with quarters for a newspaper and sat down under a metal shade canopy with the little boys. We looked at the new conductor, standing by the train, arms folded.

"Doesn't he look snappy?" I said.

He resembled a young Denzel Washington in a crisp, pressed uniform, white shirt, keys on his belt, black gloves on his hands, and some very cool-looking shades. A figure of authority.

On board he announced, "Welcome to the Texas Eagle. We do not tolerate crude or lewd or rude behavior of any kind on this train. Please be kind to your fellow passengers. We thank you."

Our way was blocked by two freights. Track work also forced slow orders. It took one and half hours to reach Dallas. At that rate, it would be well past dinner before we got to Longview. Because Hubbard had booked my tickets, I knew the folks occupying our roomettes were getting off in Dallas, so I asked the young conductor if we could get into the rooms there.

"You got it. The attendant will need just a few minutes to tidy up the rooms."

The coach seats and the train's slow progress were getting old. The lounge lizards, back from the bar, had passed out and were snoring. We needed the change, and the boys reveled in their new "first-class" digs.

We were looking forward to dinner, but when we sat down with the menus, the attendant said the dining car was out of kid's meals—no pizza or macaroni and cheese—just the build your own burger, which neither Colin nor Patrick eats. Colin stomped off back to the room—"Just make me a PB&J please"— while Patrick ate a dinner roll and then left as well. Kelly and I ordered the steaks.

"What's with the kid's menu?" I asked Chris Morley when he came by.

"We ran out on the way down. They only put in twelve pizzas."

"Doesn't the train get restocked in San Antonio?"

"Everything comes out of Chicago."

"Amtrak ever heard of H-E-Bs? Why not just send somebody over to a supermarket for microwave pizzas?"

It was a joke, but I was peeved. At $110 per roomette, they at least could have mac and cheese for the kids.

When the waitress came to take away the plates, I ordered ice cream so the boys could have dessert.

"Sorry. No ice cream. Just pecan pie."

Unbelievable. Only it wasn't.

Somewhere between Dallas and Mineola, the train pulled into a siding and sat for a full hour, a long time to look at a cornfield, but pretty as the sunset turned the tassels red and gold. I made sandwiches, had the attendant put down the beds, and the two younger boys took the upper bunks. There were stops and starts all night long, and by breakfast we were seven hours behind schedule. Out of Little Rock, while we were at breakfast, the train ran through a narrow, raised corridor of brush and trees surrounded by vast rice fields yet to be flooded. Tractors were out on the land throwing up plumes of dirt and looking like Lego toys on a big table.

The morning sun lit up the dining car, the shadows of the trees ran across the faces of the boys as they took big bites of railroad french toast and sausages. This is I how I had envisioned the trip, a beautiful morning, a hearty meal, and a bucolic landscape stretching on and on as the train clicked along, feeling its power, eating up the landscape.

At Poplar Bluff, Missouri, the depot was as pathetic a station as I'd seen—at least one still open to the public. Outside, it was bare wood, peeling paint, curled shingles, and crumbling sidewalks. Inside, there were a few bare seats, no air-conditioning, nor a newspaper rack. An old man from the sleeper wandered in and muttered, "What a dump. Meanwhile we're spending all that money in goddamn Iraq."

Out on the platform, the lounge lizards came off the train carrying suitcases for their lady friends. The one had changed her rude T-shirt, and the other looked around nervously as if watching for a boyfriend coming to pick them up. Tio leaned in for a goodbye kiss; she tried to step back but he rubbed up against her and cupped her butt in his hand. The younger guy pecked the other's cheek before she pushed him back. They grabbed their suitcases and walked off quick, ankles twisting side to side because of their spiked heels on the broken sidewalk. Shaking smokes from their packs, the two men looked at each other and broke into wracking laughs.

Days of rain had delivered a Katrina-like disaster to the upper Mississippi. Eastern Iowa and Cedar Rapids were under water, interstates flooded, freight trains backed up and delayed. As we came into St. Louis, the sky boiled up and let loose a hard rain. The Mississippi, remarkably wider than a week earlier, filled the floodplains, so all we could see were the crowns of trees where there once had been open woods. Swirling with eddies and whirlpools, the river licked the edge of the right-of-way. We were lucky to get through at all.

We all squeezed into one roomette, looking out and marveling at Old Man River.

"How wide?" Patrick asked.

"A mile, maybe."

"It looks like a lake."

An uprooted tree, a piece of Styrofoam swept by and what else?—likely tons of topsoil, ag chemicals, dead animals, sewage, and debris.

Two roomettes up, I met Jerry, a retired college professor from San Diego who had come out from California on the Sunset Limited. Amtrak workers in L.A. call it the triage train because there are so many elderly aboard. He grew up during World War II in Aberdeen, South Dakota where the local people would make pheasant sandwiches to feed the soldiers stopping through on the troop trains. In 1945, he got on board his first train with his parents. It was full of drunken, happy soldiers coming back from Europe.

"They were sleeping in luggage racks, wandering around, singing—a bunch of eighteen- and nineteen-year-olds just happy to be alive," he recalled. "There weren't any seats, so my family had to sit on our suitcases, and after a time, a couple of these soldiers gave us their seats. I'll never forget that."

Jerry, recently widowed and finding it strange to travel alone, was on his way to Chicago to visit a daughter. By Springfield, the train was eight hours behind schedule. We were not going to make it to Chicago in time to catch the last train to Milwaukee. I got the younger boys into bed and packed all the gear. Kelly watched a video, and I chatted with Jerry and then fell asleep sitting up.

At 11:00 p.m. we saw the Chicago skyline, but it took another forty-five minutes to get into Union Station. Amtrak customer service was ready for us with vouchers and a bus to a hotel. I had feared they might stick us on a bus for Milwaukee and we'd end up at the airport station at 3:00 a.m.

It was June, a weekend for festivals, and the only hotel with vacancies was thirty-five miles away in Indiana. Colin slept on my lap, and Patrick on Kelly's, and we rolled down the interstate—around cloverleaf after cloverleaf, on-ramps, off-ramps. After a while, I didn't even know where we were, just that it was two in the morning.

We were a motley bunch—Amish, nuns, old people, hip-hoppers in do-rags, a couple of business types, and me with three kids. In the hotel lobby the driver shouted out, "I will be back here at 9:50 a.m. The bus leaves at 10. Make sure to be here."

The next morning, before he got on the highway, he cued up a movie for the ride.

Colin nudged me, "Dad this isn't right."

"What's not right?"

"The movie."

It was *Kung Fu Panda* and rather blurry.

"It's out of focus, Colin."

"No, no. How did he get it?"

"Get what?"

"The movie. How did he get it?"

Kelly whispered in my ear, "Dad, it just got into the theaters two weeks ago. It's not on video, yet."

"Well then. It's probably pirated. Pretty poor copy, too."

"Pirated! Does Amtrak know about this?" Colin asked.

He's my rule man. We'd been talking about seeing the movie when we got home, and Colin wasn't going to have it spoiled by this scofflaw bus driver.

He pulled his hat over his eyes and stuck his fingers in the ears.

"Let me know when we get to the train station."

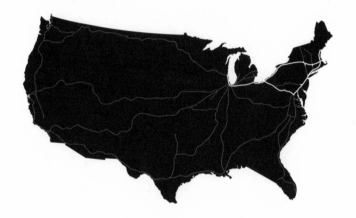

The Hiawatha
deadly days

In August, Barack Obama chose Joe Biden as his running mate, and Biden—perhaps Amtrak's most well known rider—actually mentioned Amtrak in his acceptance speech. It was stunning. The trains were full of people. And even the presidential candidates were talking rail.

In September, I headed back to Washington, D.C., and from there up the Northeast Corridor to New England, but first I stopped in Milwaukee to talk with Matt Van Hattem at *Trains* magazine. I got to Kalmbach Publishing late in the afternoon of September 12, 2008. The day was to be a turning point for passenger rail.

We chatted about the upcoming election and the recession, which by now everyone was admitting was the real thing. The poor economy had already claimed Colorado Railcar, a company that had been building tourist coaches for Alaskan Railways and self-propelled consumer coaches known as diesel multiple units. It wasn't a big player in the industry, but it was the last American car builder. It couldn't get financing to continue. Its sister company, GrandLuxe Rail Journeys, went under, too. Formerly known as the American Orient Express, the company ran truly luxurious cars on the ends of Amtrak trains. There just weren't enough people to blow money in a stagnating or declining economy.

Ironically, Matt told me, at this same time, 85 percent of all transit systems in the country were over capacity. In Chicago, Metra was taking bathrooms out of some of its commuter cars to create more ridership space.

The pending Amtrak Reauthorization Bill, which had gotten through the House and Senate with veto-proof majorities (Bush had said he would veto it), promised some capacity relief, but passage before the end of Bush's term was looking doubtful. Representative James Oberstar in the House and Senator Frank Lautenberg in the Senate were trying to put together a conference to work out the details, but Senator Tom Coburn from Oklahoma, a fierce Amtrak opponent, was using an arcane rule to keep it out of conference. On his Web site he was still complaining about the price of food and beer.

"It doesn't look like this Amtrak bill is going anywhere this year," Matt said.

"It looks dead in the water. Too bad, there are some really good things: grants to states, more money for equipment, money to develop high-speed corridors."

As Matt and I talked, 2,000 miles to the west on tracks I had ridden over just weeks earlier near Chatsworth in a Los Angeles suburb, a Metrolink commuter train carrying 220 people running on shared infrastructure collided head-on with a Union Pacific freight train. I heard about it on the radio while driving to my hotel and then watched the twenty-four-hour news networks showing the scene from helicopters hovering overhead. When I went to bed, crews working through the night with floodlights, heavy equipment, and cadaver dogs searched for the dead and injured.

Milwaukee's streets were shiny with rain when I left the motel at 5:15 a.m. and drove down the empty interstate to the downtown intermodal station. All glass and brightly lit from the inside, the station glowed like a transparent cube among the city's old masonry structures.

On the Hiawatha as the gray dawn came on, we ran past patches of flooded woods, and sprawling truck farms—long rows of cabbages as big as volleyballs. The closer we got to Chicago, the more it rained.

It was Saturday, the early train. On the Glenview platform, a pretty young Indian woman in an aqua blue sari, rouge cheeks, and a red dot on her forehead held a pink umbrella—the only color in what otherwise was a monochromatic scene. Rain pelted the windows, and the droplets adhering to the glass ran sideways in the slipstream. We barreled through several Metra stations, our whistle blaring out a warning.

Then the train came to a quick stop. The PA crackled, "We have had an incident on the tracks. We will be delayed here for some time."

Passengers' eyes met; we looked out the window into the rain, but could see nothing. Two tracks over, an outbound Metra crept by.

A grandmother headed to Michigan called her grandchild.

"I'm on a choo-choo coming to see you. But we're having a bit of trouble."

When she hung up, she told her seatmate, "I hate trains, something always happens and you wait."

The assistant conductor came through on his way to the locomotive.

A businessman in a trench coat, who had been muttering to himself, demanded, "Why are we still here?"

"Sir, we had a fatality. We hit a pedestrian."

No one said anything.

Then I asked, "Did someone run in front of the train?"

"Yes."

The businessman said, "Well, a Metra train just went by. Can't we back up and get on those tracks?"

"We can't back up. It's a crime scene behind us. The police are here, but we're waiting for the Amtrak police on their way from Union Station. They need to take statements."

"We've been here for forty-five minutes."

Some of us looked askance at the businessman.

The young conductor turned up his palms.

"Sir, it's up to the police now."

We sat like sheep. A body must have passed below my window or the wheels underneath.

I got up and wandered toward the back of the train. Two guys in the next car asked, "Hey, do you know what we hit?"

"We hit a person."

The Amtrak police had arrived and were walking up the tracks. I could see a Metra station about seventy-five yards back. The head conductor got on, hair dripping wet, his big raincoat soaked. "An ambulance just took someone else to the hospital. I don't know what that was all about."

The Amtrak cops were two burly guys in orange rain gear. They walked through the cars dripping wet, and climbed into the locomotive to interview the engineer.

An hour later, the assistant conductor came through.

"We should be under way soon. I know you are probably tired of hearing us say that."

"Sure are," the businessman retorted.

It was nearly 11:00 a.m. when we came to a stop under the sheds at Union Station. As I walked toward the front of the train, I examined the massive wheels resting on the greasy tracks. Rain dripped down the metal skin of the locomotive as if it were in a sweat. Had the other passengers done what I was doing? How macabre, but there just above a wheel, in the running gear, was a small but bright and pink torn piece of flesh.

In the Metropolitan Lounge, I got online to the *Chicago Tribune* Web site. A story appeared at 2:00 p.m. headlined "Man Hit by Amtrak Train, Killed."

It happened at the Edgebrook Metra station at 7:50 a.m. Carrying a large, heavy bag and an umbrella, he was across the tracks from the platform. He saw our train coming and apparently mistook it for the commuter train he wanted to catch. Perhaps he thought it would slow down or maybe he just couldn't see well in the rain and mistook the distance. According to a witness, he stepped onto the tracks when the train was less than 100 feet away. Of course, we weren't stopping and he didn't make it across. A woman who saw what happened became so distraught; she fell, injured her leg and was taken to the hospital.

The accident left a pall over the day. The rain and wind blew so hard, it was impossible to go out for a walk. The Chicago River ran muddy and turbid, its surface carrying garbage washed off the streets.

In the Metropolitan Lounge, passengers stood riveted to big-screen TVs where the news alternated between Hurricane Ike, which had just come ashore in Galveston, and the Metrolink crash in California where aerial footage showed firemen scrambling up ladders to get inside the shredded cars. The videos of bloodied passengers in L.A and bent-over palm trees in Texas ran over and over again. No one could tell what was happening in Galveston, but in L.A, the death toll kept rising.

The Capitol Limited
a complete washout

The storm that day dumped eight inches of rain on Chicagoland. The Capitol Limited was due out at 4:05 p.m., but we didn't board until 8:00 p.m. As I settled into my sleeping car the conductor announced the train was under slow orders owing to high water. At dinnertime, we'd yet to reach Indiana.

I ate with Tricia, an elderly woman from Peoria headed to Virginia to see her son, and Naomi, an earnest thirty-year-old Australian working for BP (formerly British Petroleum) out of its London office. Naomi's line of work is carbon sequestration. She examines opportunities for the company to invest in projects that offset global warming—a wind farm in Turkey, a reforestation project in Algiers, and, on this trip, her first to the United States, a Chicago landfill that captures and burns methane.

Naomi had work in Washington before heading home and wanted the experience of taking an overnight train. She majored in economics and art and after college set off hitching through Europe and never went back home. To her parents' chagrin, she hasn't married either.

Tricia's hands and lips trembled as she spoke, but she was sharp.

"A woman does not have to be married or have children to be happy," she declared.

"I am jubilantly happy," Naomi said.

And she was on top of her game. After Tricia left, Naomi gave me an impassioned presentation that probably went well with PowerPoint.

BP was going to change the world, and make money doing it.

"I am an American. You think I really want to drive a smaller car?" I said.

"There are nice small cars."

"Yeah, but we don't make them here. Besides, it's a big country. We need big cars."

I was being facetious, but Naomi didn't realize it. Maybe she was young and idealistic; maybe I was old and cynical.

"Well, there isn't just one answer. We have to start somewhere, don't we?"

"Absolutely," I said.

The tracks were flooded, signals out of order, and several freights halted between Chicago and South Bend. When I went to sleep that night, our train hadn't moved in two hours.

So it was not a surprise when the conductor came on the PA at 9:00 a.m. and said, "Folks, in ten minutes we will be in South Bend, Indiana. Our first stop. As you know, we are running, very, very late. It's not a pretty picture. We've had to deal with freight traffic and all this high water."

I had breakfast with Roy and Martha, from near Tillamook, the cheese capital of Oregon. Roy is retired military. Most of their seven children served. Two grandsons are in the Navy, two in the Marines. They were conservative Republicans and Catholic, making the sign of the cross before eating. Martha is getting feeble, and she's uncomfortable on airplanes. Roy wears a hearing aid, and the couple can no longer drive cross-country. Although it's a long ride from Oregon to Georgia, where they will visit a daughter, they like the train and had the handicapped bedroom in the lower section.

They were incensed at our attendant who had told them, "If McCain gets elected, we're dead. Republicans don't like us. The Democrats support Amtrak."

It sounded like our attendant. She had been sarcastic, impatient, and mostly absent so far.

Martha asked, "Is that true?"

"McCain sees Amtrak as a boondoggle," I said.

"But the Democrats are in charge now, and they had presidents before. Why didn't they fix it then?"

Good point.

After Waterloo, the sky brightened, and fans of sunlight sliced through the clouds. The train finally started to roll, rushing along double tracks. We were thirteen hours behind schedule.

Westbound freights came by in a blur. Some were piggybacks—truck trailers fastened atop flatbeds—but others were road-railers, semitrailers placed onto sets of steel wheels, or bogies, and pulled by locomotives.

A road-railer train is an odd sight, but its efficacy is unmistakable. Each trailer represents a semi truck taken off the roads. As the capacity of the nation's rail infrastructure expands, the future of such deliveries is bright.

Near Cleveland, I was joined in the dining car by a father and his eight-year-old daughter. He wore a "Go Irish" sweatshirt, matching sweats, and ball cap. The daughter had a leprechaun on her shirt. In our car's passageway earlier, I'd already run into Mom emblazoned with Notre Dame wearables.

"Who won?" I asked.

"We did," the father chimed.

"Was it wet?

"Very. It rained all day."

Aside from victory, theirs was a sad story. They had taken Amtrak from their home in Pittsburgh and secured a sleeper for the return trip. The plan was: see the game, eat dinner in South Bend, board the train at 9:00, hit the hay, and wake up in Pittsburgh. Except the train didn't show for twelve hours and the family paced the night away in the train station.

"We would have gotten a hotel, but they told us the train had left Chicago and was on its way," he explained. They had two pricy bedrooms for the day and no refund because weather delays are acts of God.

Tailgate madness was on display in Cleveland as the train eased past Cleveland Browns Stadium. Smoke from hundreds of gas grills wafted above a throng of thousands, all outfitted in various patterns of brown and orange. Browns fans waved to the train, danced on the roofs of RVs, and held up mugs of beer. It was sheer goofy spectacle, and the stadium, open at one end, resembled a giant mouth ready to take them in.

Through the afternoon, the train angled away from Lake Erie, crossed eastern Ohio, and followed the Ohio River into downtown Pittsburgh, where we stepped out onto the platform. Roy and Martha walked up and asked, "Do you have photographers taking pictures of this train for your book?"

"What do you mean?"

"For the last three hours, we've seen all these people with cameras alongside the tracks—taking pictures," Roy explained.

They were probably rail fans who, knowing the train was late and coming through in daylight—rather than at night—capitalized on the opportunity.

Roy and Martha would miss their connections to the Silver Meteor and have to wait another day in D.C., but they seemed unconcerned. They passed the time, reading newspapers and saying the rosary together. From down the hall, I could hear Hail Mary's; they were praying the Joyful Mysteries.

Leaving the city, we followed the Monongahela River to the southeast, running past warehouses and shuttered factories. The day was late. The conductor announced that the running time to Washington was six hours, but it might be eight hours owing to freight congestion. The dining car was making preparations to serve an additional, unplanned meal. It was my first experience with the beef stew; Amtrak breaks out the Dinty Moore as a last resort. We got a bowl of stew and a biscuit.

I ate with Dave and Michaela Pokraka of Chicago, recently retired and traveling to Washington for an Elderhostel program that Michaela called "Government 101." They would tour Congress and learn how bills are passed.

This was their second time on Amtrak, and they loved it.

"People talk on trains. That was one of the surprising things to us," she said.

They didn't know that Amtrak was mainly a public entity. They weren't sure who owned the tracks, which isn't surprising since the country's rail network is largely a mystery to most Americans.

Living in Chicago, the Porakas see the rail-capacity problem firsthand. Freight and Metra trains rumble by their home near the Des Plaines River. About 500 freight trains, 700 commuters, and several long-distance Amtrak trains move through the metropolitan area each day. Chicago handles 75 percent of the nation's freight, but its 16,000 acres of rail infrastructure has been described as byzantine and antiquated. It takes longer to move a shipping container through the city than to haul it from the West Coast.

The big freight railroads and several government entities have teamed up to put $1.5 billion into the Chicago Regional Environmental and Transportation Efficiency Project. Project CREATE will develop five separate rail corridors, including one primarily for passenger trains. There will be flyovers so the tracks of one railroad don't cross another. Old tracks will be converted to public use for more commuter and transit trains.

CN, or Canadian National, is getting around the whole Chicago mess by purchasing the Elgin, Joliet, & Eastern Railway, a lightly used short line that skirts to the west and south of the city. Suburbs such as Naperville, Barrington, and Aurora fought the purchase, saying more trains would lower property values and cause noise and air pollution. "It's the whole NIMBY thing. These rail corridors have been there for a long time, since the time these places were farm fields. Just because people decided to build houses there, does that change things?" asked Dave rhetorically. "We have national needs. There's no reason one area of the city should have all the trains and others none."

After dinner back in my roomette, I called Amtrak's customer service at Union Station in D.C. We wouldn't reach the city until long after the Metro trains to Gaithersburg, where I had a hotel, stopped running, so they offered cab fare.

That gave me peace of mind. I packed my gear, put down the bed, and fell asleep under two woolen blankets. We arrived at 3:10 a.m., approximately thirteen hours late. A clerk in customer service gave me $50 in cash, saying she hoped it was enough. It wasn't. Sixty dollars later at 4:00 a.m., I got to the hotel. I ironed my clothes for my appointments and watched the TV, which had the first news about the AIG takeover. I went back to bed at 5:30 a.m.

Union Station, Washington, D.C.
the big lie of profitability

When I met Don Phillips at Union Station the next afternoon, he was carrying a reporter's notebook and holding a cell phone to one ear. A compact man with gray hair and a beard, Phillips paced the lobby for several minutes, listening.

He was on a group press-conference call with Joe Boardman, the then federal railroad administrator, who was commenting on the train collision in L.A. Hours earlier, a spokesperson for Metrolink admitted its engineer had run a red signal.

Phillips covered transportation tragedies during long tenures at the *Washington Post* and the *International Herald Tribune*. These days, he is semiretired but writes a column for *Trains* magazine. He clicked the phone shut, "Man, the damn press doesn't know what questions to ask about this crash. They just don't understand it; they don't know anything about positive train control. All they can talk about is this engineer screwing up."

Such plain speaking characterized our interview, which we held in a restaurant overlooking the concourse. I told him my train had been thirteen hours late and observed how little Amtrak has changed since the 1970s.

Phillips laughed derisively, "Damn right it hasn't changed. And that's because what happened the first year of Amtrak has happened every year since—it never gets enough money, and the politicians don't try to make it work. And now that ridership has started up like a rocket, there's not enough equipment out there—and won't be for several more years."

Amtrak's problems really do go back to its creation and what Phillips called "the big lie" —that Amtrak could become profitable if you just kept tinkering with it.

"Those lies were told by the people working on the inside. They all knew better, but it gave everyone cover," said Phillips. "And Nixon signed the bill on the theory that no one would ride Amtrak anyway and then we could get rid of it."

The intent was made clear when Nixon appointed Roger Lewis, from the aviation industry, as Amtrak's first president, Phillips continued. "He didn't know how to run a railroad. His orders were to kill it or babysit it until it died on its own, but neither happened. People rode the trains back then. And just like today, they bitched and complained, but they rode the trains."

Although subsequent Amtrak presidents were railroad men, most didn't cope well with hostile administrations and highly politicized Amtrak boards. They saw their budgets cut and were forced whenever in front of Congress to give lip service to the big lie.

I heard several people ridicule the promise of former Amtrak president Tom Downs who told Congress in 1995 that by hauling some express freight along with people, Amtrak would be "on the glide path to profitability." His successor, George Warrington, spent oodles of money reorganizing the company into business units and trying to build up the freight side business. The company nearly went bankrupt trying to get profitable and had to mortgage Penn Station to make ends meet. None of these efforts made Amtrak a better railroad, and meanwhile the core business was neglected, said Phillips.

The president who most impressed Phillips was David Gunn, who pushed away the politicians, reorganized the company using a traditional railroad structure, got rid of all freight operations, fired the consultants, and invested in the infrastructure—including electrifying and upgrading the Keystone Corridor to a 110-mph service between Harrisburg and Philadelphia. On the Northeast Corridor, the catenary—some of it dating back to the 1930s—was so deteriorated the corridor was in danger of being shut down.

"Look, Gunn spent money because it had to be done," he said. "Can you imagine if the Northeast Corridor had shut down?"

The government has to take a larger role in building up the nation's rail system for both freight and passenger, he said.

Would all this change with a new Democratic administration—particularly one led by Obama and Joe Biden, who was sometimes called "Amtrak Joe"? I asked. Biden had been a strong supporter of Amtrak as a senator and for thirty years had ridden the train to work while commuting from Wilmington, Delaware.

Possibly, but don't count on it, warned Phillips. Democrats haven't been all that rail savvy in the past: "Some of the biggest cuts and boondoggles in Amtrak came during Democratic administrations," remarked Phillips.

The next morning, I went over to the Department of Transportation and met the ninth president of Amtrak, although I didn't know it then and he probably didn't either. At that time, Joe Boardman was in his last few weeks in the George Bush administration as the nation's top railroad regulator. Boardman, who had been commissioner of the New York State Department of Transportation, had been at the Federal Railroad Administration since 2003.

This day Boardman had his hands full with the California accident, and all the news was distressing. Clearly, it weighed on him. As it was later revealed, the Metrolink engineer had been text-messaging rail fans on his cell phone when he ran the signal. As well, he sometimes allowed teenagers to ride with him in the cabs—all against the rules.

The accident was due to human error, or negligence, but had those loco-motives been equipped with positive train control (PTC), a computer would have been able to tell—using a global positioning system—that the Metrolink had run a signal, and it would have stopped both trains and prevented the accident. "Now we've seen what happens when a heavily laden freight train and a passenger train come together. That freight engine moved clear into that passenger car," Boardman told me. "What is not seen by the public is the abso-lute need to have efficiency in the operation, and that cannot happen without the deployment of PTC."

PTC not only would improve safety, but make it possible to increase traffic on shared right-of-ways because trains wouldn't need as much separation in distance or time, Boardman said. Prior to this accident, he had been unable to get the big railroads and the Bush administration to agree to a timeline for PTC implementation.

Many problems needed to be worked out. PTC requires radio spectrum, which is a hot commodity in the age of cell phones and Wi-Fi. Railroads must agree on a common technology so the system works seamlessly across regions. Under shared power arrangements, railroads are swapping locomotives and allowing their equipment to be switched to tracks of competitors, so every locomotive will need to be equipped with PTC. The costs will run into the billions, and the feds will have to help out.

All of these challenges had made it unlikely PTC would find its way into the Amtrak reauthorization act or any other railroad bill in 2008. But the Metrolink accident changed everything. Shortly after my visit, new safety language was introduced by the senators from California, the Amtrak bill was rechristened the 2008 Rail Safety and Amtrak Funding Authorization Bill, and it included a requirement that PTC be installed in all locomotives by 2015. It passed both houses of Congress with big margins, and George Bush signed it, even though he earlier said he would not. But it would have been difficult to hold up a safety bill in the shadow of the California crash, and by then Bush had his hands full with the meltdown of the banking industry and looming troubles with the automotive companies.

Don Phillips later wrote that Joe Boardman was a hero because he was pushing PTC hard before the accident. Safety was about all Boardman could pursue in the Bush administration's DOT, which was reluctant to spend money on anything, said Phillips. Under Boardman's leadership the FRA had, however, established a $30-million program to provide matching grants for states doing capital improvements to set up or improve passenger services.

When I said that was a drop in the bucket, Boardman conceded as much.

"Well, we got to start somewhere. Amtrak is like a canary in the coal mine. If you can't get a passenger train through, then there are capacity problems," he said.

Boardman had been criticized for holding up money that could be used to repair damaged cars and get more rolling stock back on the rails.

"Well, we still don't have a fleet plan [from Amtrak]. Do they have a plan for capital investment, for repair of equipment? No, they don't. All we get is a broad-brush approach. Where is the detail?"

Amtrak people, I said, have told me it's hard to do long-term planning when they don't know how much money they'll get year to year.

Boardman waved his hand dismissively. Amtrak, he said, should function more like a state DOT that works up plans and projects so it is ready to act when money becomes available. What Amtrak lacks is vision, and plans to make that vision a reality.

It was a prescient observation. When Boardman took over at Amtrak, he asked for just such a vision document and finding none, he decided to write it himself.

In the afternoon, I walked over to the Smithsonian Institution to talk with William Withuhn, curator of Transportation at the National Museum of American History. The museum was under renovation, so Withuhn, a tall, curly-haired, bespectacled man, met me at a guard shack on Constitution Avenue, and we walked through dark and dusty exhibit rooms, where all the artifacts were encased in waterproof and dustproof materials—including a ninety-two-foot-long locomotive.

Withuhn, nearing retirement, specializes in railroad technology and the social history of transportation, mobility, and commerce. I asked Withuhn for his thoughts on the notion of passenger trains making a profit.

"We've been hearing variations of that since 1971—if Amtrak was reformed or if it got new equipment or got rid of certain trains, it would make a profit. It's all a crock," explained Withuhn.

Journalists, he went on, are as bad as the politicians at perpetuating the myth.

"You read these Associated Press stories about intercity passenger trains and there's always a phrase in the story about 'money-losing Amtrak' or 'Amtrak, which hasn't made a profit since 1971.'" Passenger trains, he said, do not make a profit. Neither do roads or airports. If America wants a world-class transportation system that includes rail, it has to pay for it. Rail cannot be self-supporting.

Government should guarantee Americans the right to mobility, and give them at least two modes of travel to choose from, Withuhn said. Corridor trains make perfect sense. Long-distance trains may require more subsidy, but they provide connectivity. Better bus service would be the best alternative for isolated communities not served by a train.

One of the biggest benefits of such a coordinated transportation system would be to encourage national cohesion. "It's like the model of the post office," he suggested. "We decided a long time ago that no matter where an American lives, the cost of mailing a letter should be the same."

In the 1950s, the government stepped up and created public-private partnerships to put up houses, build highways, and retool the automotive industry. It subsidized the building of roads, and citizens thought these were appropriate roles for government.

"When the idea for the interstates came along, we said, 'What a great idea. Let's pay for it,' and we did that with a tax on gas, when that tax was 15 to 20 percent of the price of the gallon. Now raising the gas tax a few cents is controversial," he said. "It was a patriotic duty to pay your fair share. I'm not sure that is the feeling out there today."

Amtrak Headquarters
broken governance and the amtrak haters

When I got to Amtrak's headquarters in Union Station the next morning, Cliff Black, Amtrak's spokesman, told me Alex Kummant, Amtrak's president, was squeezing in my appointment before a meeting with the Amtrak board, which might account for his blunt mood. Apparently, he and the board weren't seeing eye to eye. Black looked harried himself, preparing for the arrival of the *Good Morning America* show, which was being broadcast live from a train.

It was to be a brass-tacks interview, and I had at most twenty minutes. Kummant was a thin guy in his late forties with grayish, blond hair. He wore stylish designer glasses and a light-colored suit. He was polite and refined, but blunt in a refreshing way. Cliff Black looked at his watch, and set down his own little tape recorder next to mine on a conference table.

When I asked about Joe Boardman's demand for a fleet plan, Kummant dismissed the controversy as mere mechanics between Amtrak and the FRA. We have a fleet plan, he said, and his tone had finality about it.

The issues of the Cross Country Café car and the wisdom of cutting back on food service were sore subjects, too.

"Well, write your congressman," he shot back.

Some services had needed fixing, but to zero in on food service and demand changes was largely an initiative coming from what he called "the Amtrak haters." They parse up pieces of the operation and find places to be critical.

"Look, it is silly to be viewing the business in these narrow ways and not see it as a whole in terms of cost recovery. Overall Amtrak runs with pretty low overhead and does a good job of cost recovery. Do we lose money on food? Sure we do. In 1958, the Santa Fe lost money on food service, too. And here's a news flash for you, we lose money on brake shoes and on bathrooms, too."

Like food service, the long-distance trains have been budgetary targets for decades. Senator John McCain and others have pushed for their elimination. But if long-distance trains were eliminated, Kummant told me, Amtrak would have to close stations, lay off employees, sever vendor contracts, give up slots on the freight lines, and essentially lose capability to operate within regions and corridors. Rather than canceling the trains, he said, we ought to be expanding them. By running more frequencies, putting on additional sleepers, and improving what is often dismal time performance, ridership would increase substantially, as would cost recovery.

"Look, if you don't have good service, if you have lousy looking stations, and you don't have on-time performance, you won't do very well. It becomes a self-fulfilling prophecy."

Well, he hit the nail on the head with that one, I thought. It was an honest assessment regarding Amtrak's core issues. As he spoke, we could hear locomotives powering up down below in the yards. Each time a train pulled in or out of the station, the vibrations made the room tremble.

Cost recovery with long-distance trains is below that of corridor trains, but they earn back about the same amount as a typical metropolitan transit system. In Kummant's words, it's "hardly in some criminal proportion as alleged by our critics."

The cross-country trains also connect the corridors, and without them the corridor trains would be orphans. "If you blow those away, the rest of our services will generate less. The network matters," he said.

Prior to being named Amtrak's president in 2006, Kummant was an executive at Union Pacific, overseeing marketing operations and on-time delivery services. He also spent several years working in manufacturing. When the Amtrak board, flush with new Bush appointees, fired Dave Gunn and brought in Kummant, many employees saw him as a Darth Vader who would lay waste to the organization.

That didn't happen, and it became clear early on that he came to Amtrak to run a railroad, and to secure the resources needed to do so. Nearly everyone I had spoken with gave him good grades for his tenure, many expressing great surprise.

When we talked about the job, Kummant pointed out the window at the Capitol dome across the street. It was a magnificent view.

"I've been in this job two years and I can't tell you the number of times I've been threatened by a governor or congressional delegation who feel that they can call over here anytime, demand a meeting, and push their cause. The next time they threaten, I may say, 'Hey get in line. And if you want to write a letter, here are three samples to choose from. In fact, we'll write it for you and you can just sign it.'"

Before he took the job, he estimated that about 70 percent of his time would be spent dealing with the Amtrak board and Washington politics; the rest on the operations of the railroad. In fact, the machinations of Washington probably take up to 85 percent of his time, he said.

His tone indicated he was chafing under the political pressure and the oversight of the Amtrak board. When I talked to insiders later, they said a rift had developed between Kummant and several board members, particularly the conservative Bush appointees, most importantly, Chairman Donna McLean, who had once been the chief financial officer of the FAA and later a transportation consultant/lobbyist. The board felt that Kummant was being dismissive of its oversight.

It had been a fabulous year for ridership. Numbers had just been released and they were the best ever, so my core question to Kummant was, "How is Amtrak going to gear up for the future?"

"Well, that is the question, isn't it?" he countered.

He thought a moment, and gave this scenario.

First, if it gets the money, Amtrak will repair seventy to eighty Amfleet cars at the price of $700,000 to $1 million per unit. Also, it will try to add a car or two to each Acela train set to increase capacity. It may tack on a special service charge to each ticket to raise more capital for new cars and locomotives, and start a procurement process that includes design work.

Even then, it will be years before any new equipment is delivered, he conceded.

If the Amtrak authorization bill is fully funded—and it rarely is—there will be significant investment in the Northeast Corridor infrastructure. Also, the $500 million in matching grants to states should add more corridor service.

All good things and all doable, but not enough to bring much change to America's passenger-rail system, he admitted. What's really needed, he said, is to change the fundamental ways that Amtrak is funded, governed, and does business.

He clicked off a wish list on his fingers: First the federal government needs a national transportation policy that addresses not only rail but also highway and air. And if Amtrak is to be the nation's intercity rail system, it shouldn't be hostage to the conflicting interests of congressional politicians and administrations that try to kill it or just let it limp along.

Passenger rail needs a dedicated funding source, something akin to the highway trust fund, because even when Amtrak is promised money, it rarely gets the full amount. Finally, the country's entire rail infrastructure should be updated and expanded with more public monies being spent to benefit both freight and passenger trains. The freights aren't able to do this on their own. They've got a growing freight business to contend with, and then when you factor in passenger-rail demands, it makes matters worse. Public money is going to have to flow into the network.

In Kummant's estimation, it will take four to five years to put these "business fundamentals" in place. In the meantime, if America decides it really wants trains to be a part of the solution to transportation, passenger rail should be thriving within ten years.

So, are we on the edge of a rail renaissance? I asked.

"I would like to say yes. You would think that if we reached a boundary, it would look like this year. There are many voices in favor of it, but perhaps air and road travel need to get worse before it really begins to happen."

In the last ten minutes of the conversation, Black fidgeted. When I said I had one last question, he nearly shouted, "Good, good, good." Kummant didn't seem to mind; he appeared energized and invited me to come back again.

I did come back, but by then he had moved on. Six weeks after the interview, he resigned.

Philadelphia
trains with people in them

From Washington, I boarded a Northeast Regional train to Philadelphia where I had an afternoon meeting with Craig Lewis of Norfolk Southern. We sat down in his corner office in the Bell Atlantic Tower, a fifty-three-story highrise that had an expansive view of the city, including the rail yards and 30th Street Station.

He recalled the early 1990s when Amtrak was hauling freight, mostly expresstype package services, in an effort to earn revenue. NS employees would watch passenger trains leave 30th Street Station pulling twenty mail/express cars heading west on the old Pennsylvania Railroad line that runs from Philadelphia, through Harrisburg and Pittsburgh, to Chicago.

"There was Amtrak hauling goods that it got by underbidding us, and then it's out on the tracks, saying, "I'm supposed to get priority. Get out of the way, guys," said Lewis. "When we got Conrail, we thought we were buying the Pennsylvania main line to Chicago, but we had these passenger trains to deal with, and they were taking business away from us."

It was a low point between Norfolk Southern and Amtrak and all the other passenger entities.

"There was this notion that passenger service was a noble, public good, so it was OK for a freight train to sit on a siding," said Lewis. "That thinking has changed. Now I think there is an understanding on their side that if our business goals are met, if the infrastructure is expanded, we can coexist with the passenger folks."

NS understands that more passenger entities—typically states—will be asking to access its tracks. More passenger trains are on the way. So Norfolk Southern, in a preliminary way, has begun asking itself a revolutionary question: Do we want to get back into the business of running passenger trains?

At that point in the interview, I was sleepy. The sun was going down, the skyscrapers casting long shadows, and below us we could see rush-hour traffic creeping along the Schuylkill Expressway.

But I sat up when Lewis started talking about a freight railroad running a passenger train. It was a question I'd been asking myself. Would these big railroads that control most of the rail network in America, and that have been mostly hostile to passenger trains since the 1960s, actually consider moving people again?

The answer is a big maybe.

When Norfolk Southern began doing its analysis about running passenger trains, some operating people were aghast, said Lewis. But consider the alternative.

"Somebody else is going to be out there on our railroad. Are we going to have any direct control on how they promote safety, instill the culture, or train their people? The answer is no. Maybe Norfolk Southern should be doing this and getting compensated for it. This could be a business opportunity."

It was a type of out-of-the-box thinking I had yet to hear from any freight railroad. Even BNSF hadn't alluded to such a notion.

There would be a couple of important conditions, said Lewis. NS would not market the service or be dependent on the farebox for revenues. It would run the trains, providing a defined service for a defined price. The passenger entity—such as a state—also would pay for the additional infrastructure to accommodate the trains.

It's still early in the game, but NS may be willing to give time guarantees that Amtrak cannot provide. One way to do that is build an incentive structure into the business model—as do many states. Deliver the trains on time and the freight railroad earns extra money, said Lewis.

"I see us bidding to provide transportation services. If passenger service is going to happen on our infrastructure, someone has to operate the trains. What is the difference between pulling cars that have people in them and cars that have coal in them?"

When we broke up the interview, Lewis asked where I was off to next. Up to Boston to see Mike Dukakis, who was on the Amtrak board and has been a longtime advocate for passenger rail. Lewis reached around to a bookshelf and took down a framed picture of himself with a smiling Dukakis.

"He's a great guy; I was one of his campaign chairs in Pennsylvania in 1988. Tell him hello for me."

Boston

i was your governor

The next morning by 5:00 a.m. I was in a cab to 30th Street Station and then on a Northeast Regional to Boston. Unlike many cities that tore out their trolley tracks for buses, Boston kept its trains. In the late 1950s when the private trolley system was going under, the state and city stepped in and created the Massachusetts Bay Transportation Authority (MBTA). Everyone called it the T, and when I was a photography student at the Art Institute of Boston in 1975 and 1976, the T took my friends and me all over the city for just a quarter. Today, it costs a $1.50; still a bargain considering all-day parking in the city runs $30.

Around noon, I got off at Back Bay Station and caught the Green Line to Northeastern University where Mike Dukakis has taught political science since 1991. He and his wife, Kitty, winter in California where he teaches at UCLA. When in Boston, he lives in his boyhood home in Brookline and rides the T to work.

His modest office, not untypical for a faculty member at a university, was at the end of a narrow hallway. Dressed in an open shirt and khaki pants, and with a sports coat over one chair, he was coaching a student writing a paper on the shortage of primary-care physicians.

The interview started fast and never slowed down. Like the consummate policy wonk (that's not a criticism), Dukakis threw out names and statistics and anecdotes from decades of work on transportation issues.

"Are you talking to Dave Gunn? Good, he's terrific. He was doing a hell of a job at Amtrak. And the board—once Bush got his people in there—fired him because he was trying to make it work. They didn't want to make it work."

"How about Gene Skoropowski? Been on the Capitol Corridor? Great. Skoropowski is a Gunn disciple. I'd like to see Gene in this next administration."

Skoropowski, Gunn, and Dukakis—Boston natives all—were important figures in the story of how Boston kept its trains, expanded the rail system, and avoided the city's further dissection by more freeways.

In the early 1960s, Dukakis and a few other state legislators were alarmed at the master plan to bring six eight-lane expressways into the city and build an elevated inner beltway, all financed by the highway trust fund. The highways would have destroyed neighborhoods and cut their way through the Emerald Necklace, the city park system designed by Frederick Law Olmstead, the father of American landscape architecture.

The push back against the highways plan culminated with Governor Francis "Sarge" Sargent, a Republican, who in 1972 made a "gutsy decision," according to Dukakis, to cancel highway projects inside Route 128, which arcs around the western suburbs. Sargent requested the federal highway trust funds instead be redirected into the T. When Dukakis defeated Sargent for governor in 1975, he and the commonwealth's congressional delegation, most notably Thomas "Tip" O'Neill, who became Speaker of the House, took up the cause.

"It was because of that sainted man, Thomas P. O'Neill, that we were the first state in the country to use our interstate highway money for transit—because we didn't want to build highways. In those days, you couldn't bust the highway trust fund. We did it, thanks to Tip, who put an amendment in the highway bill," Dukakis recalled.

Over several years, the state received $3 billion, and Dukakis poured much of it into the MBTA, which he described as a basket case with a dilapidated infrastructure and old trolley cars.

The state extended and modernized the T. It also acquired in 1976 the entire commuter-rail system in eastern Massachusetts for the paltry sum of $35 million (which shows how undervalued rail was at the time). David Gunn told me for a few million more the state could have bought lines all the way into Maine and New York State.

Today, the commuter rail network has 200 miles of routes, and the T is the fourth-largest transit system in the country. A third of Boston residents ride it to work each day.

"We put thousands of people to work, and it was politically popular because people could see tangible benefits," said Dukakis.

When he learned that I grew up near Erie, he said, "GE makes damn good locomotives and ships them all over the world. You know the commonwealth spent hundreds of millions of dollars on rolling stock for the MBTA, and every scrap of those cars was made overseas. We used to be the greatest railroad nation in the world, and now we can't even make a damn car here. It's pathetic."

The discussion turned to the presidential election, which was six weeks away. Dukakis lamented that Obama had not been talking about rail. He'd sent memos to the campaign suggesting the candidate appear in battleground states promoting rail projects. Picture the candidate, he said, surrounded by hard hats, union leaders, and mayors.

"The pitch ought to be that we are going to end this stupid war, bring our troops home, and spend those billions of dollars putting people to work here. If we took just the money spent in Iraq in one week and put it annually into intercity rail and transit, we could have a first-class rail system. I mean you go to Europe and it's embarrassing. Great trains, and they use half the energy per capita as we do. This is not complicated."

So what is the problem with American politicians? I asked. No president—Republican or Democrat—has pushed passenger rail. Dukakis agreed and threw up his hands.

"It's the damnedest disconnect I ever saw. I sent memos to Clinton saying, 'Bill, you can be the Eisenhower of the steel interstate.' He did a few good things but . . . and my friend Kerry. John's a good rail guy, but he didn't talk about it either."

He stopped, laughed again and pointed both hands towards his chest, "Now I need to be humble about this. Look. Consider the source. If I knew anything about running for the presidency, I'd be here in another capacity. But rail is good politics. Go out and poll the public, and they all overwhelmingly say give Amtrak more money. People want more trains."

The Obama campaign never did build events around rail. The last six weeks Obama rarely mentioned rail, and even during the debate on the stimulus package, the talk was all about roads and bridges and electrical grids, not rail and certainly not Amtrak. And then in the last few hours while details were being worked out on a compromise, the president and Rahm Emanuel, his chief of staff, inserted $8 billion for high-speed rail projects. Three weeks later, Joe Biden was at Union Station to announce another $1.3 billion would go to Amtrak for car rehabilitation and infrastructure repair on the Northeast Corridor.

Dukakis's student assistant interrupted saying he had a phone call.

Dukakis picked up the receiver, "Hi, Brad. Thanks for calling back. How's my student volunteer? Yeah, I've been telling that story all over. Brad, I'm calling because Coburn has put a hold on the Amtrak bill using this crazy rule. I don't understand it, either. Both you and I were legislators, but the Senate has this silly rule.

"I don't know if you have any pull with him or know somebody who does, but this bill has huge bipartisan support, more than seventy senators voted for it—including Kay Bailey Hutchison down your way—and more than three hundred House members. It's the best damn bill for Amtrak in years."

When he hung up the phone Dukakis looked at me.

"That guy was a student volunteer of mine in 1988. Brad Henry. Now he is the governor of Oklahoma."

"You do that often?" I asked.

"Only informally."

"I suppose people do return your phone calls."

He chuckled, "Not always."

After my talk with Kummant and my sense that he was frustrated with the Amtrak board, I asked Dukakis if the governance structure was broken. The new Amtrak bill will enlarge the board and allow the Amtrak president to become a voting member. Dukakis, appointed by Bill Clinton, served on the board from 1998 to 2003 as its vice chairman.

Whether the five-member board gets larger or stays the same, it doesn't matter, said Dukakis, as long as the board has the best interests of Amtrak in mind. Too many times—especially under the Bush administration—the board was packed with political appointees, zealots who didn't know the first thing about transportation policy or railroading, he said.

"Jeez, you get people on the board who haven't even ridden a damn train. Like Bush, they wouldn't know a train if it hit them between the eyes," he said.

He recalled a time he and Tommy Thompson, former governor of Wisconsin and chair of the Amtrak board, went over to see Senator John McCain.

"We were there to talk about Amtrak, and McCain essentially threw us out of his office. Didn't want to listen. Just said, if it can't make a profit, then the hell with it. You can't solve problems with that kind of attitude, and that's the kind of folks that have been put on Amtrak's board."

Some people told me Dukakis is a bit of a foamer in his enthusiasm for rail—and during the interview he referred to himself as a "rail guy"—but as I rode the T that day and next, and compared it to the rickety, beat-up system in the 1970s, I considered it a remarkable accomplishment. The T is a convenient and modern transit system. And if you think about putting a mark on a city and making people's lives better, Dukakis's work on public transit is as long-lasting a gem as Olmstead's Emerald Necklace.

When I was leaving, Dukakis walked me down to the elevator.

"When did you go to school here?"

"'75"

He jabbed my elbow and grinned, "Then, I was your governor."

"Yes, you were."

Cambridge

mega-regions: 100 million more people

It was only September, but this was New England. Overnight frost had hit large swaths of New Hampshire and Vermont, and the air was crisp as I left the hotel on Tremont Street and walked through Chinatown to the Orange Line. I passed young Asian couples bringing children to daycare. In the playground, an old woman in a wool sweater and tights balanced on one leg and scribed circles in the air, practicing tai chi.

I was headed to the Lincoln Institute of Land Policy, a think tank in Cambridge that focuses on community development, land-use patterns, and transportation. It cosponsors America 2050, a national planning initiative to prepare for an America—forty years hence—that is likely to contain 120 million more people than it does now.

America 2050 has identified ten emerging mega-regions where cities and suburbs are so dense they often function as a single system. Some mega-regions already exist: Southern California from San Diego to Ventura to Orange County, and the East Coast from Richmond to Boston. America 2050 anticipates others, including: the Texas Triangle (Houston, Dallas, San Antonio); the Piedmont Atlantic (Atlanta to Raleigh); and the Great Lakes (Chicago to Detroit.)

I got off at Harvard Square and walked down Brattle Street, rolling my suitcase through wrought-iron gates, along ivied brick walls, and over uneven sidewalks heaved up by the roots of mature trees. The neighborhood was old and distinctly Brahmin.

The Institute is in the Lincoln House, a large colonial revival built in 1887 by Henry Wadsworth Longfellow for his daughter and her husband. His house next door is a national historic site, not only because of Longfellow's accomplishments but because the house served as George Washington's headquarters for nine months during the siege of Boston.

I sat down with Anthony Carbonell, chair of the institute's Department of Planning and Urban Form. He teaches urban planning at Harvard and the University of Pennsylvania and looked the part of an Ivy League professor with a navy blazer, white shirt, and tie.

The 2050 concept tries to show how trillions of public and private dollars could be invested in the coming decades to promote economic development, affordable housing, efficient energy usage, and mobility. Looking out decades in advance, of course, is a dicey business. Just a couple of days earlier, I'd been in a museum browsing posters of *Popular Mechanics* and *Popular Science* magazines from the 1930s and '40s whose covers showed Americans flying around in personal helicopters and being whisked to work in pneumatic tubes.

Carbonell said one trend is certain: America will add a lot more people, and the population growth won't be distributed evenly. Many people will settle in regions already urbanizing and growing fast. In these mega-regions, population growth will have a profound impact on energy usage, transportation, water-sheds, and the conversion of land to sprawl. Already, Americans have the highest per capita consumption of land in the world.

"When you look at the potential land consumption, it's staggering. If we are to absorb these people, there just has to be a more compact pattern to settle-ment and development," said Carbonell. Housing and business districts likely will be denser and centered around transit and train stations, much like the transit-oriented development I'd seen in Dallas and Emeryville, California.

"Some planners believe we've built enough big-lot houses for the next thirty years. Baby boomers are downsizing and families are getting smaller," he said. "In the future, the market will reward investors and developers in this type of denser development. We anticipate public policy will respond to the markets and the markets will respond to the policy," he said. Build a rail line and station and development will follow.

If adding more people will strain the country's resources, there will be bene-fits, too. Carbonell anticipates an urban renaissance where communities are denser but more livable. A trip to the store may require only a short walk or a hop onto public transit. Huge swaths of city space won't be set aside for parked cars. People may do more telecommuting, long-distance commuting by rail, or just live closer to work so they don't spend hours on crowded roadways.

"There's a potential to rediscover the wonders of living in a real community. We may have a higher quality of life than we have created in the last thirty or forty years," he said.

The 2050 study calls for big private and public investments in all types of infrastructure—most especially rail.

"In terms of efficiency—fuel savings, lower carbon outputs, smaller footprint on the landscape—the advantage is really rail," he said. "It has been significantly underinvested in and disadvantaged against the other modes. We once had good train service in this country. We need to recover that capacity."

Does this mean we'll have high-speed trains crisscrossing the nation tying together these mega-regions? I asked.

Probably not, said Carbonell. The amount of capital spent on infrastructure will be steered by return on investment. High-speed rail will work well within the mega-regions and in travel corridors of less than 500 miles. Don't expect bullet trains running coast to coast.

Some mega-regions will resemble Texas and California with sprawling cities connected by fast trains running through open country. Others will be more like Boston and Western Europe with dense development, easy access to trains, buses, and light rail, and more space for walking and biking.

However, you can't entirely bypass the rest of the country, even the places with low populations and no large cities, he said. The notion of "territorial cohesion" requires that transportation networks serve all parts of a country to provide connectivity and hold it together. The transcontinental railroads did that in the nineteenth century. Interstates and commuter airlines held the bond in the twentieth century. What role territorial cohesion will play for high-speed rail in the twenty-first century isn't clear.

Carbonell reminded me, "Every state has two senators, and politicians are going to advocate for their regions. Sometimes that leads to bridges to nowhere, but it will also help ensure that these lower population places aren't ignored. These issues will have to be worked out in the political and planning processes. Some guy like me at Harvard in Cambridge is not the one who will be making the decisions."

The Downeaster
maine's very own train

I caught the T again and made my way over to North Station where I boarded Amtrak's Downeaster to Portland, Maine. The Downeaster began as a citizen's initiative in 1992 when TrainRiders Northeast, an advocacy group, began lobbying the legislature for a train. The Downeaster made its first run in December 2001.

Maine never had Amtrak service. The last passenger train that connected Portland and Boston was discontinued in 1965 by the Boston and Maine Railroad, which went bankrupt a few years later. The Downeaster runs to New Hampshire on MBTA tracks and then up to Portland on Pan Am Railways, formerly the Guilford Rail System. The entire route is 116 miles.

On a lovely September afternoon, we passed through Woburn, Lawrence, and then into Haverhill where the train paused on a trestle over the Merrimack River before entering the station. These are classic New England mill towns with abandoned or converted red brick factories anchored right on the river's rocky shore in places where dams and spillways manipulated the river for power.

The Downeaster was my first train with wireless Internet. A lot of friends had asked me, "Does the train have Internet?" The Downeaster did, and I was curious to know why.

The further north and inland we went, the trees showed hints of fall, tinges of red in the maple leaves. Asters grew in the wasteland beside the tracks, their tiny blue blossoms like dots in a Seurat painting. In New Hampshire, we paused at Durham and Exeter, where students piled on to the train. And then in Maine, at the Saco-Biddeford station, then under construction, I got a good look at the Downeaster's economic influence.

In 2007, the city of Saco sold developers Saco Island, a spit of land littered with abandoned tanneries and cotton textile mills. Some of the mills closed fifty years ago, and a few buildings even predate the Civil War. With the proceeds from the sale, the city financed a new $7 million train station for the Downeaster.

Just 300 feet beyond the station, the gutted shells of the mills—their windows missing and floors removed, and pigeons flying in and out—were being reconfigured into condos and commercial space. The project will run eventually to $100 million.

The Downeaster earns $6 million annually from its farebox, about 55 percent of its operating budget, but this transit-oriented development ought to be factored in as part of the train's value. When people can reach Boston without the hassle of driving I-95 or Route 1, the train transforms southeast Maine into a commuting suburb of Boston. Already, the Downeaster's morning and evening trains are jammed with commuters.

By 2010, Downeaster service will expand from Portland north to Brunswick with a stop in Freeport, home of L.L. Bean and 150 other outlet stores. Freeport anticipates hordes of shoppers from Boston detraining and spending the day in town, blowing money, eating seafood, and filling up their shopping bags.

Until then, the Downeaster's end of the line is the Portland Transportation Center, formerly the Concord Trailways bus station. Maine enlarged the station to create a train platform and a much larger waiting room. The Downeaster runs five trains daily, each trip taking two hours and twenty-five minutes between Portland and Boston. The buses fill gaps in the schedule.

"It made sense to create an intermodal facility because we have the same purpose—to get people out of their cars and onto mass transportation. It's why McDonalds and Burger King are on the same corner—it drives traffic and makes it convenient," explained Patricia Quinn, the executive director of the Northern New England Passenger Rail Authority (NNEPRA), which is responsible for the Downeaster.

Quinn started working part-time for NNEPRA in 2001 after being in the hotel industry and customer service. She was a single mom looking for a change where she wouldn't be on call twenty-four hours a day.

She had never stepped aboard an Amtrak train before taking the job. Today, her teenagers tease her that she's becoming "one of those freaky train people" because she's constantly looking at equipment running on tracks and making detours on family vacations to peek at train stations in other communities.

NNEPRA acts as the business operations and manager of the Downeaster. It answers to a board of directors appointed by the governor. Amtrak operates the trains and provides two train sets. It staffs a ticket agent in Portland; MBTA sells tickets at North Station. The rest of the stations in between are unstaffed, and tickets are bought at self-service machines, over the Internet, or by telephone.

NNEPRA contracts out the food service to a caterer to create a unique identity for the Downeaster, said Quinn.

"Amtrak does a great job of running the train, but we wanted it to have the character of Maine. We can do that through the food—so we have clam chowder, lobster bisque, and locally made whoopie pies."

Wi-Fi was installed just a few weeks earlier when a provider came into

NNEPRA's offices with a proposal to get an entire train online by connecting with cell phone towers along the route. The cost was just $8,000, a bargain considering the benefit to passengers, said Quinn.

"Because we're a small operation with few layers of bureaucracy, we'll give good ideas a try," said Quinn.

Such streamlining saves money, and the Downeaster needs to squeeze out every bit of revenue. The annual budget is $13.5 million and with the farebox earning just under half of that amount, the rest must be made up in subsidy.

The story of the Downeaster is a revealing picture of how states and organizations struggle to find money to make passenger rail work. First, Maine had to pay for the expansion of the Pan Am Railways infrastructure to allow for ten passenger trains a day (five round-trips). Fortunately, it received a $54-million grant from the Federal Transit Administration because the Downeaster qualified as a commuter service (not an intercity train), meaning half of its passengers make a round-trip each day.

To subsidize the train's operation, Maine received money from Congestion Mitigation Air Quality (CMAQ), a federal program authorized under the Clean Air Act. CMAQ provided an 80 to 20 match. It would have expired after three years, but Maine's congressional delegation received an extension through 2008, and it is now requesting another one.

When I met with Quinn, she was on her last few months of CMAQ money. If CMAQ isn't extended, Maine has to come up with $7.5 million out of its general fund each year to support the train. New Hampshire has not kicked in any money, even though thirty-six miles of the route runs through the state and one-third of all passengers board or detrain there. Massachusetts hasn't directly funded the train either, but has been supportive by allowing the use of North Station and MBTA infrastructure. Generally, the Maine legislature and Governor John Baldacci see the train as important to the state's future. Still, Maine has a biennial budget and every two years the Downeaster potentially could be on the chopping block. In the tight budget environment of 2009, some legislators—especially those from northern Maine, which isn't served by the train—were making noise about subsidizing the train while Massachusetts and New Hampshire sit on the sidelines.

In 2008, NNEPRA received a $35-million loan from the Federal Railroad Administration to expand the service to Brunswick. The loan, to upgrade the tracks, will be repaid over twenty-five years by a revenue stream capturing half of the taxes from rental cars rented in Maine.

When I said to Quinn that this sounded like Oregon taking money from the sales of license plates to pay for the operation of its trains, she said, "We're always looking for creative ways to raise the money we need. This is just indicative of a national problem. There's no dedicated money out there for rail. We have to ask people to create some money for us."

The following day, I caught the 6:00 a.m. southbound back to Boston. The train gave a blast on the whistle, left Portland, and started across Scarborough Marsh, thousands of acres of salt marsh, tidal rivers, and flats bordered by the sea. Egrets and herons backlit by the rising sun stalked the shallows for clams and invertebrates. At Saco, a morning fog engulfed the abandoned factory buildings.

In the dining car, I bought a fruit cup and yogurt and noticed separate receptacles for plastic, glass, and cans. The Downeaster recycles—another first. In the dining car that morning were two couples, obviously good friends headed down to Boston for the day. It was their first time on the train, and they commented on everything

One woman proclaimed the train was a moneymaker for Maine.

A conductor corrected her, "This train doesn't make a profit."

"You mean Maine loses money on this? Can it do that?"

That gave him an opening and he made what sounded like a practiced presentation.

"Yes, this train is subsidized by government, but did you know this country spends $180 billion a year on the airlines and the road system? Most years Amtrak gets just a billion or so, and a lot of that goes into the Northeast Corridor—not on routes like this one. Portland to Boston would be a perfect place for a high-speed train. If we put in overhead wires and electrified the track, we could go 150 mph easy. And then we wouldn't be burning diesel in these locomotives. And people wouldn't be driving between Boston and Portland because the train would get them there in forty-five minutes. Now something like that is surely worth the investment. . . ."

And so on. I was impressed.

When he left, one of the women said, "I didn't know that airlines were subsidized by taxpayers."

Her husband said, "They must be. He certainly seemed adamant."

Lake Shore Limited
can i sit somewhere else?

†††††††

Catching the Lake Shore Limited from Boston's Back Bay Station to Pennsylvania was like old times. But unlike student days, this time, I could afford to pay extra for a seat in the business-class car.

In Worcester, Massachusetts, a burly soldier dressed in camouflage fatigues and blond desert boots waited on the platform with his little boy and waiflike wife. His duffel bag was close to my window. I could read his name and unit—10th Mountain Division—stationed at Fort Drum, New York.

She was an amalgam of Goth, punk, and grunge, purple lipstick, piercings, and tattoos. When I saw him in the café, I detected two little white scars, one just below his lip and another through the eyebrow, puncture wounds from piercing. He had a tattoo on his neck. It was the grunge generation gone to war. Yet the uniform, and maybe the army, too, had made the man. He looked all warrior.

For months, I had stared out at train platforms, watching soldiers coming home from war, lovers bidding good-bye, children running into the arms of grandparents, and friends embracing before one of them steps aboard. In my head, I made up their stories, and sometimes learned the truth if we met later in the lounge or over dinner.

But on this day under the warm sun, I stayed in my seat and dozed. We crossed the Connecticut River into the Berkshires, passing between farm fields and pastures, woodlots and wetlands, all wedged into narrow valleys between the hills. In the hardwood swamps, the dead bleached trees stood like sentinels. At their feet, rafts of duckweed floated iridescent green on black water rich with organic matter. It was the first day of fall but only the sumacs had turned, their umbrella-like canopies as red as blood.

Because we encountered no freight trains along the way, the train arrived in Albany thirty minutes early. We had an hour or so layover while our coaches and those coming north from New York City were joined together for the trip west. There was no business-class car west of Albany, so when I reboarded, the attendant assigned me a seat in a car just in from New York. I followed the Fort Drum soldier and his wife down the aisle and put my suitcase overhead. In the seat against the window, a woman wrapped in a blanket was reading a paperback novel. She was dark haired and stylishly dressed. I apologized for taking the space, explaining the train was full and seats were assigned.

Her name was Meghan and she was going home to South Bend, Indiana, having spent a few days with her family on Long Island. We talked a bit and she asked me what I did, and I said I was a journalist.

She said, "So am I."

She had been an anchor for a South Bend television station but now worked for a consortium that produced news for several stations. She told me she worked hard, producing spot news, mentoring young reporters, and doing pieces herself. Our encounter was one of those pleasant surprises of train travel, where you meet kindred spirits and have the time and inclination to converse.

Eventually, I went to the dining car and had a plate of scallops over rice pilaf. Then I bought a beer and took my laptop into the lounge to write.

The train was running hard, shimming from side to side, and rattling loudly. An assistant conductor, a stout blond, probably in her late thirties, talked— more like shouted—shop with two attendants. She was testing out to become a conductor and was recalling her first days on the job: ". . . we stalled out near Utica in a sleet storm and I had to walk up and down the train in the freezing rain. I was soaked and, it was so cold, my jacket had ice on it and weighed a ton. I was so tired when I got to the hotel, I couldn't even undress. . . ."

As an Amtrak's supervisor had told me, there's a new generation taking over the business. These are not old railroad men anymore, but women and men with tattoos and earrings. Still the work remains the same, and it isn't for the fainthearted.

Through Syracuse and Rochester, I typed at the table and then went back to my seat just before Buffalo. The car was dark, people sleeping. I stayed awake and watched the lights slip past—Dunkirk, then North East.

I got off in Erie at 2:00 a.m., just as a nightclub down the street let out, and the patrons came out screaming and singing. Bottles shattered on the sidewalk, cars peeled out, and profanities echoed off the buildings. A fight spilled into the street. I stepped back into the shadows and was glad when I saw my brother pull up.

The next few days, I visited my two brothers, stopped at the cemeteries where my parents and grandparents are buried, sorted through old family papers, and poked around in libraries and railroad museums to find newspaper clippings about my grandfather's death. My interest had been piqued by all of the train riding I had been doing over the months.

The night I left for Chicago my niece dropped me off at 11:30 at an all-night restaurant where I ate a late dinner of Lake Erie perch and walked up to the

Amtrak station when it opened at 1:30 a.m. Amtrak has never come through Erie at a decent hour.

Back in the 1970s, it was best to wait for the train inside your car and stay out of the station. Plywood covered broken windows, plaster peelings lay everywhere, and homeless people crashed out in the corners. In winter, they lit warming fires fueled by the station's wooden doors. Today, Erie's Union Station, built in 1927, is privately owned, restored to its art deco beauty, and home to a microbrewery and restaurant. Amtrak rents out just a little corner. The platform and canopies up on the tracks look as crummy as ever.

Still, it was shelter, and I was glad to be in the waiting room and off the street.

When I came in the stationmaster said, "The train is late."

I shrugged, didn't ask how late (I could always call Julie) and went over to a bench, rolled my sports coat into a pillow, and stretched out. Someone would wake me when it was time.

I closed my eyes. The stationmaster came out of his office to chat with a couple headed to Indiana who innocently asked, "Is the train sometimes late?"

I rolled my eyes beneath my closed lids—newbies.

The station manager told this story: "Two or three weeks ago, one of the dumbest things I ever saw. Train was running half an hour late, and a guy asked did he have time to go to the McDonalds over there. Don't do it. You better wait, I said. A train can make up time. Yeah, yeah, he says, and goes anyway. And when he got back, the train had come and gone." He had a couple more anecdotes, each ending with the implication that passengers were dumb as dirt. Thankfully he went back in his office, and I fell asleep.

The train arrived at 4:02. We lined up under the canopy lit by a couple of bare lightbulbs, and the attendant assigned us seats. When I got on board, I took one look at my seatmate and stopped in the aisle. He was a big man, hairy, thick all over and asleep with his mouth hanging open. A soiled Chicago Bears hat was pulled down over his eyes, and he wore a sweatshirt that I couldn't read but imagined said something like, "I've got sleep apnea. How about you?" About half of him had rolled onto my seat.

The train left the station and the attendant came up the aisle.

"Can I sit somewhere else?"

"Why?"

"You're putting two big men together." I thought I would include myself to garner some sympathy, but in truth I was nowhere near the size of this guy.

"Sir, the train is full."

I whispered, "Would you take a look at him. Come on."

She did and then began looking around the car for another seat.

"How about up there?" I pointed two seats ahead where a thin person—I couldn't tell if it was a man or a woman—was passed out against the window. She nodded.

After the conductor took my ticket, she came back and put her hand on my shoulder.

"Are you comfortable, sir?" I thought she was being sarcastic but she wasn't.

"Yeah, this is great."

"Want me to see if I can get two seats for you after Cleveland?"

I rolled my eyes. "Don't you know the train is full?"

She hit me on the shoulder playfully, "Watch it."

I pulled my coat tight and went to sleep until Sandusky when a dozen Amish swept down the aisle, the men in black coats and hats, the women in black capes and bonnets. In the dark car, they were as black as crows in silhouette. One man wore two hats, one on top of the other like nesting Russian dolls, and they made him so tall he was Lincolnesque in profile. The top hat belonged to his son, who was fast asleep in his arms.

In northwest Ohio at first light, the farm ponds shimmered like mirrors, and head-high rows of corn next to the tracks swung and undulated in the train's wake. Out in the fields, the tree islands, or woodlots, resembled rocky mono-liths, like big erratics carried south by the glaciers and dropped onto a flattened landscape. Sometimes, only a single hickory or black walnut tree stood in a field, spared for its mast crop or perhaps the quality of its wood.

In Archbold, Ohio, I moved to the café car, passing the Amish all still asleep in the front of the car. They must have had a long wait for the train. They were young couples, late teens or early twenties. Some of the wives rested their heads on their husbands' shoulders. A baby girl slept on the lap of a mother and father, and the mother had one hand firmly around her daughter's ankle.

Although I had been this way many times, I never noticed the overhead catenary alongside tracks west of South Bend. Just as I was asking myself what it could be for, a trolley pulled alongside our train. There was no locomotive, just three aluminum-bodied cars. The trolley steadily pulled ahead, and then the tracks and catenary diverged. We cut across a cornfield, and the trolley went off to the northeast along a roadway where I could see the electrified lines running off toward a small town.

The South Shore Line was one of America's last interurban trolleys. These trains were an extension of streetcar lines into the countryside. The South Shore transitioned from an interurban to full-fledged railroad.

Interurbans predated automobiles, emerging in the 1880s when large coal-fired utility stations were created in cities to light homes and power trolleys. As the demand for power grew, the trolley companies lengthened their lines, built their own power plants, and sold the electricity to rural customers.

Interurban trolleys were common all across the country, and they had some advantages over steam-powered trains that ran from station to station. The trolleys ran on streets, along roadways, and stopped at rural crossroads, allowing farmers, merchants, and factories to load directly onto the train, which frequently pulled freight cars as well as passenger coaches. Electrified trains were fast and accelerated quickly. They were cheap to operate, so fares tended to be low. But they didn't generate much of a fiscal surplus, so when roads, cars, and trucks became more prevalent, interurbans had very little margin. Those that carried freight—such as the South Shore Line—lasted longer.

World War II slowed the decline of interurbans when more people were forced onto mass transit owing to gasoline and rubber rationing. But like all trains during the war, the trolleys were crowded, overworked, and deteriorating. After the war, trucks bled away the remaining freight business. Passengers fled to the automobile. Gas was cheap, roads were good, and cars offered convenience.

As well, interurban equipment and infrastructure were in need of repair. The trolley companies and the governments that subsidized them just didn't have the money to upgrade the tracks and the equipment. And there was a cheaper alternative—buses running on new roads subsidized by the federal government. General Motors, Greyhound, and other interests in the automotive industry did everything they could to get rid of the trolleys. And tearing up trolley lines and putting in buses seemed like a good economic decision, at least at the time. A lot of politicians wanted trolleys off the roads because they thought they were a hazard to drivers.

"If you were a mayor or city manager faced with the massive cost of upgrading and even extending the trolley system into new suburbs, if you were getting complaints about run-down trolleys and bumpy tracks, then buses just made a lot more sense," said Bill Withuhn, the transportation curator at the Smithsonian.

When the Northern Indiana Commuter Transportation District formed to run the South Shore line in the late 1980s, it replaced the South Shore's vintage cars with coaches from Nippon-Sharyo, a Japanese manufacturer. Today, the railroad remains a vital transportation link for northern Indiana into the city.

We were supposed to be in Chicago within one hour and forty-five minutes after leaving South Bend, but this day it took nearly three hours. About fifteen miles from Union Station, the train halted at a siding next to a bunch of parked freight cars. For seventy-three minutes, we gazed out at an industrial wasteland of rusted cyclone fence, graffiti-tagged retaining walls, and patches of weeds shimmering with broken glass.

A conductor came through the car and said, "Freight traffic up ahead. There's no room for us to get through. We have to wait our turn."

A woman asked, "Why don't they just move out of the way and let us get through?"

PART 8
The Gulf Coast

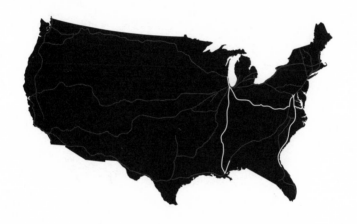

City of New Orleans
on the main line of mid-america

▓▓▓▓▓▓

When I boarded the Indian Trails bus to take me from the Upper Peninsula to Milwaukee in early December, eighteen inches of snow already lay on the ground in Marquette and that evening the town had gotten eight more inches from a squall blowing off Lake Superior. I was glad not to be driving, and not unhappy that this last trip was to the Gulf Coast, Florida, and then D.C.

I was anxious to see how the events of the past few weeks had affected train world. Obama had been elected president. The automakers had flown private jets to Washington to beg for money and left chastened. Alex Kummant had resigned from Amtrak, and Joe Boardman had stepped in as interim president, the company's fifth in four years. In October, George Bush signed HR2095 that will provide Amtrak with $13.5 billion over five years and for the first time establish matching capital-expenditure grants to states. Although small, the grant program was exactly what rail advocates had been asking for.

Everyone on the bus that night wanted to sleep except two wheezy-voiced guys who sat three seats apart, leaned into the aisle and shouted to each other over the engine noise. Eventually they quieted down, too, but because we stopped every hour—Escanaba, Marinette, Green Bay, and Sheboygan—I slept in short stretches. The sun came up just twenty miles or so from Milwaukee, and I walked off the bus directly onto a Hiawatha train.

By now Union Station in Chicago felt like home. I got my first cup of coffee in the Metropolitan Lounge, and then killed the day by walking up to Millennium Park and watching people acting silly in front of the Bean and then, after dinner, walking back under the Loop with the trains rumbling overhead.

The City of New Orleans left on time at 8:00 p.m., and as first-class passengers, we were immediately brought into the Cross Country Café for dinner. The regional menu was excellent. I ate gumbo that night.

Back in the roomette, the berth above rattled, the door shook until I wedged it with a notebook, and my body shimmied from side to side. Yet, as I warmed beneath the blankets, sleep came and Illinois passed in the night.

I woke as we left the Memphis yards, and walked down to the dining car when the train entered Mississippi. In the Delta, the cotton fields stretched out bare and dark, but with wisps of white—the detritus of the harvest—lying snowlike on the soil. At the fields' edge or in a ditch, where the mechanical picker couldn't reach, a mature plant shivered in the wind, its brown pods open to its puffy filling.

Coming into towns, we passed through neighborhoods of uninsulated shacks with sad-looking porches and junk cars in the backyards. These ruins gave way to better homes and finally the pretty downtown squares of southern towns. The pattern reversed itself on the way out. Thirty percent of all Mississippians live in poverty, and there was an evident truth to living on the wrong side of the tracks.

Teenage boys wearing do-rags and smoking cigarettes huddled around an open fire. A shiny boom box on a stump pumped out music. In Yazoo City, in the muddy parking lot of the Beer and Butts store, men passed a bottle between parked pickup trucks.

It was Sunday, and the righteous had other pursuits. Cars and pick-ups surrounded low-storied wooden and tin-roofed churches with Baptist, Redeemer, Missionary, and Zion in their names. Men and women, dressed impeccably, walked toward the doors arm in arm.

Just before Christmas in 1987, I rode the City of New Orleans when the train was full of late-middle-aged and elderly African Americans who had gone north decades earlier during what became known as the Great Migration. They'd left for the factories of Detroit, Gary, and Chicago and were coming back for Christmas to see the parents and siblings who had stayed behind.

The migration had been fed by segregation and jobs and information of a better life in the north. Pullman porters snuck black newspapers, the *Chicago Defender* and the *Pittsburgh Courier*, on board the dining and sleeping cars and in arranged locations threw them off trains. In the South, ruled by Jim Crow, such newspapers were considered dangerous and incendiary by white authorities and were nearly impossible to obtain otherwise.

The Great Migration's artery was the Illinois Central Railroad (IC), which was known as the Main Line of Mid-America. Back in the 1850s, the line's construction was subsidized by government land grants that totaled 2.5 million acres. During the Civil War, the IC transported troops and supplies into the South to secure the Mississippi River. In 1900, a small train wreck at Vaughan, Mississippi, was made infamous by a song extolling the deceased engineer John Luther "Casey" Jones. The IC's premier passenger train was the Panama Limited, an all–Pullman service that lasted until 1967 and rivaled other luxury trains of the era. The City of New Orleans was a day train with coach seats only, but Amtrak adopted the name largely on the popularity of Steve Goodman's ballad. Back in the streamliner era in the 1930s, it covered the route in sixteen hours. Today, it takes nineteen.

After Amite, Louisiana, the train penetrated cypress swamps and bayous as sprawling as those Delta cotton fields. Old-man's beard drooped from the trees, and cypress knees jutted like stalagmites from the mud. Turtles sunned on logs, and an alligator floated in the open water.

We skirted the west side of Lake Pontchartrain, and I could look across the water to the black rectangular outlines of downtown New Orleans. The closer we got, the more the buildings seemed to rise out of the water. It is a hell of a place to put a city, and there were residual signs of Katrina's effects and damage caused by storm surges: flattened swamp houses, torn-up boat docks, and rafts of plastic buckets, lawn furniture, thousands of Styrofoam floats, and all manner of debris washed up on shore. Junk hung in trees like Christmas decorations, and occasionally I saw odd circles of downed trees in the swamps from tornadic winds.

I'd booked a room at the Lafayette Hotel on St. Charles Street where the old trolley runs by every twenty minutes on its way to the Garden District. I took it over to the French Quarter, then walked down Bourbon Street and up Decatur, passing by one drunk girl lying on the sidewalk, a frenetic white boy with stringy hair pounding on two five-gallon buckets, a skinny black kid in a bowler hat tap dancing up and down a set of concrete steps, and a voluptuous girl in high heels, a G-string and see-through blouse talking to a cop on a corner. A guy in a dirty T-shirt came weaving up the street and was about to hug me until I shoved him away.

It was New Orleans after all. I found a bar where I drank beer, ate gumbo, stuffed crab, red beans and rice, and listened to live zydeco.

That night, I walked back to the hotel looking up at a crescent moon in convergence with Venus and Jupiter, the three rising aptly enough over the Crescent City. In Lafayette Park, as I stood next to a statue of Henry Clay, I thought to myself, I'll never see the like again. The next such convergence, a sliver of moon with two very bright stars (planets), won't reoccur until 2052.

Meridian, Mississippi
interstate II in fifteen years

The next morning, I boarded the Crescent, which runs 1,400 miles to New York through Charlotte and Atlanta, but I was taking a day trip to Meridian, Mississippi. We pulled out next to the Superdome, went under I-10 where high-water marks darkened the concrete pillars, then along a wooden fence spray painted with "Bama Makes History," and then past cemeteries where the aboveground tombs resembled a miniature Roman city.

Eventually, we passed neighborhoods where FEMA trailers and motor homes stood in the front yards of dilapidated houses or ones under reconstruction. Some streets still had small hills of debris neatly piled on vacant lots. Abandoned homes displayed spray-painted numbers and crosses, indicating they had been searched during the flood. The train crossed the shipping channel on a trestle and then ran along the south shore of Lake Pontchartrain where the wind kicked up three-foot whitecaps. On the other side of the train, a twenty-foot-high earthen levee ran for miles. In Mississippi, we reached higher ground and continued northeast into the piney woods, through the Desoto National Forest to Meridian, an old railroad town of 31,000 people.

Meridian has played an outsized role in the passenger-train story of late because of two native sons: Gil Carmichael, who was federal railroad administrator under George H. W. Bush, and John Robert Smith, its mayor who served as the chair of the Amtrak board from 2002 to 2006.

Stepping off the train, I faced an impressive two-story, red brick station with a balcony and tower. Retro-looking, Union Station actually was built from the ground up in the early 1990s after Carmichael had his hometown designated as the study model for developing a small-city, multimodal transportation center. He could only offer the town about $30,000 in planning money from FRA funds, recalled Carmichael.

"The mayor was kind of indifferent but John Robert—he was on the city council then—took that check and ran with it."

Smith got Louisiana State University to do some traffic studies and found more study money at the Mississippi DOT. Norfolk Southern donated nine acres along the right-of-way, and the depot project qualified for big bucks through ISTEA (the Intermodal Surface Transportation Efficiency Act of

1991), a federal program that diverted some highway-trust-fund monies to intermodal projects.

The town of Meridian began with the railroad, and the railroad made it a target during the Civil War. In 1864, Union general Tecumseh Sherman and his 10,000 troops leveled the town, tore up 112 miles of track, and heated the rails to malleability atop bonfires and twisted them around trees into what became known as Sherman's bowties.

A postwar building and manufacturing boom saw construction of an opera house, Carnegie libraries, and other turn-of-the century structures representing all sorts of architectural styles. For a time, Meridian became Mississippi's largest city, but it eventually went through a decline, including its importance as a railroad center as the industry changed over from steam to diesel and then went through its decline in the 1960s and '70s.

Smith met me at Union Station, and we drove past a number of old buildings, many beautifully restored as part of the city's arts and historic district.

"Why do you have all this great architecture?"

He grinned, "These structures survived urban renewal in the 1960s because we didn't take money from Washington. It was considered Yankee money; there had to be something wrong with it."

Smith, a confident and skilled Republican in his late fifties, was a pharmacist when elected mayor in 1993. His office is filled with memorabilia from his time on the Amtrak board. He's been to the White House, knows the players in national transportation. He paced the room as we talked.

The construction of the rail depot spurred the revival of downtown Meridian, he said.

"Today we'd call it transit-oriented development, but back then we figured if we could get a critical mass of people coming into the station, they might buy a coca cola, a sandwich, and do some shopping downtown."

As the station was being constructed, Amtrak announced it was cutting the Crescent from daily to thrice-weekly service, which in Smith's opinion "was no transportation at all." In response, he organized the Crescent Corridor Coalition of mayors between Atlanta and New Orleans and called Trent Lott, Mississippi's senior senator. "I told Trent the Yankees are after our trains again, and if you're from Meridian that means something."

Lott worked the Hill to find common ground with other pro-Amtrak senators. The mayor's coalition went to Washington and met with their congressional delegations. They reminded Tom Downs, then president of Amtrak, of the railroad's importance to small communities. There are about five hundred Amtrak mayors nationwide, Smith said.

"The trains aren't stopping out in some cow pasture; they are coming in to downtowns. Rural communities live or die with passenger rail."

Tom Downs reportedly put a banner up in his office that said, "It's Meridian, Stupid."

The Crescent cutbacks never happened, and Smith's advocacy and political skills attracted attention in Washington. Lott, working with the Clinton White House, got Smith appointed to the Amtrak board in 1997 along with Mike Dukakis and Tommy Thompson.

At the board's first meeting in Washington, Smith walked in and saw Thompson with his back to the door, looking at a big national map of Amtrak's network.

"He was saying, 'Where in the hell is Meridian, Mississippi, and when did it become the center of the universe?' I went up and introduced myself. From that point, the three of us—Mike and Tommy and I—became fast friends. And in all the time we served, there was never a partisan moment between us."

In 2001, Thompson left to serve in the Bush cabinet, and Smith was elected chair. Under his leadership, the board hired David Gunn, who was considered to be one of Amtrak's more effective presidents, reducing the number of employees, making important repairs to the Northeast Corridor, getting rid of the freight business, and making Amtrak's accounting more transparent.

"With David, there was no spin. He told everyone the same thing whether it was a journalist or a congressman," Smith said.

Gunn told Congress that Amtrak would never make a profit, nor should it be required to do so. He was the first Amtrak president to say it unequivocally and without apology. Smith's job was to massage the message, "David and I made a pretty good team. We believed in each other, and I could soften some of his more rough edges politically."

By June 2002, Amtrak, which had not been getting its full authorization, was running out of money and needed a loan of $100 million from the Department of Transportation (DOT) until Congress could appropriate more money.

Smith flew to Washington for what he thought would be a routine board meeting. However, then transportation secretary Norman Y. Mineta informed everyone that DOT would not provide the loan. It was the Bush administration's first move against Amtrak, and the beginning of another in a long line of financial crises for the railroad.

Without the loan, Amtrak would have to shut down the system. Mineta told Gunn to do it—until he was informed it would cost $90 million because of contract obligations alone. In addition, the Northeast Corridor, which Amtrak owns and dispatches, would then be unavailable to freight traffic and public-transit trains in places like New Jersey, New York, and Philadelphia.

Havoc would have resulted, but for a few days, the administration appeared willing to let that happen. Eventually Amtrak got the loan, but in the succeeding years, the administration tried cutting Amtrak's appropriation to zero, and Congress each time put in enough money to allow the railroad to limp along.

Meanwhile, more Bush appointees came onto the board to replace Dukakis and Smith, who were considered too pro-rail. One appointee, after his first meeting, asked a staff member, "What's an Acela?" He had never heard of it, nor ever ridden a train. Eventually the board forced out Gunn too, who had opposed its proposal to give the Northeast Corridor to the states or sell it to a private entity.

"I am Republican, but this is not what a board is supposed to do. There were people there who had no interest in passenger rail," Smith said.

He has stayed involved with rail issues on the national scene: giving speeches; chairing Reconnecting America, a center for transit-oriented development; and serving on a team from the U.S. Council of Mayors that briefed Obama's people on rail and transit issues during the presidential transition. Smith will leave office as Meridian's mayor in fall 2009, announcing his decision not to seek reelection while standing on the balcony of Union Station, "because this is where it all began."

During his time in Washington, Smith learned that most members of Congress don't know much about transportation and certainly don't ride trains. And many have a deep-seated bias against rail, a bias that sometimes surfaces even in the semantics employed. "Most politicians use the verb 'invest' when they discuss highways and airports, but when it comes to passenger rail, the verb of choice is 'subsidize,'" he pointed out.

"I would like some of these Amtrak haters to walk the cars of the Crescent and see the retired couples, the single parents, or the school kids going to their nation's capital for the first time, and tell them that they do not deserve this service."

Smith went to have lunch with his daughter, and I waited for Gil Carmichael, who is now a developer in Meridian, purchasing and restoring many of those old downtown structures. Carmichael, eighty, is a Republican activist who ran unsuccessfully for governor of Mississippi and a Senate seat before being named as FRA administrator in 1989.

A sixth-generation Mississippian, he has a southern, low-key folksy manner peppered with plain-talk aphorisms. At FRA, he came on like gangbusters, seeing his job as more than regulation, but as a promoter of the rail mode for both passenger and freight. In the 1990s, he founded the Intermodal Transportation Institute at the University of Denver and gives speeches today on what he calls Interstate II.

"We have this incredible railroad network that goes out all over this land from city center to city center. That's what is so amazing. It's already there," he said.

He would like to double- and triple-track 20,000 to 30,000 miles of mainline freight railroad. The corridors would be grade separated to allow for 90 mph intermodal freight and 125 mph passenger trains. Slower coal and grain trains would run on their own tracks. When possible, slower passenger trains would have a single line or share one with intermodal. Positive train control will keep the trains separated and safe. Power initially will come from diesel, but eventually the right-of-ways should be electrified.

"The railroad is the one mode that can be electrified without any leap in technology. We already know how to do it," he said.

As daunting a task as it may appear, Interstate II pales beside the alternative in transportation. Without rail, it has been estimated the country will need nine new airports the size of Denver's and will have to double the interstate highway system to meet demand.

"We could build Interstate II in fifteen years," he said.

The timeline seemed ambitious, I said.

Not if Congress and the states focus their resources. Give the freights their 25 percent tax credit for infrastructure improvements, which would boost their current $9 billion in capital expenditures to $15 to $20 billion annually. The new 80–20 match for capital projects from the federal government, outlined in the Amtrak bill, is a good start, but it needs more money.

"Rather than put billions into General Motors, we ought to be putting billions into a rail-corridor program," he said. "I think we'd have a lot more jobs when we got through. Last century was the automotive century. I think the twenty-first is fixin' to be the railroad century," Carmichael added.

A few weeks before we spoke, Congress had shifted $8 billion from the general fund into the highway trust fund because of falling revenue due to decreased driving and gas usage. That shortfall is a harbinger of things to come. Carmichael expects the traditional trust fund and gas-tax method of paying for highways is on its way out—or should be.

He knows something about highways. He owned several car dealerships before he went into government. Nixon named him to the National Highway Safety Advisory Committee, and he served on the National Transportation Policy Study Commission under Gerald Ford. The United States cannot maintain its current road system unless government doubles or triples the fuel tax, Carmichael believes. Congress screwed up by putting a cent tax on gas rather than a percent tax, leaving no inflationary mechanism and no way to recoup more dollars when the price of gas shoots up.

Vehicle miles traveled (VMT)—the amount of miles driven by Americans—has been dropping since 2007. Trust-fund revenues will fall further if Americans turn from gas guzzlers to smaller vehicle or even electric vehicles. State DOTs are worried, and some—most notably Oregon—are studying a vehicle-miles-traveled tax or a road-user fee. Cars could be equipped with onboard wireless devices that transmit mileage data to a gas pump and automatically add the tax to the price. If the vehicle does not have a device, the motorist pays a flat tax per gallon.

The technology is not that expensive, and can easily be placed on cars and trucks or retrofitted onto older vehicles. The tax can be graduated to the vehicle, too. Heavier vehicles would be taxed more because they do more damage to roadways. Carmichael believes such a taxation system is inevitable because the trust fund alone won't be adequate to meet future needs. When it comes to passenger rail, the federal government, he believes, needs to push the states to sit down with the freights and figure out how to finance additional trackage. "I may be a bit naïve but I think the freight-railroad boys are willing to share that right-of-way with the passenger folks. Public support for railroads will come through passenger trains, and it would be very smart for the freight boys to work with these states," he said.

I'd heard a version of this before, too. Don Phillips at *Trains* had said: "The freights are beginning to understand that the public doesn't give a damn about freight trains, but people do care about passenger trains. So the railroads are ready to embrace Amtrak, give it a big hug, and say 'Now, go out there and say good things about us.'"

What worries the freights is government regulation, and, in Carmichael's mind, it is an understandable fear. When the ICC was around, he said, "The railroads couldn't flush a toilet without a regulation. So we need to find a way to do this without imposing excessive regulation."

Smith walked back into his office, and Carmichael pointed at me, "He punched my button and got me going. I haven't talked like this for a long time."

I had to catch the southbound Crescent back to New Orleans, and Carmichael offered me a ride to the station. When we walked inside, he said, "Isn't this pretty? This was a model for the whole United States, and now 135 cities have done what Meridian has done."

New Orleans
rail: the redheaded stepchild

The ingrained highway culture of state departments of transportation (DOTs) and the lack of understanding of rail by legislators could be epitomized by the Southern High Speed Rail Commission (SHSR), an interstate compact between Louisiana, Alabama, and Mississippi. In existence since 1980, it hasn't moved much beyond the planning stages of bringing more frequent, dependable passenger service to the region.

I walked over to the Amoco Building on Poydras Street where the New Orleans Regional Planning Commission provides SHSR with technical expertise, a Web site, and its executive director, Karen Parsons. The position is part-time; she also works on bike-pedestrian coordination in the city, freight and port issues, and post-Katrina recovery.

"I like to say that rail and pedestrian-bike are the redheaded stepchildren of transportation. They don't get a lot of attention or dollars," said Parsons. "Right now we're not building track, just keeping options open and planning so when money is available we're ready."

Parsons is a thin, tall woman with straight hair who can see the Mississippi River and the barge traffic moving on it from her office window. She's passionate about rail, but talked quietly and with diplomacy about the three states in the compact that are, in her words, "like three different siblings." It wasn't meant pejoratively but as a way to describe their different maturity levels regarding passenger rail.

A few weeks earlier the SRHC held a "Rail Summit" at Union Station in Meridian, featuring then Amtrak president Alex Kummant, Mike Dukakis, Frank Busalacchi, and many rail luminaries. The summit was to educate legislators, mayors, and transportation officials about what could be possible with a coordinated effort, said Parsons. The rail summit addressed jobs, economic development, mobility, and demographic and social trends. The compact states have aging populations and large numbers of poor who cannot afford cars and need more public transportation.

"When you're talking to a thirty-six-year-old legislator who has never ridden a train, you really have to help them understand what rail is all about. This mode has been under-analyzed and not well understood. We have to quantify it for the decision makers—explain to them who uses trains, why they use them, and how rail relates to economics and public benefit. Our first job is to get them to want the service."

Louisiana's state transportation plan did not include rail until 2006. Mississippi's plan has no mention of passenger service. These two states fund the commission through their DOTs, but their rail divisions are small, concentrating on improving grade crossings. Alabama's DOT is prevented by state law from spending money for anything other than highways and bridges. It has no state rail plan and has yet to provide matched funds for a federal grant to study the route from Meridian to Anniston for possible passenger service.

The diaspora of New Orleans citizens after Katrina—many to Baton Rouge eighty miles northwest—spurred Louisiana's interest in a commuter train between the two cities. During planning meetings attended by thousands of citizens, New Orleans residents said they wanted more train service as an alternative to I-10. Such a commuter service, running 79 mph, would cost an estimated $110 million for capital expenditures and three years of operating subsidy.

With the passage of the Amtrak Bill HR 2095 in October 2008 and its matching grants to states, there are financial incentives for the states to initiate rail projects. The bill provides $1.9 billion ($380 million per year) for grants to states to pay for the capital costs of facilities and equipment necessary to provide new or improved intercity passenger rail. The federal share of the grants is up to 80 percent.

"Now we have a carrot to go back to these DOTs and say, if you want to compete, there is money out there for real projects," she said. "Improving grade crossings is probably their first focus, then maybe we can get them interested in two-mile-long sidings that improve freight and passenger flows."

However, that won't happen until the states update their rail plans and identify such projects. Until then, the states with developed rail plans—such as North Carolina, Illinois, and California—will most likely get the funding instead.

Like many states, the compact's members have left it up to Amtrak to provide train service, and consequently the region has never had enough reliability or frequency of train service to really make a difference in transportation patterns. When the Sunset Limited was running to Florida, it could be up to twenty hours behind schedule, crawling along at 25 mph.

Parsons said the commission supports a corridor train between New Orleans and Mobile, Alabama, running through Gulfport and Biloxi. Amtrak has given "a back of the envelope" estimate that $3 million per year would be needed in subsidy to run such a passenger service. One proposal is to bring back the

Sunset three times a week and run the corridor train the other days for seven-day-a-week service.

HR2095 mandates that Amtrak do a study on renewing the Sunset service, but neither Amtrak nor CSX is anxious to do so. The farebox recovery was just 20 percent. East of New Orleans, the train ran on mostly single-track railroad. It's not a main through-line for CSX, so it's not kept up for higher speeds. And any new service on that route would have to have positive train control, which would be expensive.

Even if capital-expenditure monies could be obtained from the feds, decisions by the three states in the compact on how they would divvy up the subsidy or if they would even agree to help fund a train at all is still a long way off, said Parsons. "The commission supports restoration of that service, but we want something different and a whole lot better. Right now, the best we've been able to do is stop Amtrak from decommissioning that train permanently."

CSX Headquarters, Jacksonville
where's the vision, where's the money?

Absent the Sunset service, I had to find another way from New Orleans to Jacksonville, Florida, where I would meet with CSX freight executives. A bus would take fifteen hours and cost $82. Airfare was just $62. It wasn't a difficult decision.

From the windows of CSX's headquarters along the St. John's River, downtown Jacksonville presented a beautiful cityscape of water, modern buildings, and sunshine. I wouldn't get to explore any of it. After the interview, I was off to Tallahassee, the state capital.

I'd come to talk with John Gibson, CSX's vice president of Operations Research and Planning, but he'd been summoned to a meeting with the lieutenant governor of Massachusetts, which was locked in a dispute with CSX over extending commuter service between Boston and Worcester.

CSX Transportation was born in 1980 with the merger of the Chessie System and Seaboard Coast Line Industries, which included such predecessor railroads as the Pere Marquette and the Baltimore and Ohio. In the late 1990s, CSX bought 42 percent of Conrail, splitting the company with Norfolk Southern when the two railroads were unable to outmaneuver one another to get it all.

Today, CSX reaches from Florida to Chicago and east to New York, running over 21,000 route miles. It provides access to every eastern port south of Washington, D.C. A third of its business is intermodal, a percentage that is likely to rise sharply in the coming years as more goods are moved from trucks to rail in order to take advantage of fuel efficiencies. In 2008, the company reported profits of $1.3 billion.

Unless a CSX train runs through their town, most Americans only became aware of the railroad through its image-building "How Tomorrow Moves" television commercials with the line, "A single train moves the same load as 280 tractor trailers, and a ton of freight can go some 400 miles by train on single gallon of fuel."

CSX was onto something with the green message, and when I met with Cressie Brown, director of Passenger and Joint Facility Agreements, it was clear the company was more ready to engage with passenger entities than I had expected. CSX has more passenger activity on its infrastructure than any other Class 1 railroad, and it knows more is on the horizon.

"It is time to take a new approach to infrastructure and decide how we can have both a strong and vibrant passenger system and also a strong freight system. They are both important to the country," she said.

When I spoke to Gibson by phone, he pointed out that the United States has never had a vision for creating an integrated passenger-rail system, nor has it tried to adequately fund one. Echoing many other critics of U.S. rail policy, he noted that the incremental approach of trying to add service here or there by putting passenger trains on networks owned and managed by the freight railroads hasn't worked.

"Congress felt that all it had to do was legislate, but not really fund a system," he said. "If the country's vision is a European-type system, we can have it, eventually. But it will require a serious investment of capital, and that outlay will come from the public, not the freight railroads."

CSX envisions something along the lines of Interstate II—separate passenger and freight tracks running side by side in the same right-of-way—which it spelled out in 2008 when the railroad applied to the U.S. Department of Transportation's "Corridors of the Future" Program. DOT would choose five projects designed to reduce highway traffic, relieve freight bottlenecks, and reduce flight delays. Joe Boardman, then at the Federal Railroad Administration, urged CSX to apply, and it drew up plans for the rail corridor paralleling the I-95 highway corridor between Miami and New York. CSX proposed building three or four main tracks through choke points, upgrading signals, and generally expanding the infrastructure's capacity. The improvements would take truck traffic off I-95 and allow for more passenger trains.

The company put considerable resources into the project, according to Gibson. But in the highway mentality of the Bush DOT, the proposal didn't have a chance. It received an "honorable mention" but no funding. All the winners were highway projects.

The I-95 corridor functions as a north-south spine for CSX's network, especially for its movement of coal, intermodal, and juice trains (orange concentrate mainly). "Already it's a strong passenger market for Amtrak, and there will be a lot more population growth in Georgia and Florida," Gibson noted.

I asked Gibson what he thought of the matching program for states in the 2008 Amtrak bill. Not enough money, he said, and too much reliance on states to step up on their own. What happens when one state is quite willing to invest in infrastructure, buy trains, or subsidize a service but the state next door is not? It will result in haphazard investment across the system, he said.

"Mainly the bill does not drive to any particular national vision, and that's what we want to see—a plan with resources that gets away from this incremental, haphazard approach," he said.

Neither is CSX pleased with the performance standards Congress made part of the bill, which requires host railroads to deliver Amtrak's trains ontime or pay a fine determined by the Surface Transportation Board (STB)—to be used to improve service on the impacted route.

The financial penalties are "draconian," in Gibson's words.

"Again Congress makes demands that Amtrak trains run on time but provides no dollars to make those standards possible," he pointed out. "You can't get stronger on-time performance without investment in the infrastructure."

As with many of the freight railroad people I spoke with during my travels, CSX is willing to accept more passenger traffic on its infrastructure but only under strict conditions. In 2008, CSX was locked in disputes with Massachusetts and Florida over liability issues regarding new commuter-passenger service. The railroad was asking for complete indemnification, meaning if an accident occurs on the infrastructure—whether it's the passenger-entity's fault or the fault of CSX—the railroad does not assume any liability. CSX holds to the "but for" position, meaning the risk would not be there but for the presence of the passenger trains, so the state or transit agency must bear the cost of the insurance.

In Massachusetts, the MBTA wants to buy 50 miles of track for $50 million to extend commuter service from Framingham to Worcester. In Florida, the state would buy 61.5 miles for the Central Florida Commuter Rail Project, also known as SunRail. In both instances, CSX won't own the tracks, but still use them. It still wants indemnification, though. The states say that puts too much risk on the public entity and unfairly holds taxpayers accountable for any misconduct or negligence by CSX.

The Florida legislature refused to agree to CSX's terms, and in April 2009 voted to kill the $1.2 billion SunRail project. It's another setback for rail in Florida. The lack of local connectivity offered by commuter-rail systems also hurts the state's chances to score federal funding for any future high-speed rail projects.

No deal has been reached in Massachusetts, where the MBTA sued the railroad in 2008 when CSX's employees allegedly failed to set a hand brake after delivering a carload of lumber to a retailer. The car drifted away and crashed into a commuter train, injuring 150 people. MBTA wants CSX to share in the liability.

So far the freight railroads and the Association of American Railroads are holding firm to their "but for" position. These liability disputes are not with

Amtrak, but with the states and the commuter-railroad operations, which don't have a lot of extra money to spend on insurance.

Amtrak carries its own no-fault liability insurance backed up by the federal government. Congress has put a $200 million cap on liability, but it has never been tested. The rare accidents that have happened with Amtrak trains have been settled out of court. However, the Metrolink crash has many of the big railroads wary. Even though Metrolink was clearly at fault, everyone expects Union Pacific, with its deep pockets, to be sued as well.

Gibson was adamant, "We're not willing to risk the franchise for the incremental dollars we get for passenger service. It's not a prudent decision for business and our shareholders."

It will likely require legislation on the state and national levels to make this issue moot, and once that happens, a big roadblock will be removed to bringing more passenger trains on line.

Tallahassee
left without a cadillac

There isn't a state in the union that could benefit more from passenger rail than Florida, and the misfortune is the state could have had a bullet train running between its major population centers today.

Because it concentrated its efforts on high-speed rail for the past twenty-five years, the state never took the incremental approach with Amtrak and the freights to build conventional service. Consequently, it has no corridor trains or any hope of getting them soon. At this point, Florida, the fourth most populated state in the country, has only three long-distance Amtrak trains running two trips per day. It also has Tri-Rail, a commuter-rail system, between West Palm Beach and Miami. It has been unable to gather the political consensus to build the Central Florida Commuter Project, a light-rail system to serve Orlando.

If you want to get between the state's major cities, you have to fly or use a highway. To get from Jacksonville to the state capital of Tallahassee, a distance of 160 miles, I took a Greyhound bus.

"We went for the Cadillac and didn't get it," explained Nazih Haddad in his office at the Florida DOT in Tallahassee. On one wall, he has a poster of the proposed Florida TGV train. It's well faded by the sun, attesting to the time that has gone by. Haddad manages Passenger Rail Development for the Florida DOT; he is also the staff director of the Florida High Speed Rail Authority, which hadn't met for years when we talked.

The bullet train would have run along the federally designated high-speed corridor between Miami, Orlando, and Tampa, cities well placed for corridor service: Orlando is 92 miles from Tampa and 264 miles from Miami.

The potential ridership for a fast train between these cities is extremely favorable; actually, it's staggering, said Haddad. Detailed studies by the authority showed 100 million city-to-city trips are taken each year in the corridor. In other words, about 300,000 trips per day in which people travel seventy miles or more to reach their destinations, mainly using Interstates 95, 74, and 4—as well as some state routes.

It isn't just residents on the roadways. Florida attracts seventy million tourists annually. Between the two groups, 98 percent are traveling intercity on these corridors by car. Air, Amtrak, and bus service make up the remainder.

"They are driving because there just isn't any other easy way to do it," said Haddad, who gets calls every week from people who want to know about train service. Tourists, for example, fly into Miami and would like to know how to get to Orlando.

"So you tell people, 'Walk over to the rental counter and get a car; you could fly, but really there isn't another choice. If you haven't developed an alternative, how can somebody make a choice?"

Bob Graham, who was Florida governor and later one of its U.S. senators, first started talking about a bullet train in the early 1980s. In 1984, the legislature created the Florida High Speed Rail Commission. The idea then was to finance the train by selling development rights along the corridor to private entities who would, in turn, leverage those rights to raise capital to build the system. No public monies would be needed. The attempt failed when it became clear the state would have to sell development rights over huge swaths of Florida to raise the capital.

"Politicians tried to come up with cockamamie ways to get private entities to do this, but like any infrastructure, it can't be done without public involvement and public dollars," Haddad said. "The systems in Japan and Europe required public dollars. Government initially built those systems."

Ten years later, in 1995, the legislature created the Florida High Speed Rail Authority that came up with a public-private partnership model. Government would build the system leveraging state dollars with federal funds and tax-free bonding. The private sector could invest money in the project, help design and build the network, and be given the franchise to operate the trains. The trains would be privately owned, much like an airline operating today in a publicly financed airport.

The system was estimated to cost $7 to $8 billion. In the late 1990s the authority and the DOT had reached an agreement with a consortium that included the Fluor Corporation and Bombardier. The consortium agreed to invest $300 million and take on the design-build-operate function. The state would float bonds. DOT would commit $70 million annually (going up 3 percent a year for inflation) to service the bonds for the next thirty years. Federal monies would pay the interest on the bonds, and the state monies would pay down the principal. When the system was up and running, operating surpluses could also be applied to the debt.

The project nearly came to fruition until Jeb Bush became governor in 1999 and killed the project his second day in office. Angry state legislators got the train on the 2000 ballot as a constitutional amendment, which voters passed. The amendment directed the governor and legislature to start building the train system by 2003. That year, Bush vetoed funding for both the project and the board, and then he led a high-profile campaign to repeal the constitutional requirement. By this time, it had gotten to be a personal battle between the two opposing camps. Bush and Tom Gallagher, the state's chief financial officer, predicted financial ruin for the state, claiming that the project would cost $70 to $80 billion and take money away from education. Meanwhile, the route had been worked out, and, the Federal Railroad Administration had signed off on the environmental-impact statement. In the election of 2004, voters repealed the constitutional amendment, although there was confusion over the ballot. Some people who voted yes thought they were supporting the train, though in fact a yes vote was to approve the repeal.

Why Bush was so anti-train is speculative. But many people say being raised in an oil family and a highway-auto dominated state, Texas, had something to do with it. The Bushes also were close to Southwest Airlines chairman Herb Kelleher, who came to Florida claiming that he had helped kill the train in Texas and he would do the same here.

Haddad said, "The rhetoric was inflammatory and misleading. It was really exaggerated tactics that were used to defeat this. The financing and the project were sound. And it really squandered a great opportunity for this state."

Florida needs some type of rail. It will soon surpass New York to become the third most populated state. It gains more than 400,000 people every year and is already reaching mega-region status. Florida's DOT has created TriRail, a commuter-rail system, between West Palm Beach and Miami, and it is building the Miami Intermodal Center next to the airport where Amtrak, buses, and rental-car agencies will be located.

After the collapse of the bullet train, Haddad and staff created a comprehensive Florida Rail Plan that would work incrementally with Amtrak and the freight railroads. Haddad isn't certain the state's DOT will move ahead. It's locked in a damned if you do, damned if you don't scenario. If it starts doing corridor-train development, which itself will cost hundreds of millions, it's unlikely to pursue a bullet train. "I can't see Florida doing both," Haddad said.

California seems to be moving ahead on both, I interjected.

"Well, California has already spent a lot of money and has service, but we would be starting from scratch. It would take many years."

In spring of 2009, when the federal stimulus package announced $8 billion for high-speed rail, the state's High Speed Rail Authority reactivated itself. There may be hope yet if Florida can pick up the pieces.

Silver Meteor
a bed and 600 miles

Back at the Jacksonville bus station, I changed into a T-shirt and jeans, and headed for the taxi stand. The train station was a $15 cab fare from the downtown bus station. So much for intermodality.

I boarded the Silver Meteor in a light rain as dusk came on. The Meteor, an overnight train that runs for 1,400 miles between Miami and New York, follows the I-95 corridor. Along with the Silver Star, Acela, and the Northeast Regional, the Meteor is one of Amtrak's successful East Coast trains, with a farebox recovery running 70 percent.

I was on my way to Virginia where I was to meet with one of Amtrak's original architects. I had a coach seat and was going just the 600 miles, but what I really wanted was a bed. A few days earlier the price for a roomette had been $400 because there were not many left. But once a train is under way and if a room is still empty, you can ask for an upgrade and get a decent price.

The conductor used his cell phone to call Amtrak.

"How's $130 for tonight?"

It was reasonable because it would include dinner, too.

The Meteor is a single-level train, necessitated by its route through the Baltimore tunnels and the tight confines of Manhattan. Its Viewliner roomettes are newer and have some advantages over those in the Superliners. There are windows at the upper-berth level so occupants of both bunks have an outside view. A slew of climate and light controls allowed me to tweak the environmental conditions. (The Superliner controls are mostly nonfunctional.) My room included a toilet and sink, crammed into an incredibly small space. For the elderly, the proximity of the bathroom is probably an advantage, but to me it was like fouling the nest. There's no privacy. If you have two people in the room, someone has to leave while the other uses the facilities. I preferred the down-the-hall common bathrooms of the Superliner.

I had a flat iron steak for dinner, bathed in the shower room, and went to bed, wanting to get my money's worth. I don't remember much that night, only a stop in Yemassee, South Carolina, where my car ended up next to a road crossing. The warning lights a few feet away pulsated and lit up my room in red light. I peered into an Edward Hopper painting. A car idled on the other side of the downed gate. The highway behind disappeared into a patch of dark woods. A wooden building, an old store front, stood at a crossroads, its display window lit up with electric candles and the words, "Jesus is Lord" painted on the glass. Perhaps it was a storefront church or the candles were Christmas decorations and the window display the owner's proclamation of faith. We didn't dwell long and the scene slid from sight.

I slept through Charleston, Florence, Fayetteville, and Rocky Mount. In Petersburg, the attendant rapped on the door and I dressed. When I stepped out into Virginia, it was cold and I had a four-hour wait in the Staple Mills Road station before I could catch the Northeast Regional to Newport News. Richmond sees a lot of Amtrak trains each day. While I waited, the station filled up and emptied out twice as people headed north to Washington. The Auto Train came through just after sunrise. The train, which runs 855 miles between Lorton, Virginia, and Sanford, Florida, had a few coaches and sleepers, but mostly a long string of automobile carriers that held cars, boats, and travel trailers. Snowbirds, especially, use the train to move their vehicles between home and their wintering grounds.

Northeast Regional train number 67 to Newport News was nearly empty. After Richmond, it turns into a local, dead-ending at Hampton Roads and heading back up the peninsula later in the afternoon. Leaving Richmond, we passed trendy apartments and lofts constructed in former cigarette factories and warehouses, an area known as Tobacco Row. During the Civil War, it was the site of Libby Prison, a notorious hellhole that housed captured Union officers. To my right ran the James River, storied in American history and affected by tides this far inland.

I'd been this way in spring, and remembered a carpet of white lilies in the cypress swamps along Chickahominy Lake, but now the vegetation had died back and browned. In Newport News, I boarded the same beat-up James River connector bus, rode through Norfolk and out to Virginia Beach, getting off at a Plexiglas bus shelter on Pacific Avenue.

"Be here tomorrow at 1:15, if you're taking the afternoon train," the driver said.

Virginia Beach
railpax: set up to fail

Rooms on "The Beach" in mid-December were plentiful and cheap. For $50, I had a Jacuzzi, a kitchen, two televisions, two bedrooms, and a balcony on the boardwalk. A nice view, too, of a wind-tossed, white-capped Atlantic Ocean that could have been a twin for Lake Superior in December. It was bone-chilling cold.

I walked down the empty strip, past shops of T-shirts—as tawdry as any I saw in the French Quarter—and then along the boardwalk before getting ready to meet Jim McClellan for dinner.

His name had popped up early in my research. McClellan was a central character in the book *The Men Who Loved Trains* by Rush Loving, a business and transportation writer who chronicled many of the cutthroat machinations of the big railroads as they went through merger mania after the Penn Central collapse. McClellan was there for some of the biggest decisions in railroading of the last forty years. Known as a superb operations analyst, he helped create both Amtrak and Conrail.

Immediately after Amtrak's creation, he went to work for the company as a long-term planner before going back to freight railroading. He retired from Norfolk Southern as vice president of strategic planning. In his seventies today, he still gives speeches on the future of railroading and spends much of his free time riding and photographing trains all over the world. He had just gotten back from riding California's Capitol Corridor with Gene Skoropowski, and he was impressed.

As we drove over to his house for drinks before dinner, he said, "California is proof of the concept. What they are doing out there works and ought to be emulated everywhere else in the country that it makes sense. Back in the 1970s, we were recommending corridors with frequent service, and all these years later, we're seeing it. It's a good idea now; it was a good idea then."

To chat with McClellan that evening was to end with the beginning, to sit down with someone who was in the room for the birth of what became Amtrak. I had heard secondhand reports, but McClellan was there. What were the decision makers thinking in 1970? What was the atmosphere in Washington? What was this passenger railroad supposed to do and become?

He prefaced the conversation by explaining that I needed to understand the political players, the interest groups, the mood of the public, and the desperate shape of the railroad industry in the early 1970s. The bankruptcy of the Penn Central, which has been losing nearly $375,000 per day on its passenger operations, had nearly brought down the American financial system. As we sat there in Virginia at the end of 2008, it was remarkable how analogous that railroad situation in the 1970s was to the debacle of General Motors, AIG, and the question of government intervention and the whole notion of "too big to fail."

"The passions ran just as deep then. Some politicians looked at the railroads and said, 'Let them die. Their time has come and gone.' You hear that about GM now. And there were others who said we can't let that happen. It would be disastrous. Government has to step in," said McClellan.

At the time he had been working as an analyst in the Federal Railroad Administration. The U.S. Department of Transportation was a new cabinet-level department, created in 1966 to encompass all things transportation from the St. Lawrence Seaway to the ICC to the Bureau of Public Roads.

Bob Gallamore, who was an economist at DOT, helped to come up with the idea of establishing a national rail corporation—an agency that would be quasi-public and quasi-private—to take over passenger operations from the railroads. The railroad unions and passenger advocates had been proposing a direct government subsidy to the railroads—in other words, a payment to keep the trains running and make up for the losses in profit. The unions wanted to preserve jobs. Passenger advocates thought it would preserve trains, but the Nixon administration saw it as unending subsidy to the railroads.

I interviewed Gallamore on the phone a few weeks after I spoke with McClellan, and he said John Volpe, the DOT secretary under Richard Nixon, and people in the Office of Management and Budget (OMB) saw the creation of a new company as the best alternative to a bad situation.

No matter what they did, the United States was going to end up with a much smaller passenger-train network. There was no way to save the nearly 400 passenger trains operating in the country. Railroads had just over a 5 percent share of the passenger market. Most Americans, in this era before the first oil shock in 1973, were driving Detroit's big gas guzzlers down the new interstate highways and getting accustomed to routine air travel, which had previously been expensive or considered a luxury.

"We hoped we could save a few trains—the ones worth saving anyway—but you couldn't save them all," Gallamore recalled. The creators of Amtrak felt that a company dedicated to passenger service would have a better chance of success than continued operation by the freight lines, he added.

McClellan, just thirty-two years old but with an encyclopedic knowledge of the network, was given the task of recommending which trains would continue and which would be cut. For a guy who loved riding and photographing passenger trains but also understood the need for efficiencies, it was a bittersweet task.

The preliminary plan that emerged from FRA called for several corridor trains and five long-hauls. A few corridors still had good ridership, including the Northeast Corridor and the L.A. to San Diego route, then served by a train called the San Diegan. It was also thought the Southwest Chief between Chicago and L.A. could break even or make a profit.

When the concept of the new company, which was given the name Railpax, was introduced to Congress, it raised a storm of controversy. Some members didn't want to lose trains in their districts. Others didn't want to spend any money that would benefit the railroads.

At first, the existing railroads were against the idea of Railpax and sharing their right-of-ways with passenger trains run by somebody else. This was not the clean break many wanted from passenger service. But these railroads were themselves under duress, facing huge deficits, said McClellan.

"A couple of railroads—the Santa Fe and the Seaboard—had a lot of angst about signing because they still liked their passenger trains. The rest were willing to do almost anything to get rid of their trains, and they eventually agreed to it," he said.

A flurry of political deal making ensued between Congress, the industry, and the executive branch. Arms were twisted and promises made. The newly formed National Association of Rail Passengers wanted a nationwide system of trains, not just a few isolated segments in the Northeast and California and around Chicago. The Nixon administration and fiscal conservatives wanted the company to make a profit as soon as possible and relieve the government of any responsibility. The most cynical of that group believed Railpax was just a transition to the end of the passenger-train era.

As we talked that evening, McClellan again cautioned me to remember the interest groups and the political climate under which any decision is made in Washington. DOT and FRA's goal was to save the railroads, not necessarily set up an efficient national passenger service.

Eventually, the interest groups came together to support the Railpax bill. In October 1970, Congress passed the Passenger Service Act, and the National Railroad Passenger Corporation (NRPC) was created.

After its creation, the new corporation hired a New York advertising firm that came up with the name Amtrak and its logo—no longer used today—called by some detractors the "pointless arrow." The federal government provided Amtrak with $40 million in working capital to get started and access to another $100 million in loan guarantees. The railroads were required to turn over passenger equipment and ante up about $100 million in capital as their share of the start-up monies. To run a national railroad, it wasn't much. Amtrak spent the federal contribution in the first year.

"It was really a niggardly amount of money to get started," said McClellan, "If you look at just the capital that was made available to Amtrak, it was really set up to fail."

But Amtrak did start running the rainbow trains, those bizarre consists of cars and locomotives from all the different railroads. A lot of the equipment was junk and needed to be repaired and refurbished. And almost immediately members of Congress—including powerful senators, such as Mike Mansfield of Montana and Harley Staggers of West Virginia, for whom the Staggers Act was named—began pressuring Amtrak to add services to their states. Other politicians complained Amtrak was too dependent on the government dole. The push-pull, love-hate relationship with Congress was already under way.

When I asked Gallamore, who became deputy administrator at FRA during the Carter administration and sat on the Amtrak board, why Amtrak hadn't been successful over these past forty years, he said he disagreed with the premise. Getting passenger service away from the freights was DOT's primary goal, and that had proved to be an important factor in the comeback of American railroads. Politically, he said, Amtrak was successful because Congress has been willing to keep funding it. Amtrak saved options for the future that would have gone by the wayside had all passenger service been allowed to disappear entirely.

But what about profitability? I asked. Whatever happened to the notion that this company would make money?

"Well we hoped by trimming it down and improving the efficiencies it could be, but when you scratch the surface, you really had to say we didn't know if it could. It was really an experiment."

I had gone back and read articles in the popular press from 1971, and found this one from *Time* that addressed profitability. It was prescient:

> Private railroaders consider this idea ludicrous, and predict that Railpax will be forced to turn to Congress for more subsidy within a year or two. Even if their freight operations are included, the much-admired nationalized railroads of Western Europe and Japan run deeply in the red. Railpax backers count on managerial innovations to entice more riders aboard trains. The average passenger may find conditions much the same for a considerable time. Railpax will pay

the private railroads to operate its trains; they will run over the same bumpy tracks and be manned by the same surly crews that have made train travel a trauma instead of a treat. (October 26, 1970)

During dinner that night in Virginia, I asked McClellan, "Was it a reasonable supposition back then that this new entity could be self-sustaining, that it would make money?"

He smiled and then turned serious, "That was another political compromise. It was bullshit. That's a direct quote. It was bullshit. OK? When we wrote the legislation, we were under pressure from OMB. Nixon wasn't going to sign it without that language. We said, 'OK, We'll call it for-profit.' Not a bad goal. But was it realistic? No."

That some politicians and Amtrak critics are still hanging on to the profit canard nearly four decades later never ceases to surprise McClellan.

"This idea that if Amtrak could just be tweaked or fussed with, you could solve all its ills is nonsense. They've been doing that for nearly forty years, and it hasn't worked. There simply is no business model out there that is going to magically solve this. If there was, you would have found it by now. There is not a private-interest solution for intercity passenger trains, there's only a public-sector solution....

"Amtrak didn't get the capital, didn't get the support, and didn't have any ongoing source of operating subsidies—and that's been the whole history of it."

Washington, D.C.

the freight-railroad boys

When I went to Washington the following day and interviewed Ed Hamberger, president and CEO at the Association of American Railroads, I had Gil Carmichael back in Mississippi to thank.

When he dropped me at the Meridian train station, Carmichael asked, "Up there in Washington, are you talking to Ed and the freight-railroad boys?"

I knew who he meant and said I hadn't gotten past corporate communication on my last visit to AAR.

"Well, you need to talk to Ed. There's some new thinking going on with those boys. I'll give old Ed call and have him talk to you."

When Hamberger and I sat down in his office, it was quite clear the world had changed for the railroad industry, just like it had for the rest of country.

Freight revenues were down nearly 10 percent (they would plummet another 20 percent in coming months). A new pro-rail administration had been elected. After the Metrolink crash, positive train control was no longer a debate. The gas crisis of mid-2008 and the automobile companies' woes showed that the dominance of cars, trucks, and highways had slipped a bit. Railroads, despite all the challenges, have opportunities.

So the script at AAR had changed.

Hamberger has been head of the AAR since 1998, a time when the organization was suing Amtrak to stop hauling freight cars on its passenger trains. He testified several times in front of congressional committees that Amtrak should pay fully allocated rather than incremental costs. Hamberger is a sharp and articulate guy, comfortable with politics, and the repositioning it sometimes requires. He wasn't unaware of the ironies of what he was about to say, and acknowledged them with some humor.

Since my last visit, the AAR had launched a phase two of its capacity study, this time to determine what the future demands of the passenger interests will be on the freight networks—most importantly, how much more room has to be made for both freight and passenger traffic. The study will quantify the benefits of more passenger trains in terms of mobility, carbon savings, and congestion mitigation. AAR plans to present this information to Congress and the new administration as a way to make its case for a 25 percent investment-tax credit in capital expenditures. In many ways, it's also making the case for more passenger rail.

"The industry is taking an aggressive stance to link its message with that of passenger-rail advocates. Perhaps we haven't been as forthcoming in the past as we could have and should have, but now we are saying: We think the country has to move forward with both freight and passenger-rail service," said Hamberger.

I'd gotten wind of this turnabout in attitude from Don Phillips and Carmichael, but it was still striking to hear it directly. It's a strategy capsulated in the phrase: "Commuters vote, boxcars don't." Delivering improved passenger service benefits freight railroads.

Although the recession has given railroads some breathing room, the industry is clearly worried about capacity. If just 10 percent of highway freight switched to the rails, the railroads would be inundated. As one executive told me, "Corporate America is ready to move a hell of a lot more goods on trains, but they won't do it if the railroads are incompetent."

Railroads aren't looking for a handout from government, Hamberger said. A tax credit would simply lower the hurdle to more private investment and speed things up.

"We are a privately owned network, financed by private investment. We pay taxes on our right-of-ways. We should be making those investments." With tongue in cheek, he said, "Besides, when the federal government gets involved in making the decisions, I've read that political considerations come into play. At least, I read that."

However, the railroads don't rule out private-public partnerships, working with state DOTs to create more slots for passenger trains. Eventually AAR would like to see dedicated passenger lines—a separate track used only by passenger trains—where there's room on the right-of-ways.

When he was through, I smiled and said—also tongue in cheek, "I've read that this relationship between Amtrak and the other passenger folks and the freight railroads has not always been so friendly."

He came back, "You know, I've read or heard that too."

We talked a bit more, and he alluded to a new advocacy organization formed by the freight railroads, environmental groups, Amtrak, the National Association of Railroad Passengers, and the States for Passenger Rail Coalition. The OneRail Coalition had been announced a few weeks earlier and it was another example of how much had changed in real railroad world.

It was a head-scratching moment when Hamberger said, "There's a recognition that we are better off going together to state and national policy makers to say we need to have enough capacity for both passenger and freight trains. That's so much better than us drawing a line in the sand and taking our football and going home. Now, we would never acknowledge that the freight railroads have ever done that, but there are stories about, well . . . difficulties."

What about the ongoing dispute over whether Amtrak pays its full share of costs, that the incremental cost structure is unfair to the railroads? I had read AAR's position paper on the way into town that morning on the Metro.

He surprised me again. Hamberger waved his hand, "Well, we have a rhetorical position on that issue, but we aren't doing anything about it."

"So are you saying the freights are going to open up their right-of-ways?" I asked.

"Under the right circumstances, why not?" he replied.

It wasn't an entirely new concept—CSX had said the same thing, and it had been hinted at by other freight railroads. Carmichael had laid it out. The right-of-ways are out there and wide enough in places to accommodate a passenger-only line, and where they are not, the right-of-ways could be widened through land purchases and condemnation. The fact that the freight railroads were saying—even inviting—the passenger entities and government to invest and retool the right-of-ways for both passenger and freight was a profound shift.

"Our perspective has evolved—I don't think we can say to the passenger folks that we don't want you on our tracks. It's just not reality."

So do you really expect that voters are going to support public monies going into rail versus highways? It's not as though we still have a train culture in this country, I said.

"Oh, come on now. Everybody loves trains. The question is how do you take all that nostalgia—the Casey Jones, Lionel toy trains, and Thomas the Tank Engine—and translate it into the public-policy arena?" Hamberger said. "That's going to take some time."

"But what we would like is that when people are out there in their cars, waiting at the grade crossing while a freight goes by, or lying in their beds at night listening to a whistle as the train comes through town, they won't be swearing under their breath about the damn train. That instead, they are glad it's there because it's good for the environment, good for America, and good for them."

EPILOGUE

Pittsburgh
on train time again

It's summer 2009, and I'm in Pittsburgh about to board the Pennsylvanian for New York City, riding on free tickets I earned with my Amtrak Guest Rewards points. I started the trip two nights ago aboard that all-night bus from Marquette to Milwaukee. Someday, I'd like to live in a place where all I have to do is walk down the street and get on a train, or even on a bus that would whisk me to a railhead in less than an hour. We ought to make it easier to live in this country without a car. More mass transit will lessen pollution and congestion, create more livable neighborhoods, curb urban sprawl, improve quality of life and increase productivity, take some of the hassles out of transportation, and give people—especially the growing number of elderly (which includes me in a few years)—an alternative mode of travel.

Because of family obligations or my teaching schedule, there were times I had to drive to Milwaukee to catch the train. And then a week or two later, I'd get off a long-haul train and find myself facing a 300-mile drive north. What a drag. What I really wanted to do was read the newspaper, nap, sit down to dinner, and not have to pay attention. After all that train time, driving seemed like such a waste.

The country needs connectivity—seamless, frequent, and dependable connections between an intercity train, bus, light-rail vehicle, or airplane. Although I avoided renting a car while researching this book, I paid some hefty cab fares just to make connections from one mode to another. Connectivity was the exception, not the norm.

Out there on the rails, the renaissance is underway. I felt it on the Hiawatha and Capitol Corridor, which weren't fast commuter trains but dependable. You see it, too, on the BNSF transcon when those Z trains loaded with UPS containers fly by the window. If intermodal today mainly moves "doodads" from Asia to Wal-Mart and the other big box stores, there's no mistaking the efficiency of fast trains carrying shipping containers and truck trailers. Intermodal increasingly will run goods and materials between American cities. Corporations already are eyeing property for warehouses and plants along rail corridors. Trucks will move goods the final miles, but long-haul trucking is losing its economics. One guy behind the wheel of a tractor-trailer driving from California to New Jersey cannot compete against a two-mile-long train of 300 containers running at 70 mph today and likely 90 mph in the future.

So goes the freight, so go the people. Despite the recession that has cut their business by 30 percent, American railroads are on the edge of something big, and it looks like the passenger folks are coming along for the ride. The decades-long rivalry or impasse between freight and passenger may be nearing an end or, at least, morphing into a different relationship. What synergies result remain to be seen.

Efficiency will be the driver. Energy promises to be more expensive in the future, and if we decide to regulate greenhouse gases and tax carbon—all that bodes well for rail. If America is looking for a greener, more efficient solution to transportation, trains are it. Sure we can and should build electric cars, but those clean cars have to run on roads.

Hard choices will have to be made. Where do we invest? What can we afford? Doubling the interstate highway system, constructing new mega-airports, and building a lot of magnetic levitation train systems? Probably not. And if we do build more trains and electrify corridors, where will the energy come from? Wind, hydro, solar, and other renewables? In part, but the country and the environmental community may have to reconsider nuclear power, too, otherwise the bulk of the energy will come from fossil fuel and that means coal—which, of course, is also good for railroads. One-third of their revenues today come from long-haul coal shipments.

The year 2008 was momentous for rail just as it was for the country, and the news kept coming in 2009 in a dizzying blur. It began with Obama and Biden riding a train into Washington, D.C., for the inauguration. That same month, at the last minute, Obama slipped $8 billion into the stimulus package for development of high-speed rail.

I called up Pat Simmons, the rail chief in North Carolina: "What can I say, Jim, but shazam!" Bill Bronte, rail chief in California, who has billions of dollars of shovel-ready projects, was feeling very confident California would get a big share. Amongst rail folks across the country, the feeling was euphoric. What was happening was beyond what they could have imagined just a few months earlier.

In March, Joe Biden announced $1.3 billion from the stimulus bill for Amtrak to replace and repair bridges, refurbish cars and locomotives, install handicapped access at stations, and a host of other badly needed repairs and maintenance. In a surreal moment during his speech at Union Station in Washington, Biden referred to Amtrak as a "national treasure." I'm sure that was hyperbole for a lot of people—me included. His better line was, "We subsidize our highways and airports more than we subsidize Amtrak. So let's get something straight here. Amtrak has not been at the trough. Amtrak has been left out."

One Sunday morning I turned on *Meet the Press* and watched Arnold Schwarzenegger and Ed Rendell, governors of California and Pennsylvania, respectively, and New York City mayor Michael Bloomberg bubble on for an hour about infrastructure, rebuilding America, and high-speed rail. They co-chair Building America's Future Coalition, an organization whose logo is a train going over a bridge. In July, the House Transportation Committee passed a draft bill calling for tens of billions of more money for high speed rail, well beyond what the Obama Administration has recommended. As well, EPA announced it wants to regulate greenhouse gases as pollutants. If Congress goes along, such regulations will have profound implications for transportation.

Daily, my e-mail inbox filled with newspaper articles and television and radio spots talking about passenger trains. The governor of Wisconsin wants to use $500 million of the stimulus funds to build a 125 mph line from Milwaukee to St. Paul. Texas asked for $1.7 billion for its bullet train project. Ohio plans to revive its 3 Cs proposal to run a high-speed train between Cleveland, Columbus, and Cincinnati. New York would like a third track across the water level route between Buffalo and Albany. Florida asked for $2.5 billion for a bullet train. Flush with the lure of stimulus money for infrastructure, states suddenly discovered rail or dusted off their old rail plans. Forty states requested funding for 278 rail improvement projects totaling $102 billion.

One afternoon, I called David Gunn at his home in Nova Scotia. He had just read of New York's proposal to triple-track the Empire Corridor. The price tag was $3 billion with nearly all the money allegedly coming from the feds. It was the first time in twenty-two years the state had updated its rail plan. Gunn knows that stretch of railroad well and told me there are cheaper ways to increase capacity before building a third track. "Most of these state DOTS are just bullshit. They don't have any substance, any experience when it comes to rail. The big risk is they'll go out and find some consultants who will do all the designing, and then there isn't enough money in Christendom to pay for that."

Channel the money to states that have already invested, created rail expertise in their DOTS, and established working relationships with the freight railroads, he advised. Develop the Chicago to St. Louis high-speed line. Give money to California, Wisconsin, and the folks running the Talgo trains out in the Cascades.

"Show Americans what can be done. The worst that could happen is putting the money into something that flops or drags on for years."

A few days later, I called Joe Boardman, who had been at Amtrak for several months as its interim president. He made it clear he wants to stay on for a few years, and had just delivered a vision document to the Amtrak board. He found good planning, projects, and talent at the company but no vision, he said. It was the same criticism he had of Amtrak when he was at the Federal Railroad Administration.

"We need to move away from any kind of excuses, and feeling bad about ourselves. Amtrak has always had great promise and good talent, and now is the time to demonstrate what is our core competency and competitive advantage—we are the people who know how to run a passenger railroad."

If states want more passenger trains within their borders, they will need to step up to the table with money, Boardman said. Amtrak for too long has been like the people's railroad, besieged from all sides, finding it difficult to say no and trying to be all things to everyone.

"Passenger rail is not just a federal responsibility. States did not stand aside during the building of airports or interstates. It's not acceptable for them to think Amtrak and the federal government is just going to come in and provide rail service. We're looking for commitment, and that means money on the table."

The DOT, too, hinted that the inside edge for the stimulus monies would go to states already putting up money, partnering with Amtrak, and working to upgrade their DOT-designated high-speed corridors. And that clearly gives the edge to the Midwest, California, North Carolina, and Washington.

In the foreseeable future, Amtrak will remain the nation's intercity passenger railroad and run those higher-speed corridor trains. With its incremental cost structure, liability insurance, and ability to get access to the freight network, it has a virtual lock on the business and is unlikely to be usurped by another provider—unless the freight railroads decide to get back into the passenger business themselves. That's not out of the question if governments compensate them for doing so. Otherwise they will keep their distance because the economics of passenger service have not changed—there's no profit in hauling people.

As for those bullet trains with their level, fenced, electrified corridors with nary a road grade crossing—well, maybe someday. I hope I'm still around to see it, but in the mean time, I'm going to Europe in a few months to run through the Chunnel on the Eurostar, sleep on the TGV from Paris to Madrid, and sample new high-speed lines being constructed in Spain.

On that last trip to Washington, D.C., I rode back to the Midwest on the

Cardinal, which runs just three days a week between New York and Chicago, taking a twenty-six-hour circuitous route on the Northeast Corridor to Washington, Virginia, West Virginia, Kentucky, Ohio, and Indiana.

The consist had a single locomotive, three coaches, a Viewliner sleeper, and a combination dining and lounge car. Getting a bedroom at a good price on the Cardinal is always difficult because the sleeper also serves as the crew car. The rooms go fast. When I went online to book one, the price was $833 for just one night. I rode coach.

A congressionally mandated train, the Cardinal has been protected by Robert Byrd, a Democratic senator and an Amtrak supporter well known for "bringing home the bacon" to West Virginia. None of the states through which the Cardinal passes contributes any subsidy to the service.

Everybody loves riding the Cardinal. Me, too. It's a pretty route, climbing through the Blue Ridge into the Alleghenies, passing over the eastern continental divide, and even going past the Great Bend Tunnel that gave birth to the "John Henry was a steel-driving man" railroad legend. It's Americana.

By no stretch will the route ever become a high-speed corridor. Should the train run at all? That's a political question, but I did find some telling stats: Kentucky's total yearly ridership on the Cardinal is about 7,000. Amtrak has six employees in Kentucky and spends about $7 million in the state annually on stations, support services, and access to the freight-rail system. Depending upon your point of view, that either argues for getting rid of the train or increasing frequency to bring in more revenue. A three-day-a-week schedule will never build ridership.

The Cardinal felt like a mom-and-pop train. A single dining-car attendant cooked and served the meals. Many of the stations are unstaffed. Passengers bought their tickets after boarding. In the lounge car, Conductor Dennis Gleason counted tickets, took dollar bills and change for fares, and helped the elderly to their seats. "You just sit back there, sir, and enjoy the ride. We will deliver you safe and sound to your family. Sir, there are refreshments in this next car. Our lounge, sir."

Amtrak ought to clone Gleason. He was a professional. He had stagecraft and presence. Before a station stop, he'd rise up, don his hat, straighten his jacket, and put on a game face, "Ladies and Gentlemen. Your attention, please. Your attention, please. We are entering Clifton Springs, West Virginia, the home of the world famous Greenbrier Resort and Hot Springs. If this is your station stop, we will be exiting . . ." His affected manner drew smiles from the passengers as he went from car to car.

All day, a drizzle fell on the bare woods of December. Little brown creeks ran fast through the bottomlands, and the trees—blackened by the rain—poked out from mountainsides strewn with rock and shale. On such a cold, wet day, the lounge was a comfy place to look out at the mountain towns and chat with other passengers over a drink and snack.

George, a gravelly voiced retiree from Queens with a rumpled New York Mets baseball cap on his head, stayed at my table a long time. He was on his way to Maysville, Kentucky, to see his son. A flight would have cost him $900. Amtrak was $96. The train was OK but, geez, it took seventeen hours, and you go through every little burg. Not much out here in West Virginia, either.

Maysville, he said, has "the biggest goddamn Wal-Mart you ever seen. You can drop off your car, do your grocery shopping. You can pay for it all in one place. There are electric carts to get you around because it is so damn big. Wal-Mart's doing OK in this economy. Kind of attracts the wrong people, though."

George wasn't reticent with his opinions.

"Obama, he's going to have to be some kind of Roosevelt. I think two terms of him might get us on track. But who in the hell would want his job?" And so on.

I was asleep in the coach seat when George got off at Maysville, so I missed that big damn Wal-Mart.

At 3:30 a.m. I woke up in a sweat. The big fellow across the aisle from me had his shoes and socks off and was down to a T-shirt. A couple who had just boarded fanned themselves with magazines. We could have been pet lizards in a terrarium with the radiators pumping out heat. Only the elderly were comfortably asleep, but everyone's blankets and jackets had been shoved onto the floor, unneeded.

I found a conductor alone in the lounge car. There had been a crew change. Dennis Gleason was gone. I said, "The heat's gone crazy in our coach. It's really hot."

"What do you want me to do?"

I thought that was obvious, but since he asked, "Well can you turn it down so it's not so hot? It's hard to sleep."

"Looks like everybody else is sleeping," he said.

I wondered how he knew that since he hadn't gotten up to look in the coach.

"Sir, it's sweltering in there."

"You know, it's the equipment. It's old," he said. "You just can't keep it regulated."

And he shrugged and looked out the window.

I didn't know whether to laugh or get angry. Then my Amtrak stoicism kicked in. I'd been through worse, but damned if I was going back to that coach. I took a seat at the next table directly across from him. Our eyes occasionally met, but we never spoke again. I rested my head against the cool window or propped my chin in my hand until the rattle of the car, the click of the rails became a white noise, and I drifted off—at least, until my head slipped down and I jerked awake.

That's how I passed the night. Freight trains rushed by in a cacophony of light and noise. Our whistle moaned and announced unguarded grade crossings, and beneath street lamps in towns or lights mounted above barn doors out in the country a fresh dusting of snow sparkled as we crossed Indiana.

America is a third-world country when it comes to passenger railroads. Someday, maybe I'll be nostalgic for these old trains. Then again, maybe not.

I know this: If the country wants a robust, well-functioning train system, it will have to pay for it. There's no way around that.

INDEX